GLAMOUR IN SIX DIMENSIONS

GLAMOUR IN SIX DIMENSIONS

Modernism and the Radiance of Form

JUDITH BROWN

Cornell University Press   *Ithaca and London*

First published 2009 by Cornell University Press

Printed in the United States of America

Library of Congress Cataloging-in-Publication Data

Brown, Judith (Judith Christine)
    Glamour in six dimensions : modernism and the radiance of form / Judith Brown.
        p. cm.
    Includes bibliographical references and index.
    ISBN 978–0–8014–4779–2 (cloth : alk. paper)
  1. American literature—20th century—History and criticism.
  2. English literature—20th century—History and criticism.   3. Glamour (Aesthetics) in literature.   4. Modernism (Literature)—United States. 5. Modernism (Literature)—Great Britain.   6. Glamour (Aesthetics)—Social aspects—United States.   7. Glamour (Aesthetics)—Social aspects—Great Britain.   8. Modernism (Aesthetics)—Social aspects—United States.   9. Modernism (Aesthetics)—Social aspects—Great Britain.   I. Title.   II. Title: Glamour in six dimensions.
    PS228.G45B76   2009
    820.9'355—dc22   2008053944

Cornell University Press strives to use environmentally responsible suppliers and materials to the fullest extent possible in the publishing of its books. Such materials include vegetable-based, low-VOC inks and acid-free papers that are recycled, totally chlorine-free, or partly composed of nonwood fibers. For further information, visit our website at www.cornellpress.cornell.edu.

Cloth printing   10 9 8 7 6 5 4 3 2 1

For my parents,
Dorothy Eleanor Brown
&
George Edwin Brown

There was a kindliness about intoxication—there was that indescribable gloss and glamour it gave, like the memories of ephemeral and faded evenings.... The fruit of youth or of the grape, the transitory magic of the brief passage from darkness to darkness—the old illusion that truth and beauty were in some way entwined.

—F. Scott Fitzgerald, *The Beautiful and Damned*

It can be said that a person who is fascinated does not perceive any real object, any real form, because what he sees does not belong to the world of reality, but to the indeterminate realm of fascination. A realm that is so to speak absolute. Distance is not excluded from it, but it is excessive, being the unlimited depth that lies behind the image, a depth that is not alive, not tractable, absolutely present though not provided, where objects sink when they become separated from their meaning, when they subside into their image. This realm of fascination, where what we see seizes our vision and makes it interminable, where our gaze solidifies into light, where light is the absolute sheen of an eye that we do not see, that we nevertheless do not leave off seeing because it is the mirror image of our own gaze, this realm is supremely attractive, fascinating: light that is also the abyss, horrifying and alluring, light in which we sink.

—Maurice Blanchot, "The Essential Solitude"

Contents

Illustrations

Acknowledgments

How does one stand to behold the sublime, Wallace Stevens asks, and it seems, on completing this book, a particularly relevant question. The generosity offered me over the years by friends, colleagues, and family has been of sublime proportion, and I am delighted to offer my thanks here.

My greatest debt is to Lee Edelman, who inspired all of this book's best thinking. He combines startling brilliance with deep kindness and warmth—one couldn't ask for a better teacher, advisor, or friend. Mette Hjort, my first graduate school mentor, demonstrated the best qualities of academic life. My thanks also go to Joe Litvak, Sonia Hofkosh, Sheila Emerson, Paul Morrison, Val Rohy, Matt Bell, and Susan Gorman, who helped me at various early stages of the project. Madhavi Menon—the best friend one could find in graduate school, or anywhere—continues to push me (to work, to play, to eat) and for that I will always be grateful. My experience at Tufts University was immeasurably enriched by colleagues, friends, and students, including Jonathan Strong, Scott Elledge, Peggy Barrett, Lisa Coleman, Rubén Salinas-Stern, Rachel Berry, Carl Sciortino, and James Railey. Nancy Armstrong, William Keach, and Stuart Burrows made my year at Brown University both possible and pleasant.

At Indiana University, I have enjoyed the immense intellectual generosity of my colleagues. Thanks especially to Susan Gubar, George Hutchinson, Jen Fleissner, Jonathan Elmer, Andrew Miller, Mary Favret, Ivan Kreilkamp, Steve Watt, Donald Gray, Eyal Peretz, Nick Williams, and Scott Herring for reading my work with acuity and remarkably good humor. I learned a great deal about poetry in many conversations with Maurice Manning. Ed Comentale has improved my experience of the profession with his reliably sharp wit. Shane Vogel demonstrated a precious form of friendship—he would read a chapter on a moment's notice and offer quick and incisive comments. Connie Furey combined insight and advice with her exquisitely wry sensibility. Patty Ingham, the rarest and best of colleagues, not only read and encouraged my work but charged my imagination on our daily walks. My heartfelt thanks for her friendship, her unstinting belief in the project and her willingness to talk through its every challenge.

I also thank Justus Nieland, Aaron Jaffe, Gil Harris, Alison Hearn, Sarah Knott, and Rebecca Walkowitz for their kindness and commentary; Jason Fickel for reading the manuscript at a critical stage; Roberta Klix, Dale Robinson, Murray Forman, Sarah Pearce, and Doug Moore for their friendship; Jack Patrick and Gary Verostko for the distraction of home improvements; and Connie, Veronica, Margaret, Fern, and Kim Munroe for wonderful evenings with profiteroles and girls on TV.

I am also grateful for a Mellon Foundation award that provided me a stimulating year at the University of Pennsylvania's Humanities Forum. I particularly want to thank Wendy Steiner, Gary Tomlinson, Mark Doyle, Anthony Raynsford, Camille Robcis, Llyd Wells, and Genevieve Abravanel for all our conversations—intellectual and otherwise.

At Cornell University Press, I benefited from the generous attention of my editor, Peter Potter, and copy editor Karen Hwa, as well as that of two anonymous readers.

Finally, thanks to my family—Dorothy, George, Bob, Judi, Kyla, Jen, Meredith, David, Louise, Alex, Michael, Peggy, Gerry, Eric, Alyssa, Mira, Jamie, and Baco—for their unfailing good cheer and gracious support. In particular, I thank my mother for her constant optimism, my father for his perfectionism, Dave for sharing his interests in chemistry and old Hollywood, Kyla and Jen for the fun we had as traveling companions, and Peg for her amazing resilience.

GLAMOUR IN SIX DIMENSIONS

INTRODUCTION

All possibility—that was the charm…, the lovely, iridescent, indefinite charm,—pure illusion All possibility—because death was inevitable, and *nothing* was possible but death.

—D. H. LAWRENCE, *Women in Love* (1920)

Chanel, champagne cocktails, the banana skirt, Hollywood—what could they have to do with the likes of Wallace Stevens and Virginia Woolf? While we may typically associate glamour with the shallow world of consumer pleasure and high fashion, glamour shapes, to a surprising degree, a wide range of modernist aesthetics. Glamour is both a formal category and an experiential site of consumer desire, fantasy, sexuality, class, and racial identity; it thus uniquely frames the pleasures that drive the art and culture of modernism. Despite our ongoing cultural fascination with those consumer products and effects associated with glamour, and particularly the glamour of the early twentieth century, the word and its conceptual grounding remain remarkably untheorized. Glamour is not just an effect of the entertainment industry; it is also part of a complex aesthetic network that binds high modernism with a range of phenomena that might include the film vamp, the Charleston, the Cotton Club's "jungle music," and even such popular 1920s hairstyles as the Eton Crop or Marcel Wave. Glamour appears both as commodity (each of the foregoing made money, after all, for *some*body) and also as something distinctly modernist, formal, and tied to less material concerns than the production and packaging of goods. Glamour, I argue throughout this book, has its own recognizable aesthetic that finds its ideal conditions in the clean (synthetic, cold, abstract) lines of high modernism and provides a way of reading the modern cultural landscape, enriching the products of mass culture and disentangling our pleasure from a wholesale acquiescence to capitalist ideology.

Take, for example, the cigarette. Ubiquitous throughout the early decades of the century, cigarettes offered themselves as small portals to a more glamorous and more modern way of being. The cigarette operated on multiple levels as an emblem of glamour, a metaphor for transformation, an example of modernism, and a commodity that banked on the illusion it sold alongside its substance. Certainly, it was, in the first instance, a product packaged and sold to turn a handsome profit: one might also point to the world of commodity luxury that supported the act of smoking, from sleek cigarette cases, ashtrays, and lighters to the extreme silhouette provided by the length of a cigarette holder. The weight of modern advertising, of course, also buttressed the business of selling cigarettes. In the 1920s Edward Bernays (the "father of spin" and nephew of Freud) threw his significant talent behind the creation of new markets for tobacco—targeting young women in particular—and conceived the spectacle of ten smoking debutantes walking proudly down Fifth Avenue. Further, ad campaigns made powerful claims about the benefits of smoking, including Lucky Strike's promise that cigarettes would help maintain one's youth against the sagging realities of human flesh. Tobacco companies pushed their products as soothing to the sore throat, as helpful in weight control ("When tempted, reach for a Lucky instead" went the slogan), and as the antidote to modern life's many stresses.[1] Bolstered by the gargantuan energies of a new marketing ethos, cigarettes offered an exhilarating and impossible combination of enduring youth, beauty, and style. Nevertheless, their success was not solely due to marketing or the addiction they encouraged: cigarettes came to signify more.

The material cigarette opened up to the smoker an immaterial realm of intensified pleasure through the fleeting draft of nicotine, tar, and a curtain of smoke. The pleasure was only partly due to the drug that cigarettes sent circulating through the body; it was also aesthetic, as smoke curled around one's fingers and snaked into the air, producing a sense of mystery and cool isolation. As one critic notes, "There's simply no more compelling way of doing nothing."[2] Slim, streamlined, ephemeral, and ultimately deadly, cigarettes produced, through their veil of smoke, a sense of style, transgression, and danger that, together, created glamour. Not only did smokers reject concerns for the body and its health, they also rejected the morality that, since the introduction of tobacco to the Western world,[3] condemned the vice that smoking signified and enacted. With the simple act of inhaling and exhaling, smoking induced transformation (this did not go unnoticed: the first machine-made cigarette in 1888 was called "Cinderella")—the wallflower became a cool loner with the singular action of lighting up. The cigarette gave one the appearance of indifference, sheltering the smoker within a safety net of smoke. It thus allowed the boundaries of one's identity to shift, providing an image at once more compelling, dangerous, and individual.

P1167-212

In the smoke-filled spaces of the bohemian café, the literary salon, and the writer's garret, cultural revolution was hatched, just as from the smoke-filled frames of film—from Josef von Sternberg's earliest vehicles starring Marlene Dietrich to golden age Hollywood—a generation of feisty women and femmes fatales was born (one thinks particularly of Lauren Bacall's smoky-voiced delivery of the line, "Anybody gotta match?").[4] Smoking suggested liberation from the tyranny of convention, proclaiming rebellion, particularly if one were a woman (think also of Edith Wharton's Lily Bart, whose smoking ultimately prevents her entry into a "good marriage"). New Women from Brett Ashley to Helga Crane to Sally Seton proclaimed their modernity and sexual independence through smoking. "Miss Nancy Ellicott," wrote T. S. Eliot in 1917, "smoked / And danced all the modern dances; / And her aunts were not quite sure how they felt about it, / But they knew that it was modern" ("Cousin Nancy").[5] Women staked their place in the new order rather than the old with their incursion into a formerly men's-only province.

Yet despite its ties to a rougher masculinity, the cigarette produced a feminized beauty, no matter who was doing the smoking, as Richard Klein, in his remarkable "ode and elegy"[6] to smoking claims: "Not merely a poem, the cigarette is a poet,—esse or—ette: the fiery cinder ash is the heart of a living being, an effemin-ette, perhaps even a feminine being, endowed with abundant resources of seduction and diverse powers to focus the mind."[7] Tied to the nineteenth-century fashions of the dandy and marking women's move toward liberation, cigarettes made visible the complex and shifting lines of gender.[8] The feminized ciga*rette* communicated the loosening boundaries of gender roles and the ambivalence this in turn engendered. The strangely masculine femininity of smoking marked it as an important cultural phenomenon and an aesthetic that may be traced more broadly throughout the literary and cultural record of modernism.[9] In fact, the cigarette foregrounds the aesthetics of modernism, from its sleek lines, to its machine-age design, to its blurring of gender roles, to its fascination with death. The cigarette thus participates in an economy that moved far beyond the financial calculations of turning an agricultural product into a manufactured good.

And glamour? The cigarette—and this further ties it to the aesthetic interests of modernism—seems to stop time, to hold in suspense the unproductive moment, rendering it static for the duration of its burning ember ("Cigarettes kill time," writes Klein).[10] Those two to three minutes are committed to nothing, except the "trivial" and "futile"[11] pleasure of inhabiting that moment. It thus is a meditative pleasure, providing the smoker a space devoted to nothing, to *the* nothing that simultaneously opens up one perceptual dimension while shutting off another. The cigarette stops the onward press of time, throws off its switch, as long as it continues to burn. One steps out of the world and its demands, creating an artificial hush, at least in the solitary act of smoking.[12] Here is glamour: an experience that moves one out of the material world of demands, responsibilities, and attention to productivity, and into another, more ethereally bound, fleeting, beautiful, and deadly. Glamour, like the act of smoking, thus transcends any simple structure of the commodity, rising into the realm of formal aesthetics, modern philosophies of space and time, the shifting lines of identity, and the dazzling effects of the surface.

George Hurrell's glamour shot of Jean Harlow makes this point in visual terms, emphasizing the formality of stasis over movement, beauty over productive activity, deathliness over vitality. Laid out against a background of shimmering plastic, Harlow's hair and flesh likewise appear artificial, synthetic, and otherworldly. The oiled sheen of her face, the white lustre of her circle of hair, and Harlow's half-closed eyes simultaneously beckon and repel the viewer. Here the face is sculpted from light, it is stylized and static, as if no breath could animate the features that are rendered cold, bloodless, and beyond anything merely human. Even the left hand that clutches the shoulder disappears into darkness, as if the fingertips themselves would be too stark a reminder of the sensory dimension of human activity.

The Harlow image neatly frames the negative aesthetics of glamour. Glamour, this book argues, coalesces in the modern period as a negative aesthetic that extends to multiple cultural forms. Glamour is cold, indifferent, and deathly; it relies on abstraction, on the thing translated into idea and therefore the loss of the thing itself, curling away from earthly concerns as if in a whiff of smoke. Harlow is, of course, human, yet her appeal is produced not through the depiction of warm humanity so much as through the cold chemical wash of the photographic bath. Harlow's glamour depends on the distancing effects of technology and the modern desire necessarily mediated by technology. Glamour chills, then, even as it promises the impossible. Here we find another connection to the modernism that favors blankness, the polished surface, the stance of impenetrability (as true in architecture and design as it is in literature), the suspicion of the nothing behind it all— yet somehow, this blankness is transmuted into something that is seductive, powerful, and often simply gorgeous.

While I am most interested in theorizing glamour as a critical term to reassess our understanding of modernism, glamour does have a historical lineage. Indeed, one might find precedents for glamour in a number of cultural practices, products, and figures from earlier centuries. Marie

Antoinette jumps to mind, as does Byron, Baudelaire, and Sarah Bernhardt. One also pictures Chaucer's French-speaking, luxury-loving Prioress, the jewel-laden courtiers of the Renaissance, and the Orient-inspired fashion of the eighteenth and nineteenth centuries.[13] The late-nineteenth-century discourse of aestheticism stands out as the most direct antecedent to glamour. There is no question that aestheticism provides a foundational narrative on which modernist literary form will build and against which it will react, and it is Oscar Wilde who most perfectly signifies a turn toward glamour as a powerful new aesthetic.

Wilde's attention to style, seduction, and idleness made him the charming center of a new cult of the self, exquisitely styled and remorselessly immoral. If smoking signified a new deathly modernity, Wilde may have been the first to recognize it. Wilde, as Regenia Gagnier tells us, "captured the essence of modern economic man when he named the cigarette the perfect type of a perfect pleasure: it left one unsatisfied."[14] In his sensual appetites, and the bold formulation of a new taste culture, Wilde sketches out the lineaments of glamour, combining luxury with a certain attitude of bored pleasure. This stance required money both for its necessary idleness, and the sumptuous commodities that provided its appropriate setting. If aestheticism "signals art's increasing involvement with commodity culture and consumerism" and "bears the weight of modernist anxieties about mass culture,"[15] we may see it as centrally forming modernism's oscillating attraction and aversion to the culture of the commodity.

Aestheticism, like immoralism, exists outside a framework of good and evil, satisfying itself, rather, on the sometimes risky pursuit of pleasure.[16] Yet the subject is still central, selfishness its key to pleasure: more pertinent to glamour is the move away from insistent subjectivity to the impersonal style that modernism promoted and that would, as I will show, resist the subject altogether. The convergence of the discourses we might associate with the fin de siècle—commodification, seduction, unproductive leisure, and a nascent form of celebrity—signals a shift, therefore, into the aesthetics of glamour. I do not doubt the possibility of tracing glamour's constituent features across history through a variety of genres from medieval romance, to eighteenth-century drama, to Romantic poetry, to the aestheticism and appetite for scandal of the fin de siècle. I argue, however, that it is not until the modern period that these combine into an ideal form, a form that demands the pervasiveness of technology in everyday lives, the draining of life into black-and-white images, stylized form, and a literature that so frequently—and lyrically—circulates around abstraction, loss, and a central, structuring emptiness.

Literary Glamour

We do not generally think of literature, even modernist literature, as glamorous—the authors sometimes, certainly their salons and expatriate cafés, but not the writing itself. This, however, is a mistake, for literature set the terms for what glamour was in the early twentieth century, translating it from older notions of the sublime into a streamlined and coherent aesthetic, visible in any number of early century media. By resituating the literary throughout the modern cultural landscape, one might see how reading glamour extends the power of the literary—especially in its attention to form—to translate the world around us. In the wide array of modernist criticism produced since the new modernist studies declared itself in the 1990s, there has been an undiminished concentration on the representational powers of literature, from the "things" that arrange and shape modern subjects, to the (usually cosmopolitan) spaces that create or contain them, to the various ideological structures such as nation, race, and gender that produce them.[17] Critics have also observed the role of the marketplace as the space against which modernism has traditionally been defined.[18] My work differs from these studies by offering a synthesized account of how glamour during the period inheres in the very problem of modernist form.[19] Glamour emerges as form, yet goes unrecognized in the scholarship, bearing no cultural capital, categorized simply by its perceived links to a profit-making industry. Yet glamour, I contend, is at stake in any discussion linking literary form to modern mass culture, and indeed names their interrelation. Glamour points to the *formal* difference of modernism and in that difference locates an array of modern pleasures. In other words, glamour emerges with the modernist attention to aesthetic form and subsequently becomes visible, even most familiar, in the worlds of entertainment and mass culture. In the following pages, I trace the power of glamour not solely to the image, then, but to a range of aesthetic objects and to language itself, or the literary expression that works to seduce, enchant, and revise our experience of cultural texts.

Why is form so central in the literary formulation of glamour? Angela Leighton's work on form is helpful here: the word itself, she writes, is "an abstraction from matter, removed and immaterial; but it is also subtly inflected towards matter. As a word it holds off from objects, being nothing but form, pure and singular; at the same time, its whole bent is toward materialization.... Form, which seems self-sufficient and self-defining, is restless, tendentious, a noun lying in wait for its object."[20] Leighton traces the connections between the formal interests of aestheticism and those of modernism and contends that "form" fits especially well the creed of modernism: "the word inflects easily to the hard, sculptured quality, to the sense of art as an almost mathematical defiance of reality, rather than a copy of it."[21] Leighton's construction of form lends itself to the immaterial effects produced by glamour, whose object recedes behind the veils of its ephemeral effects, defying reality and producing instead a desire that will remain wholly unsatisfied. Glamour inheres in neither object nor subject, but is produced, most intangibly, in the space between them, in their interrelation. The difficulty of defining glamour, then, is explained here, in the space between subject and object, object and effect, materiality and immateriality. Glamour is both wispy and capacious: it is difficult to catch hold of, yet its effects pervade modern culture and writing. Glamour is *both* elusive *and* generative form with the magical ability to shape and reshape the objects before us, to make them better, more tantalizing, by pressing them into an inhuman dimension.

If critics have generally ignored the concept of glamour, modern writers at times explicitly invoked its magical powers, finding in its effect an expressive capacity akin to that of literature; among those who actually use the word and invoke its power are Joseph Conrad, D. H. Lawrence, and Virginia Woolf. Indeed, Woolf links the powers of fiction to those of glamour when she describes her androgynous subject's "rarer gift": "[Orlando] possessed, now that he was in the prime of life, the power to stir the fancy and rivet the eye which will keep memory green long after all that more durable qualities can do to preserve it is forgotten. The power is a mysterious one compounded of beauty, birth, and some rarer gift, which we may call glamour and have done with it."[22] Woolf, with characteristic irony, blithely sweeps away the concepts that most concern her: the enduring nature of fiction and the glamour of Orlando. As Woolf's example shows, glamour not only upsets the firm lines dividing masculine from feminine but also has the photographic power to rivet the eye, stir desire, and alter memory, holding a piece of the past continually in the present. Glamour here allows one the illusion of duration, of stopping time to draw in, like a puff of smoke, the possibilities of a moment.

The word "glamour" itself has thrived even as long as the ebullient career of Orlando. *New Fowler's Modern English Usage* provides the following etymology:

The word, which was brought into general literary use by Walter Scott c. 1830, was originally Scottish and etymologically was an alteration of the word grammar with the sense ('occult, learning, magic, necromancy') of the old word gramarye. It then passed into standard English with the meaning of 'a delusive or alluring charm,' and, nearly a century later (in the 1930s), was applied to the charm or physical allure of a person, especially a woman, first in American English and then in British English and elsewhere.[23]

The word "glamour," according to *Fowler's,* first referred to a state of learning as well as to the inexplicable effects of magic. Learning and magic, apparently in communication with past generations, evocatively combine to alter and corrupt "grammar." Each of these early terms has a strong bearing on the works of twentieth-century moderns, whose various interests included the evocation of ancient myths in contemporary narrative, the possibilities for new and magical surfaces to words, and the breaking up of the domination of grammatical structures. We see here how glamour emerges in language and is, from its earliest instance, linked with magical transformation, like the transformations sought by modernist writers: Woolf's "luminous halo,"[24] for instance, or Stephen Dedalus's "radiance of the esthetic image…apprehended luminously by the mind which has been arrested by its wholeness and fascinated by its harmony."[25] These writers reach not for the shallow gift of illusion in literature, but rather the refiguration of the world, from filth to resplendence.[26]

The visual world, of course, is at stake in this project of magical transformation. With the device of a focused observer, often with a highly aesthetic eye, many novels created the sense of a fascinated voyeur framing (in the shape of his or her own fascinations) the events of the narrative. Nick Carraway, early in *The Great Gatsby,* sets up the trope of a single-window view onto events from which he can record, and sublimate through writing, his obsession with his spectacular neighbor, Jay Gatsby. Virginia Woolf writes with her "eyes fixed upon a certain object" in her essay "The Leaning Tower" and uses the trope of a window to frame a section of *To the Lighthouse.* Young Marcel's eyes are transfixed by a lesbian embrace in the famous window scene of *Swann's Way* (and he will later watch Jupien and Charlus through a window). Helga Crane, who feels only alienation within a social structure she recognizes will not allow her the position of detached observer, looks out a window in *Quicksand* and makes a decision that will propel the narrative events (and of course the window in *Passing* will be the most important, and deadly, of thresholds for Clare Kendry). The camera also frequently provides a trope for visualizing narrative events and will introduce a technologized frame, implicitly devitalizing in its mechanical vision. Christopher Isherwood in *Good-Bye to Berlin* writes: "I am a camera with its shutter open, quite passive, recording, not thinking....Someday, all this will have to be developed, carefully printed, fixed,"[27] and John Dos Passos, in his trilogy, *U.S.A.*, creates the narrative frame through the camera's eye.

Modernists saw the formal potential in photography and borrowed its logic to remake language and literature. Michael North develops the connections between modernist writing and image, arguing that "the new media did influence modern art and literature at a very base and material level, as alternate methods of inscription, and for this reason they offered to modernism a formal model and not just another type of subject matter."[28] For North, the camera provided not just a new representative function but a greater hope "neither linguistic nor pictorial but hovering in a kind of utopian space between, where the informational utility of writing meets the immediacy of sight."[29] This boundary-defying effect with the power to remake the lines of reality into something better, and possibly utopic, helps us to see photography not simply in terms of mimetic function, then, but as a modern and almost magical blending of word and image that introduces the potential for new expressive form. While the new medium of photography was sometimes disparaged—ranging from Woolf's dismissal of the photographic (particularly in the form of the snapshot) to Lawrence's more characteristically volatile expressions of antipathy—the medium's visual forms of representation found ways into modern narrative.[30] Not only do cameras and photographs appear in many such narratives, but their influence becomes visible in the texts' more theoretical interest in memory and its authorship, the ways that memory might be shaped, and the past improved on, even enchanted, through the static and technologized frame.

Bad Glamours

If modernist writers took part in an aesthetics of glamour, they were not blind to the use of glamour as mystification. The moderns demonstrated an interest in the ways the mind could be captured, the ways the effect produced by an object could have the spellbinding and sometimes dangerous ability to arrest the thinking subject. Conrad, in *Heart of Darkness*, makes the link between glamour and what he will figure as a fascination associated with the unreasoning mind. The novel's narrator, Marlow, recounts meeting a bepatched youth who is utterly devoted to Kurtz, the colonial-run-wild: "Glamour urged him on, glamour kept him unscathed....I did not envy him his devotion to Kurtz, though....It came to him, and he accepted it with a sort of eager fatalism. I must say that to me it appeared about the most dangerous thing in every way he had come upon so far."[31] The youth's dangerous fascination with Kurtz is figured as glamour, as the effect produced by a fantasy so encompassing that it shields the boy from knowledge of physical threat. We can recognize the implicit warning here: glamour makes one blind to the willful power that characterizes Kurtz and the colonial system. This, then, is glamour in its ugliest guise.

One might easily find ways to condemn glamour as the streamlined vehicle of capitalist, colonial, or fascist ideology. Glamour offers a way to aestheticize politics, to make, for example, fascism compelling in its clean militaristic lines, its stylized symmetry, and its extreme indifference to human life.[32] The potential for channeling glamour's attraction for insidious ends accounts for Theodor Adorno's fury against the forces that produce its effect; he discusses the glamour effect in popular music and limits its cultural power to the uniform result and pernicious delusion of industrial production.[33] Adorno, in his collaborative work with Max Horkheimer in *Dialectic of Enlightenment,* more famously criticizes the enslavement produced by the culture industry: the culture industry and enlightenment culture more broadly infects, they declare, "everything with sameness" (94), a deadening sameness that benefits only the institutions of capitalism. While it is impossible to argue with the notion that capitalist ideology and its multiple agencies profit from selling glamour, glamour reaches more widely than Adorno's critique admits. When relegated solely to the service of capitalism and its system of commodity production, we lose glamour's aesthetic power, as well as its range of pleasures from the disruptive, to the unproductive, to the immoral or revolutionary, none of which will be neutralized in the face of the entertainment industry.

Likewise, in Laura Mulvey's account, glamour is a deliberate effect of Hollywood and its vision of itself as the "democracy of glamour." She shares, with Adorno, a distrust of the illusion sold under its sign. Consumption, according to Mulvey, was the end-goal for everything and everyone produced by the Hollywood studio system and therefore the focus was on the creation of irresistible surfaces: "the embellished surface conceals and enables a sliding of connotation from the eroticised feminine to the eroticisation of consumption."[34] Feminized glamour emerges as a "fantasy space" that masks a kind of terror, concealing a horror of female sexuality and the material body. I would add that glamour, while masking the horror associated with the organic and particularly female body, offers us a new dimension, one tied up in aesthetic value and a move away from the pressing realities of the flesh. Glamour is morally and politically suspect, as all pleasures inevitably are. Can one enjoy its illusion without succumbing to the worst of our culture? The fascination with glamour is also a recognition of the seductive *possibilities* of the feminizing aesthetic, from the androgyny of the New Woman to the stylish legacy of the dandy (maintained in suave cigarette-wielding stars such as Cary Grant or William Powell). The attention to glamorous figures signifies an attraction to rather than a horror of feminized effects. The feminine indeed carries significant cultural weight in the period, but we refuse to see it if we discount glamour. We give up something vital when we castigate glamour and the illusions to which we happily fall prey. Glamour and commodity—yes, but not only, and not necessarily.

The essay collection *Bad Modernisms* makes the claim that "to this day, no other name for a field of cultural production evokes quite the constellation of negativity, risk of aesthetic failure, and bad behavior that 'modernism' does."[35] "Bad glamours" are not, like bad modernisms, all bad: rather, they walk a line, indifferently.[36] Rather than condemning glamour by focusing on its nefarious links to profit-making and political repression, I am interested here in considering glamour beyond good and evil, as a negative aesthetic that courts danger, finds in it powerful creative potential, yet is not entirely subsumed by any political or moral ideology. In this, glamour is not unlike the sublime, that eighteenth-century symbol of negativity and delightful terror. The sublime experience produced a moment when the subject might reach outside the limits of being and feel something extraordinary and unlimited. Yet, the Kantian sublime did not survive into the twentieth century, suffering instead the fate of all transcendent subjects in a newly secular age. But did the sublime simply disappear? Out of the rubble, perhaps, from the heap of broken images, could be cobbled a dim reminder, an image of impossible desire, a fantasy of proximity, through glamour. Glamour might be understood as a magical remainder—whatever might be left of the sublime—in the early decades of the twentieth century; although this is a consumable and degraded version of the earlier aesthetic and affective category, it nevertheless shares an aesthetic forged in negativity.

D. H. Lawrence offers a vision of sublime negativity in his novel *Women in Love*. He also offers a more complicated and ultimately more interesting version of glamour than that dismissed by Adorno, tying it explicitly to industrial production, the perversion of modern vision, and the magnetic and often violent attraction that defines the relationships between his characters. Lawrence indeed gives us an illustration of the very *queerness* of glamour: glamour arises from a blending of attributes, from the attraction of men in particular to the modernization he so frequently, and vociferously, curses. Lawrence sees the effects of technology as destructive, dehumanizing, and as producing simulacra rather than real people: we are continually reminded, by Lawrence, that the world is a "ghoulish replica,"[37] a dumb show, jerking along. Gerald, "the God of the machine" (193) and "industrial magnate" (182) of *Women in Love*, becomes a symbol in Lawrence's novel for what Jean-François Lyotard in his work on the sublime calls the efficiency-worshipping modern world, the kind of technocapitalism that is destroying humanity, using photography as its tool.[38]

Glamour becomes an explicit part of the descriptive vocabulary in the novel, as the Brangwen sisters walk away from Gerald, who has, in the novel's most famous scene, made his horse submit to the industrial age: "The girls descended between the houses with slate roofs and blackish brick walls. The heavy gold glamour of approaching sunset lay over all the colliery district, and the ugliness overlaid with beauty was like a narcotic to the senses" (97). Gudrun, still under Gerald's spell, casts her eyes over the village: "'It has a foul kind of beauty, this place,' said Gudrun, evidently suffering from fascination" (97). They pass the miners' dwellings:

> There was in the whole atmosphere a resonance of physical men, a glamorous thickness of labour and maleness....There were always miners about. They moved with their strange, distorted dignity, a certain beauty, and unnatural stillness in their bearing, a look of abstraction and half resignation in their pale, often gaunt faces. They belonged to another world, they had a strange glamour, their voices were full of an intolerable deep resonance, like a machine's burring, a music more maddening than the siren's long ago. (98)

The miners' voices are mingled with the technologies of modernization that have demanded their labor. Glamour, predicated on the violence of modernization from which men may still emerge with a dignity imbued with beauty, promises both access to the past and relies, at the same time, on the corruption of the present, signified by modernization. The miners are swept into the mists of glamour with Gerald; the deathliness of industry covers them, and the beauty of impending tragedy (theirs on an everyday and invisible scale) imbues them with a distorted dignity that is, for Lawrence, homoerotic.[39] Glamour here is not explicitly feminized, but poignantly male as the devitalized men are forced to submit to the larger forces of capital. Their position, however, is indirectly feminized as they bear the weight of industry, their pale suffering rendered in the poetic gaze of the narration.

Glamour, then, emerges out of industrial waste—the waste of men's lives that feed the industrial machine—and produces a desire strangely akin to the siren's song that fascinates Lawrence and queers his narrative. In a letter written in 1916, Lawrence reveals more about his fascination with this glamour of men. He describes his own physical examination for service in the military (the British military so desperate by this time for bodies that it would consider Lawrence for service despite his obvious tuberculosis) in terms of its veil of longing that will dissolve into something else, unwanted and horrifying: "And even this terrible glamour of camaraderie, which is the glamour of Homer and of all militarism, is a decadence, a degradation, a losing of individual form and distinction, a merging in a sticky male mass. It attracts me for a moment, but immediately, what a degradation and a prison, oh intolerable."[40] Lawrence's horrified characterization of the all-male environment is notable for its combining of hardness with softness, the organic and inorganic, and the loss of individuality into the whole that is both compelling and terrifying. Lines soften here, like a camera's soft focus blurs the line between the subject and its immediate environment.

Lawrence is, as always, moved and aroused by the idea of male intimacy; yet he is also deeply ambivalent about the removal of clear lines of demarcation that define the individual and make clear the province of masculine authority. The risk, of course, for Lawrence is that of being feminized. Instead, he takes care to erect those lines once more in his ejaculation, what a "prison, oh intolerable," invoking the boundaries of prison walls where he finds none. This then is Lawrentian glamour—hardly noble, though perversely dignified, holding onto the ideals of a classical world, filled with the possibilities of male-male intimacy, yet strangely feminizing. Glamour is terrible in its reliance on the possibility of a sticky homoeroticism: this, after all, is camaraderie, and a camaraderie that fails in *Women in Love,* to the deep disappointment of Birkin, yet Gerald's glamour remains, fatal as radium, as "living metal" (346), as a sign nevertheless of possibility, of the pleasures inherent in illusions. Deathliness is at the heart of all pleasure, as my epigraph from Lawrence's novel suggests, and glamour—the illusion itself—frames both the pleasures and the inevitability of death that amplifies their effect. I have come to a vision of glamour that seems to bear little resemblance to the Harlow image with its framing of polished and unproductive beauty. Yet I offer this discussion of Lawrence because he names glamour as an effect of industrial violence that feminizes those it subjects: glamour emerges from narrative desire, from the beauty that overlays the ugliness of modern life and persists in feminized form, creating a beautiful and deathly aesthetic effect from the industrialized landscape. In Lawrence we find the sublime recast, maintaining both horror and pleasure, and unfolding against a modernized background.

Glamour's Spectrum

The title of this book alludes to the multiple dimensions of modernism, in both the sense of the multiple modernisms that we now locate in various cultural fields and also the dimensionality of modernism, its solid forms buttressing the nothing, a world without god, a sense of cultural vacancy. In choosing six dimensions, I invoke the Greek for six, *hex,* and its magical implications, including the casting of spells, the bewitchment or enchantment that shares a common root with glamour. This group of six, or *hexad,* together offers a new reading of modernist aesthetics that dwells on the enchantment of modernism's multifold surfaces. Perception, violence, photography, celebrity, primitivism, and cellophane: these are not symmetrical dimensions, but each tells us something about the perception, consumption, or framing of glamour within modernism. *Glamour in Six Dimensions* thus draws together a disparate group of modernist fascinations and productions and traces in their interrelations an important and overlooked aesthetic central to modernism. I largely confine myself to the texts of Anglo-American modernism in this book and do not include, despite their connections and rich scholarly potential, European literature or the works of the avant-garde.

I begin the book by outlining the negative aesthetics of the sublime and locating its trace in the twentieth century as an aesthetic of glamour. Glamour is a coming to terms with loss—the loss of the ability to feel, among other things—and the reformulation of feeling itself within literature (a subject to which T. S. Eliot applied himself with much energy). Whereas the sublime overwhelmed the subject with inarticulable emotion, glamour emerges only in restraint: the poetry of Wallace Stevens, I claim, not only produces the formal elements of glamour through its emphasis on wintry conditions, the nullified mind, and cool precision but also in its emphasis on the power of seeming: "Messieurs, / It is an artificial world."[41] Stevens evokes the sublime, as many critics have noted, but it is a reformulated and highly disciplined sublime, that, while producing "negative pleasure,[42] does so through the extinction of the reasoning mind on which the sublime rested, leaving only the "luminous flitterings" of glamour. I turn, in this chapter, not to visual perception but to the perception of scent and the development of Chanel No. 5 to explain the move from object world to immaterial experience that so interested Stevens.

Whereas chapter 1 examines glamour as a discipline that demands restraint, chapter 2 turns to the violent fascinations on which glamour depends. Two works that center on self-consciously modern writers motivate my reading of the violence of glamour: first the most glamorized novel of the twentieth century, *The Great Gatsby*, and second, Katherine Mansfield's lesser-known short story, "Je ne parle pas français." I investigate the violence that defines the Jazz Age and drives each work. Violence both appears in the murders and various brutal acts that accelerate, according to Fitzgerald, in the boom years of the 1920s, and it also becomes thematically central in these two stories. Indeed violence emerges as an effect of language itself. Nick Carraway will attempt to cover over the painful absence at the heart of his narrative (the dead Gatsby) through the lyricism and self-conscious polish of his prose. Mansfield, rather than offer us the veils of prose that make death bearable, creates a story based on unbearable cruelty: the story unfolds as a modernist parody of the seductive power of language and its dependence on cruelty to achieve its desired and glamorous effect. Mansfield would never know of the swift rise of fascism in the decade following her death, yet her work often suggests an understanding of the beautiful façade, the carefully controlled narrative that would mask a political era's sometimes casual and sometimes formal brutality. Glamour and fascism would come to work together, perhaps inevitably, in the 1930s as the work of Leni Riefenstahl, to offer one example, clearly demonstrates. Fascism studied the use-values of glamour, the power of the image, and engineered an affective vortex into which a population—or at least its majority—might be pulled. I do not look to the explicit turn to fascism taken by modernists to whom its glamour lent so much charm. Instead in this book I confine myself to the emergence of glamour as textual possibility, as a mode of capture and arrest that fascinated, yet did not yet turn from fascination to fascism.

Fascination may also be said to define the moderns' relationship to visual technology. Although photographs appear and are discussed more explicitly in a number of Virginia Woolf's polemical texts, I show, in chapter 3, how she invokes the expressive power of photography in her novel *Mrs. Dalloway.* This power is not borrowed from photography's representational capacity but from its grammar; that is, Woolf investigates the relationship between the arrested moment, the past-conditional tense (the what-might-have-been) that the photographic image frames and the desire that infuses our everyday experience. I argue that Woolf, much like nineteenth-century photographer Eadweard Muybridge, finds new mechanisms for locating the interrelations between motion, time, and the constant press of desire. Woolf will provide a view into an enchanted and illuminated past through modernist form that, paradoxically, borrows from a photographic present; Woolf thus produces what she calls "the glamour of the past" in written form.

In chapter 4, I turn from the theoretical and literary investigation of glamour and photography to the popular rise of personality or celebrity in the century's second decade. While Eliot advocated the extinction of personality in poetry, and Woolf recognized a novelistic shift in human character, Hollywood was busy producing its own innovations in the human form: in or around 1910, personality was born, giving rise to a new culture of celebrity. I focus on Greta Garbo as a figure who both emblematizes the twentieth-century turn toward personality and, at the same time, a turning away from all human attributes in her sleep-walking indifference. Garbo's impersonality in the guise of personality becomes a formula for celebrity and crucial in the production of glamour.

In 1925, Josephine Baker joined La Revue Nègre, created her infamous *Danse Sauvage,* and stunned audiences with her jungle-inspired gyrations. Viewed as both ebony statue and frenetic savage, Baker opened an era that would glamorize the primitive. Various and sometimes ambivalent expressions of the primitive emerge in the 1920s, specifically in the works of Harlem Renaissance writers Wallace Thurman and Nella Larsen, Claude McKay, Langston Hughes, Harlem Renaissance patron, Carl Van Vechten, and Baker herself. Why did the primitive mobilize the interests of this range of self-conscious moderns? The usual answer has to do with its commodification, the recycling of racism, and the big bucks of slumming at the Cotton Club. In chapter 5, I instead consider the fantasy structure that supports the interest in primitive aesthetics by African Americans who risked the most in invoking the primitive. Rather than reject popular images of orientalist or Africanist primitivism, Larsen, Thurman, and Baker mobilize the notions of authenticity, originality, and depth they make available, turning to the primitive, paradoxically, as an antidote to modern racist culture.

From primitives to plastics: the 1930s saw an explosion in the production of plastics that designers viewed as the new synthetic language of the twentieth century. In chapter 6 I focus particularly on the ubiquitous presence of cellophane, which was persistently linked with glamour, from its first commercial use in the early twenties as a wrapper for products such as perfume and cigarettes to its emergence on the modernist stage in the 1934 production of *Four Saints in Three Acts.* We have lost, in the decades since the modernist period, the ability to read the early-century semiotics of plastics: here I consider the status of cellophane as cultural force, including its appearance on the avant-garde stage, in the lavish MGM musical set, as a backdrop to celebrity photographs, and in the commentaries of magazines such as *Fortune, Esquire,* and *The New Yorker.* Cellophane, I argue, offered itself as pure surface, as the plastic without depth that gave the modern imagination new ways of seeing the mundane world, transforming it through its sparkling, if empty, play of light. As I began with the degraded remnant of the eighteenth-century aesthetic of the sublime, I end here with the aesthetics of plastic, poised on the brink of its own degradation in wartime mass production and postwar consumables.

The war did not extinguish the taste for glamour and, indeed, glamour continues to exert its cultural attraction and market force. Yet glamour has transformed: we recognize it as a vintage effect, visible for example in the couture worn at the Academy Awards (Nicole Kidman's vintage gown, Charlize Theron's platinum bob), the boyish sophistication of George Clooney that brings Clark Gable to mind, the numerous bars called Gatsby's, and so on; glamour is now always tied to a past that we adorn with glamorizing fantasy. The moderns certainly linked glamour with nostalgia (Lawrence imagines the glamour of childhood in his poem "Piano"), yet in the postwar era this is its only mode, even as it appears in the guise of parody or excess—in the androgynous theatrics of 1970s glam rock, for instance, or in the figure of the drag queen (such as Divine or RuPaul), in the skintight glitter of silver lamé, or in glamour's now most appropriate venue, Las Vegas. Our appetite for the extraordinary, excessive, and otherworldly has not changed, but our vantage point has as we pick up speed, create new aesthetic modes in new media, and consume vast amounts of digital information. Glamour, produced in the glance backward, now cedes itself to the future, where it may acquire new dimensions in a different language.

1 : PERCEPTION

and we breathe
An odor evoking nothing, absolute.

—WALLACE STEVENS, "Notes Toward a Supreme Fiction" (1942)

Fragrant Portals

Coco Chanel's meeting with the chemist Ernest Beaux in 1920 inaugurated a synthetic revolution in the making of perfume. The outcome was Chanel No. 5, the most significant perfume of the twentieth century, as perfumers generally agree. Chanel—whose sense of smell was so acute, she claimed, she could smell the hands of those who picked a bouquet's flowers—had already by 1920, created a fashion empire that she now wanted to extend into the realm of scent. Known for the simple lines of her designs, unencumbered by the whalebone and bustles of earlier fashion, Chanel brought women's clothing into the twentieth century.[1] She would do the same for perfume, although her foray into scent would move her into a less tangible—and highly lucrative—sensual realm.[2] A woman's fragrance, she believed, should reflect the multiple dimensions of women's modern-day lives; she aimed for a scent that was multiply layered, paradoxical, and, she said, "composed."[3] For this, she turned to Beaux, whose expertise in fragrance chemistry could offer her knowledge of new materials for her product. Chanel's intuition was right, as it frequently was: Beaux introduced her to aldehydes, a chemically derived compound that would provide the metallic tone and "champagne sparkle" that would characterize her perfume. In its move away from the simple florals that had defined perfume until this point, Chanel No. 5, when introduced in 1921, announced its modernity in a new and complex chemical language. The perfume was the first to rely on a mixture of synthetic and organic scents, at least eighty of which went into its secret formula.[4]

Chanel No. 5 was positioned to appeal to those glamour-seekers of the period who were seduced by the power of the modern (a.k.a., the new). No. 5 indeed shares many of the aesthetic and material occupations of modernism, including a move away from the mimetic interest in representation, in this instance from the reproduction of a single, recognizable scent, such as rose, lily of the valley, or lilac, all of which became associated with an older generation and its cloying scents. Chanel's perfume, according to the perfume critic and scientist Luca Turin, began the "abstract school of perfumery" and would, with Coty's Chypre,

> set the standard for perfumes without any obvious natural reference point and enable the autonomous development of perfume as Pure Art. From distilled garden roses, we were suddenly amidst synthesized Carbon atoms. It was like jumping from Delacroix's neoclassic people with arms that looked like, well, human arms into a nonhuman, natureless Kandinsky world of triangles, dots, and machine-tooled blobs.[5]

Chanel understood the age in which she lived, and her choices, from the chemical recipe of No. 5, to its industrial and abstract name, to the plain pharmaceutical bottle in which she packaged it, reflected a modernism in line with machine-age design and the avant-garde (even as it tarried with the bourgeois) and would appeal to those with an interest in haute style, as did her clothing. Chanel's flaçon (often referred to as the "Chanel Square"), contrary to the ornate bottles of competing perfumes, was notable for its simplicity, its uncolored glass, and its tiny label with clean modern font (black against a white background). Not only did the bottle break from tradition, the name itself marked new ground: No. 5 offered no visual image, no metaphor, no description of the contents of the bottle. Instead, it announced nothing, save for the perfume's clinical, or industrial, modernity.

Theories circulate about the naming of the fragrance. Was it Chanel's birthday (the fifth day of the fifth month), her lucky number, or did she choose sample 5 out of the five or ten samples presented to her by Beaux? It is tempting to think that the name is a reference to Shakespeare's sonnet number 5, a reference that would need to remain hidden so as not to pull the fragrance into a web of dreary association, tying it to the conventions of the past and breaking its hold on the new. Shakespeare's No. 5, just as Chanel's, articulates the remarkable power of perfume in the face of "never-resting time" to enliven the senses, creating beauty in an otherwise barren world. "Hideous winter" is responsible for the landscape, bereft of fertile life, yet mercifully for Shakespeare's speaker, there remains a trace of beauty in "summer's distillation," a fragrant elixir, captured in glass:

> A liquid prisoner pent in walls of glass,
> Beauty's effect with beauty were bereft,
> Nor it nor no remembrance what it was:
>> But flowers distill'd, though they with winter meet,
>> Leese but their show; their substance still lives sweet.[6]

Against the deathliness, the sensual absences forced by winter, is the memory of summer in all its fleeting beauty. With the whiff of floral sweetness, one might refurnish the trees with their "lusty leaves," and return to the earthy fragrance of a lost season. The perfume thus distills the essence of summer, preserving beauty and allowing for a sensual awakening even amid the annihilation of snow and ice. Of course, it may be mere fantasy to think Coco Chanel—poor, uneducated orphan from the south of France—would have had any occasion to read Shakespeare's sonnets; nevertheless the coincidence is rich with potential.[7] At any rate, Chanel had no interest in preserving the flowery remnants of summer. She aspired only to its seduction; Chanel No. 5, rather than packaging summer in a bottle, instead captured the essence of winter, the cold chemical abstraction of the modern world over the warm vitality associated with nature and with tradition. The modern world (or at least the world of modern artistry) favored chemical winter over redolent summer and found in it the spare blankness of creative possibility.[8]

With the drop of a golden liquid, applied discreetly to the hollow of the neck, the inside of the wrist, behind the ear, Chanel No. 5 opened a fragrant portal into an intimate—and modern—dimension of experience, built equally on the senses and on fantasy. The secret behind this sense experience was the aldehyde base developed by Beaux. Turin writes that at "a then unprecedented concentration greater than 1 per cent, these [aldehyde] molecules lent an abstract, marmoreal, blue-white radiance to what otherwise would have been a lush but relatively tame floral."[9] A perfume like marble? Like radiance? The adjectives Turin chooses emphasize the perfume's inhuman elements, its distance away from the warm vitality one might associate with the floral or animal world. Further underscoring the cold deathliness of aldehyde, the *Oxford English Dictionary* defines it as a "colourless volatile fluid with [a] suffocating smell." Yet, in combination with other scent molecules, aldehydes have also been described as adding, paradoxically, an airiness to the fragrance. Important, then, to the perception of Chanel No. 5 is the distance it takes one away from the human, its coldness and abstraction registering a new aesthetic dimension. While the synthetic properties and production of aldehydes hardly seem to be the stuff of glamour, here I make the case that their characteristics—variously described as brilliant, chalky, powdery, metallic, sparkling, white, cool, and foil-like[10]—share with glamour a surprisingly cold and luminous vocabulary. The perception of cold notes, the inhuman appeal of Chanel No. 5, lent it, somehow, a glamour that was enhanced (and only partly created) by the perfume's marketing.

In thinking about the aesthetic perception of perfume, one necessarily considers the shift from base material to sensual effect; the power of Chanel perfume, after all, is not in the bottled liquid but in the scent that emanates from the body, the transmuted thing no longer in the form of the object. The product becomes the matter of sensual perception and enters a new perceptual dimension. The transformation from mere object (the bottled perfume) to aesthetic effect (for it is, I will argue, an aesthetic at work here) is my subject in this chapter. Perfume may be a commercial product, manufactured primarily to turn a profit, but it operates, nevertheless, in a world of artistic value and according to aesthetic principles. Perfume relies on abstraction (and Chanel No. 5 has, since its introduction, been described as having an abstract smell) and relies on a combination of scents that communicate a message, that make an impression, that offer transformation to its wearer. Glamour emerges here, in the transformation from object to effect, in the act of perception, in the shift away from the concrete and humdrum to the insubstantial and extraordinary. As much about the intellect and its pleasures as the body and its desires, glamour produces distance, an inhuman sheen, and what one might term negative pleasure, the pleasure of the immaterial, the pleasure associated with *not* having, a pleasure, then, that flirts with the aesthetic possibilities of negation.

The movement between material object and ethereal effect—or what I am calling glamour—was a central pursuit of a number of modernist writers, most prominently among them, Wallace Stevens. Here I consider the aldehydic effects of Stevens's poetry and argue that his work offers a compelling literary counterpart to the sense dimension, aesthetic possibility, and molecular complexity opened by fragrance. Stevens is a poet fascinated by the process of aesthetic transformation and he pursues the shift from mere sensory object to magical emanation through the force of an invisible ordering structure. Stevens's "words of the fragrant portals" bring us into relation with the "dimly-starred"[11] possibilities of aesthetic ordering, of producing both beauty and meaning, however fictional, in the world around us. In "The Idea of Order at Key West," for example, Stevens produces a world that achieves shape through a language that shimmers only insofar as we arrange it. While the distance between a commercially marketed perfume and difficult modern poetry may seem vast, the two are linked by the centrality of perceptual transformation, the distance, again, one travels from the "meaningless plungings" of the base material world to those "ghostlier demarcations"[12] that make themselves felt on a different plane or in a different key than that of everyday living. This is, in part, what the French philosopher Mikel Dufrenne refers to when he distinguishes between the work of art and the aesthetic object in his major work *The Phenomenology of Aesthetic Experience.*[13] While the work of art remains a "thing" in the stable realm of the object world, the aesthetic object has lost its objecthood, transcending its base material as it moves into a realm of affectivity, of feeling, what Dufrenne refers to as the "sensuous" (translated from *sensible*).

I begin with the sensuous experience of perfume because it offers the clearest representation of the move between the object and the sensuous (although Dufrenne remains in a clearly delineated world of the art work, one where poetry comfortably makes its home, and not in that of what he calls the "minor arts," where he would situate perfume).[14] The sensuous stands for the effect of the work and is, then, what matter becomes when perceived aesthetically. Perfume, once applied, suggests no matter; it is no longer part of the "brute sensuousness" of ordinary perception, but becomes instead the sensuousness unique to the aesthetic object:

> It is necessary that the object exert a kind of magic so that perception can relegate to the background that which ordinary perception places in the foreground. The sensuous fascinates me and I lose myself in it. I merge into the shrill melody of the oboes, the pure line of the violin, the din of the brass. I merge with the thrust of the Gothic spire or the dazzling harmony of the painting. I merge with the word and its peculiar countenance and the savor which it leaves in my mouth when I pronounce it. I am lost—literally, "alienated"—in the aesthetic object.[15]

The experience of the sensuous, just as the experience of fragrance, is transformed into the aesthetic once it exceeds the object, when it floats free of it and becomes, instead, almost pure affect. The boundaries of the subject shift in the experience of this affect and one is made alien to oneself as one merges with its presence. This may seem an implausible stretch for the experience of perfume, although scent and subject obviously must merge, both when one applies fragrance and when one smells it. Further, the drift toward the inhuman scent of Chanel No. 5, the coldness of its particular chemical base, reaches for the alien and aims to deliver a particularly modern lostness from ordinary human experience.

Stevens takes up very similar issues in his work. From his earliest poetry, written largely in the second decade of the century and collected in the volume *Harmonium* in 1923, to his mid-career poems of the 1940s and his late poems of the 1950s, Stevens mined the process by which an ordinary experience could be transformed into a rich, multidimensional aesthetic experience. Through a lexicon of coolly shimmering elements, he would introduce a poetry devoted to the fleeting, vaporous, or volatile effects of language. In fact, poetry's power, according to Stevens, is its ability to disappear, to make itself inarticulate through the very strength of its articulation: "There is always an analogy between nature and the imagination, and possibly poetry is merely the strange rhetoric of that parallel: a rhetoric in which the feeling of one man is communicated to another in words of the exquisite appositeness that takes away all their verbality."[16] Stevens, like other modern poets, is interested in the centrality of analogy to the poetic process;[17] indeed he views analogy as an "imaginative dynamism"[18] that makes poetry possible. Poetry, in Stevens's estimation, expresses feelings without the obstruction of words and their thingness; by entering into the realm of the aesthetic object, poetry, one might say, self-vaporizes. This is, remember, similar to Dufrenne's comment when he describes reading poetry: "I merge with the word and its peculiar countenance and the savor which it leaves in my mouth when I pronounce it." Here, then, as elsewhere, we find parallels (through the power of analogy) between the aesthetic effect of poetry, and particularly the poetry of Wallace Stevens, and the sensual effects of fragrance from 1) the concept of *sillage,* which refers to the lingering effect of the perfume, the transference to a pure aesthetic in its wake, or its enduring trace ("I do not know which to prefer, / .... / The blackbird whistling / Or just after"), to 2) the reliance on abstraction ("*It Must Be Abstract*"), to 3) the idea of absence that leaves, nevertheless, a powerful impression (the "Nothing that is not there and the nothing that is").[19]

Stevens thus poses a significant challenge to a modernism that sought to produce the object in all its thingness (one thinks particularly of his fellow American modernists William Carlos Williams and Gertrude Stein). Rather than serve an objectivist practice of privileging the material world and material word, Stevens works to dematerialize, to diffuse the physicality of language in order to give access to a greater spectrum of aesthetic, and therefore affective, possibility.[20] In so doing, however, he does not deny the material pleasures of words (what Dufrenne refers to as their countenance and savor; Stevens, in fact, revels in this), nor does he produce a simple rendering of language as transparent. Instead, he grants language its power to transmute the object world before us, to create it, recreate it, and to seem, at times, to lift us out of it.

Free-Floating Aesthetics

Consider the following lines from "The Poems of Our Climate":

> Clear water in a brilliant bowl,
> Pink and white carnations. The light
> In the room more like a snowy air,
> Reflecting snow. A newly-fallen snow
> At the end of winter when afternoons return.

The cool crystalline image of flowers, brilliant bowl, clear water, and reflecting snow are, one might say, aldehydic in their sparkling perfection. The "day itself / Is simplified" by the coldness, the purity of the porcelain bowl, "With nothing more than carnations there." Stasis is compelling here, reducing the world to beauty frozen in place, without any messy human residue.[21] This is the realm of the abstract, the idea floating like a flower in a bowl of brilliant water. Stevens moves outside the everyday world and its dusty reality, into the abstract, here signified in his chilled verse.

Yet, a caveat. The poet acknowledges that "one desires / So much more than that" in his second stanza:

> Say even that this complete simplicity
> Stripped one of all one's torments, concealed
> The evilly compounded, vital I
> And made it fresh in a world of white,
> A world of clear water, brilliant-edged,
> Still one would want more, one would need more,
> More than a world of white and snowy scents.

The world of white and snowy scents is the beckoning fantasy, the uncomplicated sheen of perfection for which we long, the beautiful stasis that, in its austerity, demands nothing from us, allows us to exist simply, without the complications and demands that go with human living. The poem continues, "the imperfect is so hot in us," in fact, the "imperfect is our paradise." Heat will be tied to human failing—a nod, perhaps, to the myth of

Eden—and the flaws that embed us in a human world, despite our fascination with the pristine and inhuman which inspires us to fall into the lostness of the aesthetic object from time to time, to find peace in an empty room with its unchanging, almost deathly, carnations. While Stevens claims that abstraction is the imagination's extreme achievement,[22] he also explains in a letter that "the abstract does not exist, but it is certainly as immanent: that is to say, the fictive abstract is as immanent in the mind of the poet, as the idea of God is as immanent in the mind of the theologian. The poem is a struggle with the inaccessibility of the abstract.... There is a constant reference from the abstract to the real, to and fro."[23]

It is the to and fro that produces the movement in this poem, and others. The recovery of the vital I—the I who is complicated, irreducible, tormented, flawed, real—does not diminish the power of absence, of the flowers' elegant and abstract chill. Indeed, there is something in the oscillation from the knowledge of that I and the alienation, the letting go of the I, available in the purely, cleanly, blissfully beautiful that provokes our pleasure. This may sound like a version of Kant's negative pleasure, that experience of vibration as the subject, the vital I, gets lost in a realm beyond comprehension and then recovers in the assertion of the human dimension, and in Stevens's case, human imperfection (in Kant's scenario the vibration occurs between attraction to the restful and repulsion from the overwhelming). I return to Kant and his discussion of negative pleasure below; for now I want to point out the movement Stevens creates between a desire for pure absence (the negation of brilliant water, the vacuity of white and snowy scents) and the recognition of a more fleshly human need, the impulse to place the self back in the scene, to acknowledge its more heated desires.

We find another version of this tension, or vibration, in section VII of Stevens's long poem, "Notes Toward a Supreme Fiction" (from the second sequence titled "It Must Change"):

> After a lustre of the moon, we say
> We have not the need of any paradise,
> We have not the need of any seducing hymn.

The lustre, in its unearthly glow, replaces any thought, or need, or earthly paradise; it is the snowy room, complete in its austerity, its distance from humbling human need. We need no man-made hymn, because the seduction is complete in the inhuman world, in the luminosity of the moon. Here, under the lustre of the moon, the lover achieves a kind of "lunar synthesis."

This is Eliot's term from an early poem that Stevens admired, "Rhapsody on a Windy Night":

> Along the reaches of the street
> Held in a lunar synthesis,
> Whispering lunar incantations
> Dissolve the floors of memory
> And all its clear relations,
> Its divisions and precisions…[24]

The lunar synthesis in Eliot's phrasing makes coherent the chaotic fragments of modern life; its lustre softens and diffuses the hard lines and logic of the daylight hours. In Stevens's poem, the cold lunar light dissolves human need itself, replacing what Eliot calls the "floors of memory" with free-floating bliss, an existence apart from earthly concern:

> It is true. Tonight the lilacs magnify
> The easy passion, the ever-ready love
> Of the lover that lies within us and we breathe
> An odor evoking nothing, absolute.
> We encounter in the dead middle of the night
> The purple odor, the abundant bloom.
> The lover sighs as for accessible bliss,
> Which he can take within him on his breath,
> Possess in his heart, conceal and nothing known.

The seduction of the moon is so strong that it obtains an emphatic sense of truth. It *is* true, this is *all* we need. The odor exists without association, evokes nothing, signifies only the vastness of space, the luminosity of the moon, the absolute that is beyond human intelligibility. The lover sighs, merging with the aesthetic object, taking in the scent, possessing it without the complications of thinking, of connecting, of associating the smell with a broader world of experience. Rather, it remains hidden away and outside the realm of knowledge. But Stevens adds an element of ambiguity when he writes "as for accessible bliss," that is, as *if* for bliss, the simile itself forestalled, reminding us how inaccessible bliss actually is. The lover sighs for something she can breathe, merge with, and keep, despite the necessary ephemerality of such an experience.

The last tercet introduces the overarching thematic of change (each section of "Notes" has a governing imperative: "It Must Be Abstract," "It Must Change," "It Must Give Pleasure"). The poem moves from lover to scholar, who approaches another kind of bliss than that of abundant bloom. The scholar instead finds pleasure in knowledge, and writes

> the book, hot for another accessible bliss:
> The fluctuations of certainty, the change
> Of degrees of perception in the scholar's dark.

The change that brings pleasure is here a change in degree, the tiny shift or fluctuation in knowledge (not even an increment) that greets a scholar's theories and alters one's perceptions ever so slightly, while not altering the dark from which one works. Here, Stevens has moved us out of the realm of the aesthetic object (the purple odor) to the reaching after knowledge, the desire for certainty in a radically unstable world. Stevens remarks that "underlying [the Notes] is the idea that, in the various predicaments of belief, it might be possible to yield, or to try to yield, ourselves to a declared fiction. This is the same thing as saying that it might be possible for us to believe in something that we know to be untrue."[25] Knowledge itself is largely a fiction in the vast expanse of what we do not or cannot know, the obscurity that defines our lives. To merge, then, however briefly, with the gorgeous scent, the static bowl, the pristine flower, offers a stab at bliss, if only fleetingly.

Stevens will continually take us into the pendulum-swing from the real to the illusory and back again, adding his emphasis (and his desire) to the side of illusion, or fancy, or escape. The latter, of course, is used generally to dismiss the objects of pleasure to which one turns in reprieve from the real, as Stevens once acknowledged in correspondence: "About escapism: Poetry as a narcotic is escapism in the pejorative sense. But there is a benign escapism in every illusion. The use of the word illusion suggests the simplest way to define the difference between escapism in a pejorative sense and in a non-pejorative sense: that is to say: it is the difference between elusion and illusion, or benign illusion. Of course, I believe in benign illusion. To my way of thinking, the idea of God is an instance of benign illusion."[26] There is no moral failing in turning to the perfection of carnations, the lustre of the moon, or the savor of words as a kind of aesthetic salve. Neither is it avoidance, or elusion, of the world's pressing realities. In fact, Stevens places clear emphasis on the benign aspects of illusion—benign here to be understood as a fortunate and gracious attribute rather than simply a harmless one. Stevens had once stated that "the imaginative world is the only real world, after all. It is shocking to have to say this sort of thing."[27] The power of human experience rests not then on the concrete plane of human life, with its objects and sharp corners and things to bump up against, but in an expressive realm associated with the vaporous effects of literature and exquisitely apposite language. Why is it shocking to make this claim? Either, it is shocking to have to state such a banal or obvious truth, or it is simply a shocking statement, one that many might not understand as true. Perhaps in today's critical climate we may find it less shocking to discover the degree to which we live in a world comprised of language, of image, of mental (and ideological) construction; nevertheless this is the necessary illusion to which Stevens will continually turn his attention, and attempt to understand through his "Notes" that investigate (and approximate) a "supreme fiction." Whether an idealized fiction that shapes our lives, or the creation of the aesthetic object in the form of a poem (he writes that the supreme fiction *is* poetry), Stevens accounts for our need to surpass the realm of the material to access the necessary pleasure of illusion, just as one reaches for accessible bliss.

Section IX of "It Must Change" advances the idea that the poem primarily documents movement between realms, the to and fro between particular and general, human and transcendental, material and ethereal: "The poem goes from the poet's gibberish to / The gibberish of the vulgate and back again." Rather than provide a set of certainties about the poem, however, Stevens continues with a series of questions:

> Does it move to and fro or is it of both
> At once? Is it a luminous flittering
> Or the concentration of a cloudy day?
> Is there a poem that never reaches words
> And one that chaffers the time away?
> Is the poem both peculiar and general?
> There's a meditation there, in which there seems
> To be an evasion, a thing not apprehended or
> Not apprehended well. Does the poet
> Evade us, in a senseless element?

The lack of apprehension refers to both parts of the poem itself and also the world at large. The poem contains pleasures that, as Stevens's readers would have to agree, are not easily apprehended, or cannot be apprehended. The poem also obscures and conceals parts of the world itself. The illusion of "luminous flitterings" is presented against the molecular reality of a cloudy day, and we see the poem achieve both at once. The meditation is aesthetic as the poet muses about the poem, and this stance, the poet understands, risks seeming escapist. The senseless element, a realm where the body and its senses have no place, seems the ultimate evasion of material concern. Yet life depends on the back and forth, the escape and return, the abstract and the real. The senseless element, like "the odor evoking nothing, absolute" extends human capacity to create meaning, to remake earthly parameters, rather than to limit ourselves to the "divisions and precisions" of the object world.

This may, at least partially, explain Stevens's elemental interests in those base and transmutable components that structure human experience. Chemistry, in its capacity to reorder molecular structures, provides such a pattern for the creative mind: one finds in "The Reader," for example, that "the sombre pages bore no print / Except the trace of burning stars / In the frosty heaven."[28] One reads the elemental alphabet, coolly, just as Phosphor might:

> It is difficult to read. The page is dark.
> Yet he knows what it is that he expects.
> The page is blank or a frame without a glass
> Or a glass that is empty when he looks.
> The greenness of night lies on the page and goes
> Down deeply in the empty glass…[29]

The page offers little to the realist ("Look, realist, not knowing what you expect"). Rather, the page is all surface, an empty glass, that nevertheless registers depth. Inscrutable layer atop inscrutable layer—the greenness of night, the page, the empty glass—converge in the act of reading the world around one, adding up to nothing comfortably concrete for the realist or the materialist who might search the surface for information, but will find only the illusory depths of reflecting glass.

Sublime Variations

Stevens is interested in the process of poetic fusion that leads the reader into the realm of the sensuous, and turns, at least in some sense, toward the table of elements to augment his creative imagery. He has a modernist partner in this enterprise. Eliot famously returns us to the lab in his early and influential essay, "Tradition and the Individual Talent," when he claims that poetry should "approach the condition of science."[30] The cold precision of scientific models, the dynamic exchange between chemical elements, and the irrelevance of the personality carrying out the research together create a standard for the modern program that Eliot advocates: "I therefore invite you to consider, as a suggestive analogy, the action which takes place when a bit of finely filiated platinum is introduced into a chamber containing oxygen and sulphur dioxide" (40). The platinum acts as a catalyst in the transformation of the two gases, although it will not be altered in the chemical reaction and the sulphurous acid that results will contain no trace of the motivating metal. The analogy draws from Eliot's conception of the poet, whose mind he contends "is the shred of platinum," the catalyst whose timely presence creates a remarkable transfiguration of the elements. Further down the page, however, the mind of the poet becomes the chamber itself in a slippage that recreates the poetic process. "The poet's mind," Eliot continues, "is in fact a receptacle for seizing and storing up numberless feelings, phrases, images, which remain there until all the particles which can unite to form a new compound are present together." The mind, here, is both catalyst *and* cauldron, motivator and container of its dynamic energy. The slippage between mind and space, the subject and the environment, or subject and object, suggests something about poetic perception, and the turn to science provides Eliot a way of discussing the poetic process in cool clear (even aldehydic) tones, without relying on Romantic precedent, soppy sentimentalism, or needless incursions into the poet's psychic life.

While the action taking place in Eliot's analogy is not exactly that of chemical sublimation—no solid is literally transforming into a vapor—the crucible in which the transformation occurs may be traced in the genealogy of the word *sublime*. One etymology indicates that the word *sublime* "turns up first in English as a verb in medieval alchemy. Something that had *sublimed* had been converted by heat from a solid directly into a vapour, considered to be an ethereal or higher form of nature. As it happens, a number of substances important to alchemy sublime, including sulphur, white arsenic, amber and camphor; the device in which this was done was a *sublimatory*."[31] Whether sublimation (whose Freudian path from drive to art is easily enough located), sublimatory, or the sublime, Eliot points to a transfiguration that shifts the poetic register to something beyond this world, or at least beyond human experience in this world, which suggests, as does the "extinction of personality," an encounter with the sublime.[32]

The sublime: that experience of being dumbstruck, followed by, at least in literary history, the profusion of words with which one attempts to record the experience. In the by now well-known words (at least among scholars of the sublime) of Thomas Weiskel, this experience promises transcendence of the human, a leap out of the limiting boundaries of subjectivity, into something vast, unknowable, and exciting.[33] This, I would venture to suggest, is what Chanel tried to tap into, what Stevens taps into, and why the category of the sublime continues to exert its fascination through the twists and turns of literary histories, theories, and understandings of what it is to be a human subject in the swelling pool of ideologies, discourses, theologies, and other meaning-making systems. The obliteration of the subject—what Eliot approximates in the eradication of authorial presence—resembles the sublime effect, especially in the form of the self-surrender that Eliot describes in his essay on Dante: "It is very much like our intenser experiences of other human beings. There is a first, or an early moment which is unique, of shock and surprise, even of terror; a moment which can never be forgotten, but which is never repeated integrally; and yet which would become destitute of significance if it did not survive in a larger whole of experience; which survives inside a deeper and calmer feeling."[34] While this undoubtedly evokes the sublime (although the sublime conventionally requires a natural rather than human source), Eliot makes a curious comment in his essay on tradition: "If you compare several representative passages of the greatest poetry you see how great is the variety of types of combination, and also how completely any semi-ethical criterion of 'sublimity' misses the mark" (41). His beef is less with the category of feeling, per se, and more with the Romantics who wrote poetry under the injunction "Look into your heart and write." But what does he mean? Is it the ethical criterion at all, or the measure of its semistate that Eliot dismisses? Or is the sublime simply not modern enough?

Rather, Eliot prefers the language of the laboratory—objective, experimental, and based in the combination, molecular reaction, and transmutation of substances. Eliot's chemical metaphor induces something that might be called sublime perception in its poetic intensity and in its power to redraw the boundaries of the perceiving or poetic self. The convergence of subject and object is thus central to poetic activity, both in terms of the creation and perception of the poetic image (and one is once again reminded of Dufrenne merging with those words his tongue savors).[35] To further clarify this idea, Eliot explains that "it is not the 'greatness', the intensity of the emotions, the components, but the intensity of the artistic process, the pressure, so to speak, under which the fusion takes place, that counts" (41). Fusion, the blending of different elements into one under a pressure equal to the explosive molecular refiguration produced by the chemist, is key then to the poetic process. Poem, poet, and process combine in Eliot's extended metaphor which thus manages to relegate emotion to a supporting role, necessarily transfigured in the escape from personality, the human, the details of a particular life that distract from the poem's overall effect. Now, we know that Eliot does not extinguish the idea of the poet altogether—in fact, one might read the essay as extended aggrandizement of his own role—yet, his metaphor underscores the newly assigned significance of scientific restraint, the poet stepping (at least performatively) away from personality, his presence leading only to his absence, and into the chemical fusion of language.

The negation of the poet in the clinical space of the laboratory therefore leads to the production of vital poetry, which is lifted away from the deadening past, and recreated in the sublime fusion of elements. Poetic production depends on poetic negation, and in the process one encounters what I earlier referred to as negative pleasure, the rapid movement between extremes of negation and production, erasure and presence, that have, since the eighteenth century, defined the experience of the sublime. There are, of course, many ways to imagine negative pleasure: beginning with historical precedent, the term originates in Kant's third *Critique* where he describes the mind as "not merely attracted by the [sublime] object but is ever being alternately repelled."[36] The somehow satisfying movement between attraction and repulsion "does not so much involve a positive pleasure as admiration or respect, [but] rather deserves to be called negative pleasure" (83). This pleasure is "produced by the feeling of a momentary checking of the vital powers and a consequent stronger outflow of them, so that it seems to be regarded as emotion—not play, but earnest in the exercise of the imagination." He later clarifies that "the mind feels itself moved in the representation of the sublime in nature, while in aesthetical judgments about the beautiful is in restful contemplation. This movement may…be compared to a vibration, i.e. to a quickly alternating attraction toward, and repulsion from, the same object." (97). The negation in Kant's formulation may be, to use his word, "repulsion," yet it not only sends the self fleeing toward the affirmation of reason but also opens a chasm of negative possibility, an abyss of sorts into which the subject looks and does not find the comfort of a mirroring image.

The negative space of that overwhelming blankness, the thing that resists conceptualization yet offers pleasure, is at the center of Stevens's poetic oeuvre. The material thing frequently dissolves and becomes abstract and unreachable in Stevens. Most famously, and elliptically, addressed in "The Snowman," the nothing offers pure creative potentiality: "One must have a mind of winter," the poem begins, in order to behold the barren, frost-laden, and glittering world. The mind emptied of warm human inclination must accustom itself to the sights and bare-blowing sounds of an icy climate for "the listener, who listens in the snow, / And, nothing himself, beholds / Nothing that is not there and the nothing that is" (54). Listening itself becomes a frozen activity that shares with "glisten" the hard encrustation of winter. The senses are disciplined in this poem to give up the heat of the sun and softness of juniper bows (here they are "shagged with ice," just as the spruces are rough in the sun's "distant glitter"); rather, the senses must recalibrate to absence and the perils it presents to form itself. Even the title is undone over the course of the poem, as man faces a vast emptiness of mind and loses definition—he is "nothing himself"—against the blankness of white.

Stevens's negative pleasure remains unresolved by Kantian notions of reason. Rather, the snow man, the man with the mind of winter, must face the terrifying void, the multiple forms of nothing (there and not there) and, perhaps, find pleasure in a newly clarified perception. There is no safety net in Stevens's conception, no comfort to be found in the reasoning mind, little to promise haven from the nothing. Yet, there is pleasure. Indeed, incomprehension, whether in the face of the natural sublime or one of Stevens's poems, has its delights. Is it simply the experience of giving oneself over to the formless confusion that might describe at least the initial encounter with the vast, the powerful, or the difficult? For Kant, it is the vibration between confusion and cognition, the profound unsettling met with imaginative strain, that provokes pleasure. Incomprehension leaves little but the object for one to contemplate, in the case of poetry, the sounds of the words or their shape on the page. In the to and fro, then, the mind moves from the solid—whether sublime mountain or illogical syntax—to the abstract as one grapples with meaning. Certainly this describes the experience of reading Stevens, in its confused exhilaration and frustrated cognition, although cognition will not, as in Kant's conception, win out. The Kantian subject comes to rest on the simple certainty of the superior human faculty to encapsulate an experience via the rational mind. Stevens allows us no such certainty. From the object world of words on the page one moves, then, into the more unstable realm of the aesthetic object, the perception of the sensuous where boundaries shift, and subjects and objects merge. The nothing emerges where there is nothing substantial to grasp hold of, and the subject loses its definite form as even a snowman inevitably must. Here then is the pleasure of negative space, where nothing is guaranteed, meaning is elusive, and all that is solid melts into air, to borrow from Marshall Berman's borrowing from Marx.[37] The pleasure of the negative has therefore to do with the movement between reality and illusion, attraction and repulsion, and the desire for a subjective nothing, a self freed of human need, the extreme of impersonality.[38]

Can the sublime occur without a subject, or without the authorial presence that Eliot claims, and Stevens infers, must disappear? Certainly not in Kant's sublime scenario, or Burke's, or Wordsworth's. Yet in the twentieth century, the subject occupies a much more shadowy position; no longer the actor of the egotistical sublime, for example, the subject is relegated to the peripheries of history through the rise of such revolutionary discourses authored by Nietzsche, Darwin, Marx, Freud, Einstein, and so on. One generally reads modernism as a clinging to the subject despite the onslaught against it by the rising tide of discourses that threaten to evacuate it of its human content, or at least its humanist centrality.[39] While the death of the subject is a commonplace in late-twentieth-century formulations, in the early century the subject suffers, more accurately, a mortal wounding. To return to the question of whether there can be a sublime without a subject, or at least a vital subject, one might consider the proliferation of theories of the sublime in the twentieth century—the female sublime (Yaeger), the postmodern or technological sublime (Lyotard), the camp or hysterical sublime (Jameson), the "stuplime" (Ngai), and so on—and think perhaps that the twentieth century allows for that possibility.[40] The idea that something like a sublime effect still lingers is not therefore new, yet the terms have changed as the self is demoted, along with any absolute claims about the reasoning mind.

Stevens, particularly, has been hailed as the twentieth-century poet of the sublime (originally, and most influentially, by Harold Bloom), since his work speaks to the transcendent power of the aesthetic, to the limits of reason (his lines "one must resist the intelligence, / almost successfully," are frequently and fondly quoted), and since he overtly invokes the sublime in poems such as "Esthetique du Mal" and "The American Sublime": "How does one stand / To behold the sublime," the latter asks.[41] Certainly one can easily enough think of Stevens as a liminal poet (drawing from the same root, *limin*, as the sublime) formulating his poetic theory in the break between the Romantic and the modernist conceptions of poetic form and meaning (he writes: "The poem lashes more fiercely than the wind, / As the mind…destroys / Romantic tenements of rose and ice").[42] Rather than rehearse this particular interpretative history of Stevens's work, one that situates him in relation to the Romantic past rather than a modernist present, I want to suggest that Stevens is more pointedly a poet of glamour, devoted to the inhuman appeal of language and the aesthetic object.

Wallace Stevens? Glamorous? This sounds preposterous, of course, when considering Stevens the man, spending a lifetime in Hartford and contemplating the details of the insurance business from his desk at the Hartford Accident and Indemnity Company. But if we take Eliot's claims seriously and remove the biographical information, thinking only of the aesthetic universe created by Stevens, we find the "luminous flitterings" and the "senseless element" that bring us the modern aesthetic (and chemical) experience of glamour. Glamour depends on the beautiful, as the sublime does not, yet it is, one might say, the beautiful sublimed, made constitutively remote, abstract, and drawing on the immense sense of nothing that renders life itself empty of any essential meaning.

Glamour, with its sheen of indifference, pulls the subject/object out of the human world (sometimes with the aid of twentieth-century consumer culture, although this does not interest Stevens), harnesses the sublime's proximity to death, its reliance on the outermost reaches of human life, the dividing line where death rushes to meet life. Glamour, however, involves a certain textual frost, the cold surface, glistening and apparently impenetrable, and an increasing distance between subjects and their desires. If the sublime is, in Weiskel's words, a "stunning metaphor," glamour maintains the capacity to stun, to harness the lustre of the moon, the brilliance of the water, the polish of the surface. Glamour emerges, somehow, in the flux between the visionary moment produced by a sublime encounter and the momentary visions produced in the fragments of modernist literature that offer escape to the imaginative through the particular and exquisite power of the aesthetic (and its "lunar synthesis"). Glamour becomes, then, in the modernist period and particularly in Stevens's poetry, a production in literature, a coming to terms with whatever might be left of the sublime in the rush of the century's early decades, yet introduces the sheen of cold science, the technology of the machine age, a fascination with surface and stasis, and presents the subject on the brink of something terrifying, arresting, and potentially—even probably—annihilating. Of course, glamour doesn't pull one out of anything—whether human desire, the system of capitalist relations, commodity production, social hierarchies, etc.—even if it arrests our attention momentarily and takes us out of ourselves and our mundane realities. Glamour in fact resituates us in the powerful web of discourses that define modern life but offers that vibration, the fleeting sense of possibility that we encounter in the aesthetic object, and provides its own kind of negative pleasure. Stevens thus presents us with a clarified and exquisite perception that channels the power of absence and removes the outmoded self; the result is, paradoxically, a newly resuscitated poetic voice that reaches for the senseless and artificial element of the aesthetic object, both out of this world and in it.

The Discipline of Glamour

Messieurs, / It is an artificial world.
    —WALLACE STEVENS, "Extracts from Addresses to the
    Academy of Fine Ideas"

While the sublime is defined, in Kantian terms, by formlessness, glamour by contrast is acutely formal, requiring the mediation of the aesthetic object (whether in the form of the work of art or the "minor arts" that Dufrenne dismisses) to produce its effect. Kant remains fairly ambiguous on the role of art in the experience of the sublime (he favors the natural world),[43] but glamour is solely artificial, man-made, a human production. Glamour is thus defined by limit, by those boundaries that create and confine the illuminated lines of its object. The work that defines the early Stevens (playful, modernist) against mid- to late-career Stevens (meditative, philosophical) maintains nevertheless the sparkling strain and "seeming" of glamour. Indeed glamour—calling up the etymological roots of the word in illusion (or delusion), magic, the captivating spell—unites the poems across the poet's lifetime of writing. Glamour shares, therefore, a great deal with beauty, a category produced in symmetry and engendering a sense of calmness according to both Burke and Kant. Glamour, however, cannot be equated with the beautiful. Its ground is illusion, or its stronger cousin, delusion, and elevates the false, the world of "seeming" (beauty, rather, is conventionally tied to Truth or the Good).

Where the sublime overwhelmed the subject with inarticulable emotion, glamour emerges in restraint, the discipline of cool formalism, the detachment founded in wintry conditions, the clarified mind, and verbal precision. Stevens's most extreme example—it would seem an exercise if it were not so beautiful—of the move into the vaporous realm entirely detached from the thing itself is his long poem, "Description without Place," in which he meditates on the aesthetic cut free altogether from its object: "It is possible that to seem—it is to be" begins the poem which then sets us into a world floating free of its material referents:

> It was a queen that made it seem
> By the illustrious nothing of her name.
> Her green mind made the world around her green.
> The queen is an example…This green queen
> In the seeming of the summer of her sun
> By her own seeming made the summer change.
> In the golden vacancy she came, and comes,
> And seems to be on the saying of her name.[44]

The queen, by virtue of the word that defines her as queen, fashions a world of seeming around her. The cool luminosity of her name produces out of the "golden vacancy" (271) a sense of what is, the seeming that is all we know of the world. In the metonymic magic of her presence, queen, crown, and fame recreate the world: "An age is a manner collected from a queen" (stanza II, p. 271). An age—whether that be historical, aesthetic, cultural, or any number of the ways an age comes to be defined—is a matter of perception, the effect of the mirage we might call "queen":

> In flat appearance we should be and be,
> Except for the delicate clinkings not explained.
> These are the actual seemings that we see,
> Hear, feel and know. We feel and know them so.
>   (stanza II, p. 271)

Seeming has actual consequences—we see, hear, feel and know them—in the lived world.[45] Indeed, Stevens had, early in his career, addressed the actuality of seeming: "Let be be finale of seem" he writes in "The Emperor of Ice Cream."[46] This poem presents unromanticized death, the horny-toed corpse under the sheet, in opposition to the "concupiscent" (79) life force of those who prepare the wake. "Let be be finale of seem": the line suggests that only in death does seeming end. "Be" attains its nullifying force, the simple fact of organic life, in the demand "Let be be." In life, however, there is only seeming (in fact, the seeming brings objects like curds to life with the adjective "concupiscent"). In a poem devoted exclusively to life rather than representing the actuality of death, one might imagine this reversed to "Let seem seem finale of be." Either way, the word "finale" reminds us that we are indeed living on a stage ("Of Modern Poetry" will extend this metaphor), the theatrical production that binds our disparate strands of narrative until the curtain closes, and the sheet comes down over the body.

Strangely, Harold Bloom and Helen Vendler—two figures who loom largely in Stevens criticism—discount the importance of "Description without Place" (indeed, Bloom writes that the poem "is nobody's particular favorite and is never going to be....The puzzle...is why he wrote it" and Vendler calls it a "great falling-off of power" and worse).[47] Yet what their dismissive critiques overlook is the way the poem addresses the making of history as a continued cultural fiction and includes historical figures such as Nietzsche and Lenin: history can only be a production of seeming in its account.

> Description is a revelation. It is not
> The thing described, nor false facsimile.
> It is an artificial thing that exists,
> In its own seeming, plainly visible,
> Yet not too closely the double of our lives,
> Intenser than any actual life could be.
>   (stanza II, pp. 275–276)

Historical memory draws out the most intense strands of a long and complicated narrative, hardly mirroring the lives lived but amplifying and sometimes glorifying them. The language that records human life may even improve it, make it alive with "its own seemings":

> In a description hollowed out of hollow-bright,
> The artificer of subjects still half night.
> It matters, because everything we say
> Of the past is description without place, a cast
> Of the imagination, made in sound;
> And because what we say of the future must portend,
> Be alive with its own seemings, seeming to be
> Like rubies reddened by rubies reddening.
>
> (stanza VII, pp. 276–277)

Circular logic marks the final simile of the poem. What we say of the future will be embellished, made more vivid, like the rubies that increase in intensity through the burst of alliterative language that turns the rubies back on themselves, improving them through their own concentrated power that is, in the end, the power of poetry itself. It thus appears that poetry opens up a perceptual dimension in which glamour—the seeming with the capacity to alter past, future, and the glittering rubies before us—becomes possible, and that glamour forms itself in the concentrated intensity of poetic perception.

I want to turn back to an earlier Stevens, his poem "To the One of Fictive Music," written in 1922 and published in *Harmonium,* to develop this point. The "One" of the title works as a composite, a fusion of the "sisterhood of the living dead" who are called forth as "Most near, most clear, and of the clearest bloom."[48] The concentration of women—who seem to be muses, although Stevens would not commit to this reading[49]—in the first lines of the poem seems to crystallize, however, in the fifth line as a queen (again) is presented in telling negation: "no thread / Of cloudy silver sprinkles in your gown / Its venom of renown, and on your head / No crown is simpler than the simple hair." The queen, Stevens suggests, is natural, simple, and earthy, yet the images presented—even if in negation—are those of silvery threads, a venomous gown, the royal crown. The absent markers of royal privilege share the stage, framing the queen's natural features against their sparkling and more compelling emptiness in the second stanza: "none / Gives motion to perfection more serene / Than yours."

The poem ostensibly provides an argument for presence. "Music is intensest which proclaims / The near, the clear and vaunts the clearest

bloom," the third stanza continues, celebrating one version "that is sure, /
Among the arrant spices of the sun, / O bough and bush and scented vine."
Yet, the poem will not commit to the certainty of warm spice and fragrant vine and instead steps away in the final stanza, favoring this time the
remote:

> Yet not too like, yet not so like to be
> Too near, too clear, saving a little to endow
> Our feigning with the strange unlike, whence springs
> The difference that heavenly pity brings.
> For this, musician, in your girdle fixed
> Bear other perfumes. On your pale head wear
> A band entwining, set with fatal stones.
> Unreal, give back to us what once you gave:
> The imagination that we spurned and crave.
>
> (83)

The image of the wholly desirable queen is again delivered through negation: the "one" appears as a series of *nots* (*not* too like, too near, too clear).
Rather, the poet tells us, she should remain at a distance, faintly obscure,
foreign to our everydays, bearing "other perfumes," those that are inhuman
and unreal. We are, of course, back where we began, with the inhuman scent
of perfume, a version of Chanel No. 5 and the "lostness" it promises from
mundane, unimaginative life, through its deathly presence (whether evoked
by fatal stones or aldehydes). By now I hope it is clear that the Chanel perfume operates in dual registers in my argument: it both works metaphorically in order to explain the cool synthetic effect of Stevens's poetry, and
it points to a particular historic moment, shared with the publication of
Harmonium, thus situating their shared aesthetic within a specific cultural,
and modernist, context.

Difference and the danger it implies, in poetic image or girdled perfume,
is necessary to aesthetic pleasure, Stevens seems to suggest, whether that
pleasure comes in the figure of the muse or the even greater formless "unreal." Here, the "one" who is defined against the "vital I" who speaks, is desirable in her "strange unlike" as she loses form and floats free from the
semantic constraints of muse or queen. This becomes clear in the stanza's
final two lines, which address the figure now as the "Unreal." The poet no
longer presents the "one" in any semblance of human form; rather it is to
the "unreal" that he speaks, imploring it to give back the gift of imagination,
without which we can only see in the certain terms of "most near, most
clear, and of the clearest bloom." Clarity leads to description, to a kind of

literalism with few affinities to the poetic or the sensuous. If description without place (that is, what Stevens means by the phrase) is the work of abstraction, the moving away from the object with the aid of the imagination into the unreal, then the poetic—and here we may conceive this in wider aesthetic terms—finds itself in that space of alienation, the movement away from place, the greater interest in the distant or only faintly discernible. This is negative aesthetics, or form without form, cast in sound from intangible acoustic waves (and here again we have a structure that resembles the simultaneous presence/absence of perfume) that combine into "fictive music," doubly intangible, doubly sensuous. And glamorous. Since one cannot actually *have* the glamorous object, the object will necessarily remain beyond reach and in the realm of the unreal: to possess it would be to annul its glamour.

Perception itself reaches across multiple realms, linking the imaginative with the aesthetic with the sensual. The glamorized object and glamorizing subject merge in perception, in the moments where the subject sees, breathes, or reads and becomes part of its aesthetic sphere (the domain of the sensuous) in the move into abstraction. For Stevens, the imagination that we spurn in our irritable reaching after the clear bloom of fact[50] is precisely what we need to make a more livable life that, paradoxically, depends on the deathly or artificial: it is the "artifice within us" ("Imagination as Value"),[51] that "genius" that mediates modern experience and the perceptual field, that we require. "We do not hesitate, in poetry," Stevens says elsewhere, "to yield ourselves to the unreal, when it is possible to yield ourselves" ("The Noble Rider and the Sound of Words").[52] The measure of a poet "is the measure of his power to abstract himself, and to withdraw with him into his abstraction the reality on which the lovers of truth insist. He must be able to abstract himself and also to abstract reality, which he does by placing it in his imagination."[53] The "lovers of truth" sound faintly distasteful here, limited by their singular and impossibly idealistic passion for truth that allows no room for seeming. The imagination conceived spatially as a vast container in Stevens's example, becomes, as in Eliot, the laboratory dish in which the fusion will take place. The work of the imagination—just as the work of Eliot's analogy—is to abstract and thus transmute the real into something more right than real ("sounds passing through sudden rightnesses," he writes in "Of Modern Poetry").[54] Rightness here is an aesthetic term, pulling the elements together for an airy instant until they again float free, uncontained by categories of meaning or truth. In the sudden rightness, there is an exquisite moment of fusion, where nothing is barbed or jagged, where bliss seems accessible, before the elements again disperse.

Again, Dufrenne is useful in understanding the layers of aesthetic under-standing: imagination lies at the root of perception, he suggests, rather than exists apart from it. In aesthetic experience, then, imagination is involved only in collaboration with perception (if an imaginative act meant a refusal to perceive, the aesthetic object would disappear).[55] Dufrenne writes that "there is an imagination which derealizes and one which realizes. The lat-ter gives full weight to the real by assuring us of the presence of the hidden and distant" (357). Indeed, "we reach the real through the unreal" (357); this, of course, sounds a great deal like Stevens.[56] "To sum it all up," the poet comments late in his career, "for me the most important thing is to realize poetry.... It is simply the desire to contain the world wholly within one's own perception of it. As it happens, in my own case, and probably in yours, within perceptions that include perceptions that are pleasant. The philosophers, of course, dismiss all pleasurable perceptions; if they don't, the socialists do."[57] Just as in the glass on glass of Phosphor's reading, Ste-vens imagines perceptions within perceptions, thus realizing poetry as an act of imagination and perception, a vibration, a negative aesthetic favoring the hidden (or absent) and distant. There is no material for the socialists to worry over, no truth or common good for the philosophers to debate about, just the aesthetic that buoys us up, takes us to the edges of subjectiv-ity, and makes us realize the world more perceptively, lifting us—exquisitely, impossibly—out of ourselves.

2 : VIOLENCE

She was dark, you know, and yet she had that white skin. There's a kind
of flower called freesia—when the petals are very white they have the
color of her skin. And there's a strong sweetness to it—strong and ghostly
at the same time. It smells like spring with the ghosts in it, between
afternoon and dusk. And there's a word they call glamour. It was there.

—STEPHEN VINCENT BENÉT, "Glamour" (1935)

Violent Fascinations

F. Scott Fitzgerald, with characteristic quippyness, charts the rise and fall
of an era in his essay "Echoes of the Jazz Age," from "the general decision
to be amused that began with the cocktail parties of 1921" to something
that by 1927 appeared much darker. Noting the widespread neurosis of a
generation (epitomized in the buoyant letter of a friend who fails to note
his new address at a "nerve sanatorium") and a marked increase in tragedy,
Fitzgerald writes:

> By this time contemporaries of mine had begun to disappear into the dark
> maw of violence. A classmate killed his wife and himself on Long Island,
> another tumbled "accidently" from a skyscraper in Philadelphia, another
> purposely from a skyscraper in New York. One was killed in a speak-easy
> in Chicago; another was beaten to death in a speak-easy in New York and
> crawled home to the Princeton Club to die; still another had his skull crushed
> by a maniac's axe in an insane asylum where he was confined. These are not
> catastrophes that I went out of my way to look for—these were my friends;
> moreover, these things happened not during the depression but during
> the boom.[1]

Yet, despite the murder, tragic accidents, suicide, and acts of unspeakable
brutality, this is the age that Fitzgerald, and generations since, imbue with a
lost and poignant glory. Glamour, it would seem, comes out of the darkness
and feeds not only on the gloom of the ghostly spring, as Stephen Vincent
Benét finds in the word glamour itself, but also on the violence and cruelty

that Fitzgerald captures so forcefully in his obituary for the Jazz Age. With the end of the First World War, violence was transmuted, cloaked in the appeal of an age more associated with parties than with tragedy. In this chapter I read two works that center on the particular violence of glamour (apart from the battlefield) and argue that they, in fact, enshrine glamour as the ghostly rumble or deathly effect through which we perceive beauty, a beauty indistinguishable from illusion: first, *The Great Gatsby,* arguably the most glamorized novel of the twentieth century, and second, Katherine Mansfield's lesser-known short story, "Je ne parle pas français." While Fitzgerald's book is saturated with the longing for a prior golden age, and Mansfield's story, rather, is soaked in self-conscious irony, each work comments on the darkly seductive power of language: Nick Carraway as he writes his memoir of the late Gatsby and Mansfield's narrator as he relishes the cruelty he has authored. Glamour then will be created in language whose deathly effect becomes thematically central as each of these works comments on the writing that covers over a fundamental and painful absence. Violence here does not appear with the literal force of a blow to the head or a bullet sustained on the battlefield; violence instead inheres in representation itself and becomes part of the affective texture of the works. Glamour, emerging from the language of these fictions, appears as form, as a kind of formal violence that acts as a veil and distracts the reader's attention away from the pain that drives the narratives. Glamour, this chapter will show, emerges from *and* depends on that dark maw of violence that characterizes the Jazz Age and feeds its pleasures.

No novel, of course, more famously thematizes glamour than *The Great Gatsby:* young Jimmy Gatz from North Dakota transforms himself from a rural boy with few prospects into an urbane millionaire through a teenage disciplinary regimen, the dream of marrying a girl well outside his social standing, and a fantastically lucrative connection with a black-market underworld.[2] The transformation also results from a five-year apprenticeship aboard Dan Cody's yacht, where he was employed in "a vague personal capacity" and learned how to exploit the "savage violence" of brothels and saloons while not mirroring that violence as Cody "the pioneer debauchee" (106) did. The Jay Gatsby who surfaces years later in West Egg, Long Island, is a spectacularly sober figure who owns an extravagant car, an opulent mansion where he hosts lavish parties attended by movie stars and other celebrities, and whose wealth nevertheless sparks rumors of danger, murder, and organized crime.

While the thematic representation of glamour emerging from the extreme wealth the novel depicts has informed popular readings of *Gatsby,* it hardly explains the reach of its seduction: Fitzgerald's novel stands in for the glamour of the 1920s and celebrates a certain, if corrupt, depiction of American opportunism and the belief in the transformative power of individual agency. But this reading of glamour elides the trauma that Fitzgerald recounts in his essay and that gives *Gatsby* its force, and fails to explain the lingering power of desire that the novel portrays. Neither does this version of glamour account for the violence of the text. Physical violence appears throughout the narrative—there are three car accidents, a broken nose, a fatal collision, a rumored murder, a shooting, and a suicide—although the danger barely ripples the sedated surface of the novel's glamorous world. Violence in fact appears in multiple forms: through the physical brutality that punctuates the text (even Gatsby's name has violence embedded in it: "gat" is slang for "pistol"), the social violence on which the power of Gatsby and the Buchanans depends, the violence of fascination that arrests the narrative gaze in the novel, and the ruptures in the text itself that will betray its own vulnerability to penetration despite the high polish of its surface, thus raising the larger question of surface and textual depth. Fitzgerald's novel creates a world based on surfaces as it produces the idea of the novel itself *as* surface—that is, flat, reflective, and without the psychologizing depths that might compromise its brilliant exterior. This insistence on externals, the necessary illusions in a world characterized by multiple levels of violence, is elemental to the novel's glamour, even if we discover the exterior is a ruse to compel the attention away from the novel's central anguish.

The glamour that clings to and defines *The Great Gatsby* does not therefore emerge only from the spectacle of glittering parties but from Fitzgerald's formal decisions, including the lyricism that exists alongside the novel's violence, and conveys the intense desire of its narrative voice. The novel may ostensibly narrate Gatsby's impossible desire for Daisy Buchanan, but it is the voyeuristic yearning of its narrator that produces the far more interesting expression of desire. Not that he admits to it: Nick Carraway has carefully established himself, from the earliest pages of the novel, as a singularly upstanding member of the privileged class who is privy to the secrets of "wild and unknown men" (5). These confidences, he claims, are unsought and largely unwanted since the "intimate revelations of young men or at least the terms in which they express them are usually plagiaristic and marred by obvious suppressions" (6). The irony is, of course, that the story he narrates offers a slow and extended revelation of the secret to Gatsby's glamour and his own (obviously suppressed) seduction by that figure. Nick carefully assembles a tale built of gorgeous facades, spectacular parties, and the mysterious figure of Jay Gatsby, yet what the fascinated narrative covers over, with the help of its lyric layer of prose, is the trauma that motivates its telling and drives it forward. The prose throws an anaesthetizing chill over the painful events as, for example, in the novel's penultimate act of cruelty, the car accident that moves the plot inexorably toward its conclusion. Gatsby's car is about to kill Tom Buchanan's lover, Myrtle, and Nick writes: "and so we drove toward death in the cooling twilight." The figure of cooling twilight—the light draining, the heat dissipating, the horror building—finds a lyrical equivalent in the mode of narration. Here, the movement toward death is beautiful and divorced from any perceptible feeling. Language operates not just as distraction, then, but also as a crucial component of the cold movement toward death.

The Great Gatsby is a story about fascination and its all-consuming transport, even if Nick, in his desire to see himself as a detached and highly sensible observer, repeatedly denies his fascination for his neighbor: "Reading over what I have written so far, I see I have given the impression that the events of three nights several weeks apart were all that absorbed me. On the contrary, they were merely casual events in a crowded summer, and, until much later, they absorbed me infinitely less than my personal affairs" (62). Of course, Nick doesn't record these other affairs and he cannot erase the impression that he has succumbed to the charm of Gatsby's parties (indeed, he will later write, "I spent my Saturday nights in New York because those gleaming, dazzling parties of his were with me so vividly that I could still hear the music and the laughter faint and incessant from his garden and the cars going up and down his drive," 188). Gatsby's parties are the moth-attracting light ("In his blue gardens men and girls came and went like moths among the whisperings and the champagne and the stars," 43), the "swaying shiny point" that Roland Barthes, commenting on the effects of fascination, suggests "makes your head swim."[3] Fascination, the dominant mode of perception in the novel, grips Nick despite his repeated insistence on his stance as disinterested observer.

Fascination, etymologically linked, as Ackbar Abbas writes, "with dubious practices like witchcraft and the casting of spells which deprive one of any power of resistance... now connotes the irresistibly attractive. However, the old meaning has not been completely obliterated. We are reminded time and again that in the allure of fascination lies a lure."[4] Fitzgerald's text works through the ambivalence that Abbas notes in the state of fascination. Nick is drawn to the image, fetishizes it, and is mesmerized by its glossy surface: "My incredulity was submerged in fascination now; it was like skimming hastily through a dozen magazines" (71). At the same time, he attempts to maintain a critical voice, an interpretive interest in the veracity of Gatsby's story, even as he falls under its spell. Nick, who is self-conscious *and* enthralled, appears to react against the collapsing of reason that fascination would seem to precipitate. In Jean Baudrillard's account, fascination "does not stem from meaning, it is rather exactly proportionate to the alienation of meaning....Meaning is morally outraged by fascination."[5] Certainly Nick, his sense of reality and illusion collapsed, looks to the language of morality to provide him meaning, even if that meaning is itself only an illusion. Nick's relentless search for meaning through a carefully contrived account of the summer's events will be ruptured by the ghostly desire that surfaces in his narrative and disturbs his own careful ordering of events.

Early in the novel, Nick tells us that his tolerance has limits, that he wants "no more riotous excursions...into the human heart" (6). Yet, just as quickly, he makes a crucial caveat: "Only Gatsby, the man who gives his name to this book, was exempt from my reaction—Gatsby, who represented everything for which I have an unaffected scorn....No—Gatsby turned out all right at the end" (ellipsis added). Moral attention, stasis, and reactionary posturing may seem to present the only comforting solution in the face of loss—of meaning and of Gatsby—but Nick will not give up his fascinated stance when it comes to Gatsby and thus remains on precarious ground. We know that Nick's attitude to the world is defined by those "fundamental decencies"—he refers to the opinion of others, fantasizes about meetings "that no one would ever know or disapprove" (6, 61)—yet here we also recognize an intense interest that Nick tries to dismiss, even as he narrates his own potentially compromising fixation. Nick creates an elaborate deflection from two painful facts in the highly polished surface of his story. His story both shields him from the fact of his own desire and the violent loss of its object. Sublimation certainly, but here I am interested in the aesthetic choices our narrator (whether Nick or Fitzgerald) makes in order that he may inhabit the stillness of the glossy surface, the formal choice to find compensation for an unbearable loss in the pleasures of the surface.

Gatsby's Body

Fitzgerald will move between the material and immaterial realms in his tale of desire and its repression. Indeed, Gatsby is less a body in Nick's account than a successful series of gestures, an immaterial fantasy shaped by Nick who will cover over the materiality of Gatsby's body—and the harsh reality of its violent end—through an insistence on the beautiful effects of a static world; in so doing, he produces a glamour that veils Gatsby's loss and masks the penetrability of the carefully constructed surface of the novel. Creating Gatsby as an aestheticized object, Nick can retroactively undo the painful impact of his death. While Jay Gatsby no doubt signified glamour in life, in death he will become its pure emblem—unreachable, the locus of unspeakable desire, yet static and ultimately empty, the lost and irrecoverable object.

The description of Gatsby's murder late in the novel provides the clearest account of the narrative attention to this void. There is no grandiose gesture here, just a defeated retreat through yellowing trees as Gatsby makes his way toward the pool that had so lately been the scene of his spectacular parties. Myrtle is dead, Daisy has returned to Tom, and Gatsby now faces his own colossal failure:

> He must have looked up at an unfamiliar sky through frightening leaves and shivered as he found what a grotesque thing a rose is and how raw the sunlight was upon the scarcely created grass. A new world, material without being real, whose poor ghosts, breathing dreams like air, drifted fortuitously about…like that ashen, fantastic figure gliding toward him through the amorphous trees. (169)

The account, delivered through the omniscience of Nick's fantasy, gives us a view into the natural world, imagined as surreal and grotesque in Gatsby's last vision, bereft now from illusion. Materiality, the solidity of forms, evaporates just as quickly as the novelty of the new. The appearance of familiar images—sky, leaves, rose, trees—as distorted and shapeless objects casts them into a dreamscape laced with horror. The unreal landscape appears populated by ghosts: we know the ashen figure is George Wilson, gun in hand, his dreams of a new life aborted when Gatsby's car slammed into the body of his wife. The shot that kills Gatsby as he floats in the pool will not be described. Instead, the image of dream-breathing ghosts—somehow real *and* unreal, material *and* immaterial—describes the paradoxical and wistful production of the novelistic world.

Nick finds Gatsby framed by the pool, floating on a pneumatic mattress whose novelty once amused his guests:

> There was a faint, barely perceptible movement of the water as the fresh flow from one end urged its way toward the drain at the other. With little ripples that were hardly the shadows of waves, the laden mattress moved irregularly down the pool. A small gust of wind that scarcely corrugated the surface was enough to disturb its accidental course with its accidental burden. The touch

of a cluster of leaves revolved it slowly, tracing, like the leg of a compass a thin
red circle in the water. (170)

Gatsby's body is here not directly described, it is simply the weight, the burden carried by the floating device, a ghostly accident, barely disrupting the
surface of the pool. The leaden circles that circulate so strikingly (with the
ring of Big Ben) through *Mrs. Dalloway* (which I discuss in greater detail in
chapter 3) and mark both the movement of time and the fixing of its effect,
appear here as the thin red line of circling blood. The curving red line is
figured as the rendering of a mechanical utensil, a compass, tying Gatsby's
blood to the tracing of Nick's pen as it circles around Gatsby's painful absence. Gatsby's blood, the only material sign of his body and its murder that
Nick provides us, spreads like ink on the page. The reality of the dead body
is practically effaced by the lyricism of Nick's description; paradoxically, the
lyric phrasing circles what it will not name, the painful image of Gatsby's
corpse. The body will not appear, only its tranquil setting, beautified and
lyric; no ugliness is allowed to penetrate the poetry of Gatsby's final scene.

The vagueness of Gatsby's body in this scene builds on the long-standing
struggle Fitzgerald had to give his character definition. Indeed, Maxwell
Perkins, Fitzgerald's editor, had earlier worried about the vagueness of
Gatsby's material presence. He commented on reading the novel in manuscript form: "Gatsby is somewhat vague. The reader's eyes can never quite
focus upon him, his outlines are dim. Now everything about Gatsby is more or
less a mystery i.e. more or less vague, and this may be somewhat of an artistic intention, but I think it is mistaken. Couldn't *he* be physically described
as distinctly as the others"?[6] Fitzgerald responded by saying he would repair
Gatsby's vagueness by making him more "pointed,"[7] yet later corroborates
Perkins' impression in a letter to John Peale Bishop after the novel's publication: "You are right about Gatsby being blurred and patchy. I never at
any one time saw him clear myself—for he started as one man I knew and
then changed into myself—the amalgam was never complete in my mind."[8]
Fitzgerald calls this *Gatsby*'s "lack"[9] in a letter to his friend Edmund Wilson,
referring to criticism of the story's triviality: "the lack is so astutely concealed by the retrospect of Gatsby's past and by blankets of excellent prose
that no one has noticed it—tho everyone has felt the lack and called it by
another name."[10] Fitzgerald is referring to the weak emotional backbone
of the novel and his (in his mind) inadequately drawn account of the love
between Daisy and Gatsby, yet his nervous boasting about the impenetrability of his writing, his "blankets of excellent prose,"[11] is telling. While Woolf
worried that readers would not recognize the value of her prose because

of the "glitteriness" of her writing,[12] Fitzgerald hoped glitter might provide him some cover. Beautiful writing can distract from, if not ultimately cover, the lack that Fitzgerald associates with weakness and inadequacy and in fact becomes the name for that lack.

Yet, despite his confidence in the distraction he can create through writing, Fitzgerald does mention his "distress" and the bad habit he calls "word consciousness—self doubt"[13] in letters that refer to his writing process. An exasperated letter to Perkins in 1921 makes plain his grievance with the very substance of writing that is always compromised by the fact of the body: "Excuse the pencil but I'm feeling rather tired and discouraged with life tonight and I havn't [*sic*] the energy to use ink—ink the ineffable destroyer of thought, that fades an emotion into that slatternly thing, a written down excretion. What ill-spelled rot!"[14] The material (and permanent) mark on the page, Fitzgerald remarks in disgust, is figured not just as the body's waste matter excreted in ink, but as that "slatternly thing," the stain of the sloppy and sluttish woman. Thought is thus contaminated by its material product and perverted, feminized, and seduced by the desire that fades and destroys the purity of the idea through the filth of the word. Even Fitzgerald's self-disgusted expression—"What ill-spelled rot!"—suggests a frustration with the mechanics of his composition (his poor spelling), a decay he apparently cannot expel. Fitzgerald's remarks, written no doubt in hasty irritation, betray not just his fear that his writing is shit but also his frustration with the inevitable contamination of thought by the body. Writing, in giving expression to the body's filthy materiality, defiles the pure image and threatens the unfaded idea he wants to represent. Words thus threaten the purity of the image—in the novel's case, Gatsby—incorporating the body in ways that defile the very thing they hope to maintain, commemorate, or linger over.

Far from expressing simply tired annoyance, Fitzgerald's letter brings the workings of language to the surface, drawing from remarkably similar images as those used by Jacques Derrida when he refers to Ferdinand de Saussure's approach to writing as clothing or artificial exteriority. He writes: "What is intolerable and fascinating is indeed the intimacy intertwining image and thing, graph, i.e. and phoné, to the point where by a mirroring, inverting, and perverting effect, speech seems in its turn the speculum of writing.... Representation mingles what it represents." This is, in that view, a "dangerous promiscuity and a nefarious complicity between the reflection and the reflected which lets itself be seduced narcissistically."[15] The language Derrida employs reflects the concerns expressed by those—especially those like Nick—who fear the seduction of writing that steals from the subject its status as autonomous and rational and damages a depth associated with the purity of origins through the distraction of the surface, figured in Fitzgerald as both base materiality and the distraction from that materiality. It is the perceived sanctity of origins that is at stake in the suspicion toward language according to Derrida: "In this play of representation, the point of origin becomes ungraspable. There are things like reflecting pools, and images, an infinite reference from one to the other, but no longer a source, a spring. There is no longer a simple origin.... There is an originary violence of writing because language is first, in a sense...writing" (99). Representation cannot be understood as having a referent that remains untouched by representation: referent and representation reflect, distort, and contaminate the other in an infinite and promiscuous dialectic that undoes and commits violence on any notion of a pure source or origin. Gatsby's pool, its surface inscribed by the trace of his blood, thus may be seen as signifying the violence of language itself, Gatsby himself as the ungraspable origin.

Writing *Gatsby* a few years after his tired outburst to Perkins, Fitzgerald would attempt to suppress the pleasures and anxiety of writing in this narrative whose overt subject *is* seduction. Although he aligns himself with Gatsby in what he admits is an uneasy amalgamation, Fitzgerald expresses sentiments that likewise characterize his narrator: Nick of course describes Gatsby in technologized terms—hard, precise, machine-like, yet sensitive—"as if he were related to one of the intricate machines that registers earthquakes," counterpoising this to the "flabby impressionability which is dignified under the name of the 'creative temperament'" (6). Careful to distinguish Gatsby from the flabby or effete, Nick suggests his own ambivalence about his position as a narrator whose creative temperament betrays itself mirroring Fitzgerald's own well-recorded ambivalence about his "softness" ("I'm sick of the flabby semi-intellectual softness in which I flounder with my generation," he writes in the same letter to Perkins quoted above). Nick attempts to establish his manly disdain for effete prose when he declares that he was "rather literary in college" while denying any creativity in the "series of very solemn and obvious editorials [he wrote] for the 'Yale News'" (8). Thus Nick aligns himself with obvious and masculine prose that gives away nothing: in so doing he tries to remove his body from the text, thereby nullifying its embarrassing desires that could unmask the controlled authority he assumes.[16]

Yet the body inevitably floats back to the surface. Nick, for example, commenting on his own narration, breathes life again into Gatsby: "So I take advantage of this short halt, while Gatsby, so to speak, caught his breath, to clear this set of misconceptions away" (107). At the time of writing, of course, Gatsby is dead; Nick halts his narration to give Gatsby his breath, to infuse him with life. Later, when he describes the aftermath of his death, he writes that Gatsby "lay in his house and didn't move or breathe or speak hour upon hour" (172), as if he there was still hope he might get up and fill the house once more. Gatsby's body, present and not present, haunts the language and very writing of the text, its breathlessness inducing the writing. In fact, writing, in *Gatsby,* seems to require breathlessness; Fitzgerald comments that all good writing should not breathe: "All good writing is swimming under water and holding your breath."[17] Barbara Hochman notes that "Nick himself is repeatedly 'breathless' when 'compelled' into spellbound attention, not to 'worlds,' but to 'words.'" She comments that "by repeatedly underscoring the illusion-destroying, disenchanting effects of bodily presence, the novel demonstrates the strategic advantages of written over spoken language.…the act of writing becomes an act of separation, of distancing."[18] The novel may be about the loss of illusion (Fitzgerald wrote to a friend in 1924: "That's the whole burden of this novel—the loss of those illusions that give such color to the world so that you don't care whether things are true or false as long as they partake of the magical glory"),[19] but in writing illusion returns and produces an even greater effect. Faced with Gatsby's confidence in reliving the past, a past that he will attempt to reproduce with the exactitude of a photographic image, Nick writes: "Through all he said, even through his appalling sentimentality, I was reminded of something—an elusive rhythm, a fragment of lost words, that I had heard somewhere a long time ago. For a moment a phrase tried to take shape in my mouth and my lips parted like a dumb man's, as though there was more struggling upon them than a wisp of startled air. But they made no sound and what I had almost remembered was uncommunicable forever" (118). Nick's voice—and breath—might fail him, but his writing, although it might *expose* him, does not fail. His communication through the record he constructs seems designed to give breath to the breathless body, to mask its absence and cover over the lack that Nick's limitless desire both suffers and enjoys. One most effectively masks the painful effects of absence and desire, Fitzgerald finds, by creating a glassy surface that cannot be penetrated, as the illusion of Jay Gatsby was ("'Jay Gatsby,' had broken up like glass against Tom's hard malice and the long secret extravaganza was played out," 153) or as Gatsby's body would be by the fatal bullet.

Through his chronicle of the summer, then, Nick attempts to exert a retroactive control, but a control that is tenuous at best as he tries to maintain his dispassionate and squarely masculine stance. Tracing, metaphorically, the thin red circle of Gatsby's body is thus a dangerous activity and Nick's fascinated storytelling places him in anxious proximity to the curves and lines of what he might construe as feminine prose. When Daisy suggests that he reminds her of a rose, "an absolute rose," Nick responds: "This was untrue. I am not even faintly like a rose" (19). While humor motivates Nick's response, one might read anxiety as well. To be a rose is to be an object, feminized and made decorative, and is not without an element of the grotesque, its soft lines too easily aligned with those of a woman, as Nick's image of Gatsby's last vision indicates. Nick's quick response to Daisy's remark suggests that he hears that he is the rose, that he could be made into the fetishized object whose delicate lines are most conventionally associated with women, and specifically women's genitals. Gatsby's wound, bleeding rose-like into the water, could represent Nick's own. The anxiety of castration—Nick's fear that he is the rose bleeding into the water—is, in Freud's theory, countered by the creation of a fetish. The fetish object substitutes for loss, serving as a mask to distract from the absence of the missing object: the fetish remains, according to Freud, "a token of triumph over the threat of castration and a protection against it. It also saves the fetishist from becoming a homosexual."[20] The portrayal of Gatsby that Nick narrates and anxiously enjoys serves a fetishistic role: he can invest the object of his fetishizing desire with the power to protect him from loss, although the portrait only points to the very absence that occasions it.

The creation of a fetish also offers Nick protection from his own desire and the feminizing effects of glamour that threaten to overwhelm his own masculine stance as impartial observer, providing him a fantasy of distance from the lack he associates with the female body and mirroring Fitzgerald's own need to distance himself from what he imagines to be feminine prose. "The fetish," writes Gilles Deleuze, "is not a symbol at all, but as it were a frozen, arrested, two-dimensional image, a photograph to which one returns repeatedly to exorcise the dangerous consequences of movement, the harmful discoveries that result from exploration."[21] The fetish creates a surface onto which desires may be safely projected, and in *Gatsby* that surface is the image of Jay Gatsby, vague and shadowy, as he appears in the form of narrative. Certainly the novel is distinguished by its fanciful prose as in this passage in which Nick (whose omniscience as narrator appears only in moments of fantasy) imagines Gatsby in bed at night, again on a mattress laden with fantasy:

The most grotesque and fantastic conceits haunted him in his bed at night. A universe of ineffable gaudiness spun itself out in his brain while the clock ticked on the wash-stand and the moon soaked with wet light his tangled clothes upon the floor. Each night he added to the pattern of his fancies until drowsiness closed down upon some vivid scene with an oblivious embrace. For a while these reveries provided an outlet for his imagination; they were a satisfactory hint of the unreality of reality, a promise that the rock of the world was founded securely on a fairy's wing. (105)

The blanket of prose is thick here, covering over the naked desire (note the wetness, the tangled clothes, the embrace) of the narration. The ideological fantasy of glamour that is safe, tied to luxury consumer items, and invested in the capitalist desire for limitless supplies of money is both embellished and overturned in this passage by the sheer seduction of its excess: there is something grotesque and ineffable in the fantasy, something linked to a world without restraint or rules, but one ruled by the force of seduction.

Emily Apter and William Pietz offer a reading of fetishism in which the stasis that defines the fetish produces a paradoxical effect: "Fetishism as a discourse weds its own negative history as a synonym for sorcery and witchcraft (*feitiçaria*) to an outlaw strategy of dereification...a consistent displacing of reference occurs, paradoxically, as a result of so much fixing. Fetishism, in spite of itself, unfixes representations even as it enables them to become monolithic 'signs' of culture."[22] In its associations of sorcery and witchcraft, fetishism shares something with glamour. Glamour, with its etymological roots in magic, enchantment, and the casting of spells, is also that thing that cannot be fixed or contained. Its emergence from stasis, even from the necromancy that marks its earliest usage, produces a space of desire that appears to be vivifying, although this space itself is an illusion. Modernist literature may be most fascinated with the possibilities of creating life in a medium that bestows death and represents its own state of fascination as a violence enacted on the person it engages through stasis, arrest, and the proximity to death. The modern intuition that language is equal to lifelessness (one state of breathlessness), that textuality can only provide an illusion that will be repeatedly upset by its own ghosts and spectres, is thus manifested by the novel's insistently smooth writing.

Superficial Aesthetics

Many critics at the time of the novel's publication noted the hard, impenetrable quality of the surface in Fitzgerald's novel, and this effect, as I have been suggesting, was not accidental. While immersed in its writing, Fitzgerald himself remarked to Perkins: "This book will be a consciously artistic achievment [*sic*] + must depend on that as the 1st book did not."[23]

The critics for the most part concurred that the book was an artistic success: described as "brilliant," "glittering," "sparkling," "carefully devised," "restrained," as casting a "calculated glamour" with the extraordinary "power to throw a spell over the reader," reviewers claimed the novel to be a mixed success, praised its "rare and beneficent essence we hail as charm," but questioned its triviality and "hardness." The story, writes one critic, "for all its basic triviality, has a fine texture, a careful and brilliant finish. The obvious phrase is simply not in it. The sentences roll along smoothly, sparklingly, variously." Another writes, "He envelopes his characters in a glamorous texture." While the novel's narrative received some critical attention, it was its surface that critics seemed to find most compelling. One critic suggests that there is no place for accident in *The Great Gatsby:* "It is beautifully and delicately balanced; its shapeliness is the more praiseworthy for the extreme fragility of the material. It is an almost perfectly fulfilled intention. There is not one accidental phrase in it." Although there may be no accidental phrases, the review continues, "In reproducing surfaces his virtuosity is amazing....He is more contemporary than any newspaper, and yet he is...an artist. But he has not, yet, gone below that glittering surface except by a kind of happy accident, and then he is rather bewildered by the results of his own intuition."[24] The reviewer claims that Fitzgerald's writing dazzles not just the reader but the author himself and thus his rationality is too blinded to produce the stuff of a great, or substantive, novel. Fitzgerald's prose, reflecting the technologized world that characterizes its cultural moment, elicits critical dismissal because it does not provide substance, a body that can be viewed. Writing is conceived of as *mere* surface adornment, and Fitzgerald's writing is faulted for not being transparent but polished and flashy, deflecting the gaze from the meaning it should instead reveal. In creating prose that casts such a brilliant reflection, the critics suggest that the novel's writing ultimately threatens to dumbfound, even mortify (in the sense of control or subdue) the reader, the text, and the author with its distracting gleam.

These reviewers correctly recognize the novel's primary concern with surface appearance and the all-pervasive image that dominates the novelistic landscape, most explicitly in the billboard gaze of Dr. T. J. Eckleburg.[25] Fitzgerald's aesthetic strategies work to both fashion and direct the gaze in writing and to create characters as luminous screens *and* impenetrable objects who play to the desires of those around them by engaging (and arresting) the eye, even as they do so with apparent indifference; Fitzgerald thus creates characters as images, not drawn with psychological realism, but as effects who gain shape through fixation, repetition, and highly contrived gesture. Gesture is neither spontaneous nor natural, but analogous to the image of an image (and so on) captured on film. We know that, as far as Nick is concerned, personality is an "unbroken series of successful gestures" (6) whose success is based on how well the gestures convince or produce a desired effect. Personality, then, is another manifestation of the spectacle, where every interaction is mediated by the image, and every subject is shaped by a version of itself that is produced for and through the gaze of others.[26]

The characters of Tom and Daisy Buchanan and Jordan Baker are also presented only insofar as they create an image, make an impression, or fill the frame. Bodies, like that of the gold-hatted, high-bouncing lover of the novel's epigraph, are used to maximum effect, posed with their desires externalized. First Tom: "The front was broken by a line of french windows, glowing now with reflected gold and wide open to the warm windy afternoon, and Tom Buchanan in riding clothes was standing with his legs apart on the front porch" (11). Tom's wealth, virility, and power are emphasized in this picture that reads like a photographic still. Jordan and Daisy are introduced in a similarly posed way; the dreamy quality of the scene emphasizes their movie-set presence: "The only stationary object in the room was an enormous couch on which two young women were buoyed up as though upon an anchored balloon. They were both in white, and their dresses were rippling and fluttering as if they had just been blown back in after a short flight around the house.... Tom Buchanan shut the rear windows and the caught wind died out about the room, and the curtains and the rugs and the two young women ballooned slowly to the floor" (12). Floating, as if on helium-filled balloons, their forms are subject to the momentary whims of the air currents that buoy and sustain them. Air is not life-giving but trapped, propping them up in their environment of static perfection. The women are detached, characterized by an empty and abstracted ennui, without appetite and bearing only some vague association with mortality. Their figures are fixed and immobile like "silver idols" (122): Jordan Baker "was extended full length at her end of the divan, completely motionless, and with her chin raised a little, as if she were balancing something on it which was quite likely to fall. If she saw me out of the corner of her eyes she gave no hint of it" (13). Jordan's eyes do not return one's gaze, do not bestow subjectivity on her observer: instead, she is both the narcissistic vision of woman as consumed by her own image and the image of the image in an age mediated by mechanical reproduction.[27]

Daisy and Jordan, presented as flat and impenetrable images, their remoteness signifying their distance and inaccessibility, talk with a "bantering inconsequence" that is "as cool as their white dresses and their impersonal eyes in the absence of all desire" (16–17). As objects, they are as artificial, as impermeable as the photograph or the photographic apparatus. Their sedated luxury is underscored by Daisy when she greets Nick: "I'm p-paralyzed with happiness" (13). With little investment in anything but the image they project, they float throughout the narrative, bumping up against the desires of others, yet never feeling the impact. Daisy, the ostensible object of Gatsby's quest, whose voice of "warm human magic" (115) ripples throughout the text, is hardly more material than the green light that shines across the bay and becomes her enchanted substitute in Gatsby's fantasy. Daisy's voice exudes luxury, all that money can buy, and with every word she bestows the power of wealth on her listener. This indeed is Daisy's charm. Not simply situated in her own wealth, her good looks, or her youth, it rests in her ability to make her admirer rich. To hear the rolling cadences of money in Daisy's voice is to be transported (as in the scent of Chanel's perfume), to assume the wealth, for the moment, as one's own.

Gatsby works to imitate the effect of Daisy's voice through a gross display of his own wealth. Part of Gatsby's mislaid plan of seduction is to create grand exhibitions that will represent his worth synecdochically to Daisy. At times, this strategy achieves some success, as when Daisy bursts into tears on seeing his collection of beautiful shirts: "'They're such beautiful shirts,' she sobbed, her voice muffled in the thick folds. 'It makes me sad because I've never seen such—such beautiful shirts before'" (98). His car will produce, he hopes, a similar effect as it is designed to draw attention to his wealth—it is one of his most garish possessions, what Tom dismisses as a "circus wagon" (128)—and is meant to signify, therefore, his utter desirability. The automobile conjoins technology, sexuality, and the sexual fetish and will, Gatsby wagers, act as an irresistible substitute for him. It also exemplifies the lessons taken from his mentor, Dan Cody, whose yacht (the *über*-fetish) "represented all the beauty and glamor in the world" (106) to the young Gatz, who would, aboard its railed deck, become Gatsby. In one of the novel's early scenes, Nick is introduced to the gleaming lines of Gatsby's glamorous car and is impressed, excited, and somewhat horrified by the vehicle's ample proportions:

> He saw me looking with admiration at his car.
> "It's pretty, isn't it, old sport." He jumped off to give me a better view. "Haven't you ever seen it before?"
> I'd seen it. Everybody had seen it. It was a rich cream color, bright with nickel, swollen here and there in its monstrous length with triumphant

hatboxes and supper-boxes and tool-boxes, and terraced with a labyrinth of windshields that mirrored a dozen suns. Sitting down behind many layers of glass in a sort of green leather conservatory we started to town. (68)

Gatsby watches Nick look at his car, apparently imagining his admiration at its swollen and lengthy dimensions. The car is spectacular in its excess and, mirroring a dozen suns, repudiates the gaze of unwanted lookers through its maze of glittering surfaces that reflect the narcissistic image of its occupants. At the same time, the car invites stares ("Everybody had seen it") even as it deflects the gaze through its mirroring glass. The multilayered surface of glass not only establishes the distinction between inside and outside—a boundary the novel is most invested in exploring and ultimately maintaining—but also refutes and undercuts any sense of physical integrity and thus foreshadows its catastrophic trip through the valley of ashes. When the car's gargantuan libidinal excess meets the erotically charged body of Myrtle Wilson, two worlds will collide—one associated with the flat, breathless surface and the other with an overly material, warm-breathing and sensuous body. The car indeed becomes the agent of penetration, and Gatsby's body will in some sense achieve the substitution he sought but without the effect he intended.

The desensitized world of the novel—its embrace of modern technology, meaningless appetite, and bored abstraction—favors the distancing effects of technology over the closeness of bodies like Myrtle's and will stage the showdown between them in the valley of ashes, steel against organic and messy materiality. The narration has not looked kindly on Myrtle, who is represented by Nick as always too close, as if her body in its very sensuality pressed in on him: "Myrtle pulled her chair close to mine and suddenly her warm breath poured over me the story of her first meeting with Tom" (40). She blocks the light with her "thickish figure," her dress is "stretched tight over her rather wide hips" (31) and her voice is coarse and loud, unlike the "deathless song" (101) of Daisy's favored voice. Nothing about Myrtle is "deathless" and when her life is extinguished on the dusky road, it will be represented in the text with only the simple phrase: "the business was over" (144). "The 'death car,' as the newspapers called it, did not stop; it came out of the gathering darkness, wavered tragically for a moment and then disappeared around the next bend" (144). The outcome, unlike Gatsby's collision with a fatal bullet, is graphically depicted as if the novel itself wanted to repudiate the messy and organic substance that would detract from its glamour: "The mouth was wide open and ripped at the corners as though she had choked a little in giving up the tremendous vitality she had stored so long" (145). Reduced to a messy and liquid heap in the road, the business is over: Myrtle dies in that flash of light, metal against flesh, her breast torn from her body, her mouth ripped at the corners as if in payment for the blatancy of her embodiment. Fitzgerald exerts on Myrtle the death he will not narrate, that of Gatsby, making hers the body to be penetrated, and making her stand in and pay for the overt desire that Fitzgerald has everywhere suppressed in the exchange between Nick and Gatsby.

It is at the party with Myrtle's inelegant friends around him that Nick, in a well-known passage, narrates: "Yet high over the city our line of yellow windows must have contributed their share of human secrecy to the casual watcher in the darkening streets, and I was him too, looking up and wondering. I was within and without, simultaneously enchanted and repelled by the inexhaustible variety of life" (40). The window, appearing throughout the novel, blooming with light, framing and confining its objects for viewing, will allow Nick to maintain that sense of distance, even as it frames the erotic pleasure he derives from the act of looking itself. Framing himself in relation to windows, Nick makes clear he sees himself as distinct from the scores of party-goers and glamour-seekers that populate the novel, and that difference resides in his belief in his detachment, his judicious and dispassionate view of Gatsby untainted by the gossip surrounding his mysterious wealth. The fantasy of a window view affords him some sense of safety, of distance from his own compromising fascination as he participates with the doubled and self-conscious position of consumer and participant, voyeur and object within the frame. The window provides Nick a sheltering screen and the sustained elation through watching, keeping the enchanted and repulsive events available and in view, yet safely, he mistakenly believes, in the distance. The window here also "dramatizes the isolation of the onlooker," writes Michael North, although the view is never neutral.[28] In North's argument, Nick requires visual experience that is mediated, as if by a camera, that maintains the illusion of distance, so that his pleasure will not be compromised. Indeed, "Fitzgerald thus associates Nick, as a character and as a narrator, with a modernized visuality that undoes the old association of vision with reason and authority by emphasizing all the ways that visual pleasure misleads and disarranges" (127).

In response to the threat of dissolving boundaries that would destroy the coherence of his narrative, Nick (and Fitzgerald)[29] writes an account that defies its own penetration—making the desire invisible, and thus unreadable. The surface of Fitzgerald's apparently impermeable prose is nevertheless ruptured at revealing moments. One such moment of puncture occurs as Nick recounts those alluring evenings when crowds gathered at Gatsby's.

The puncturing event is a memory so overwhelming as to float unmoored out of the past and into the present tense:

> The bar is in full swing and floating rounds of cocktails permeate the garden outside until the air is alive with chatter and laughter and casual innuendo and introductions forgotten on the spot and enthusiastic meetings between women who never knew each other's names. The lights grow brighter as the earth lurches away from the sun and now the orchestra is playing yellow cocktail music.... The party has begun. (44–45)

The present erupts into the past, as if Nick could once again inhabit those lost moments, creating a moment of *punctum,* Roland Barthes's term for the prick that disrupts the carefully constructed surface and makes one experience the upheaval of the smooth photographic image. The *punctum,* a term associated with the visual image but here resonant with the visually conceived form of the novel, breaks the surface—disrupting the logic of its own temporal representation—and, in textual form, emblematizes Nick's wound, his desire to return to the past, or to make it present with all the strength of his former unwitting illusion. Nick's text opens up, triggered by the electric fantasy of the evening as it *happens,* with continuing riotous promise, and reveals the wound, the "sting, speck, cut, little hole" (27) that is the accident that, Barthes writes, pricks and bruises in its poignancy.[30]

A further textual rupture that collapses past and present with the insistence of the gaze occurs as Nick discusses Gatsby's obsession with the past, his desire to "fix everything just the way it was before." Nick writes, "His life had been confused and disordered since then, but if he could once return to a certain starting place and go over it all slowly, he could find out what that thing was..." and trails off with ellipses that his next paragraph takes up: "...One Autumn night, five years before" (117). Nick shifts into an omniscient fantasy of the first kiss between Gatsby and Daisy, then shifts back into his own narrative, this moment suggesting his own wish to fix the past like a photographic image that he can go over slowly, to savor if not understand the past pleasure that continues to confuse and disorder his life. The ellipses, their points punctuating the text, themselves puncture it and signal the omission that, through repetition, becomes visible, as in a scene in which the narrator focuses on the body and the stain it leaves behind. On a "broiling" day, Nick makes his way to East Egg from the city, his "train emerging from the tunnel into sunlight," a woman perspiring beside him, and a hot conductor collecting tickets: "My commutation ticket came back to me with a dark stain from his hand. That anyone should care in this heat whose flushed lips he kissed, whose head made damp the pajama pocket over his heart!" In this strange passage where heated bodies and their flushed lips combine, we follow Nick from his hot and solitary journey on the commuter train to the Buchanans' front door, where he waits with Gatsby, their meeting apparently substituted by those elliptical punctuation points. The next paragraph begins with an ellipsis:

> ...Through the hall of the Buchanans' house blew a faint wind, carrying the sound of the telephone bell out to Gatsby and me as we waited at the door.
> "The master's body!" roared the butler into the mouth-piece. "I'm sorry Madame but we can't furnish it—it's far too hot to touch this noon!" What he really said was "Yes...Yes....I'll see." (121)

Nick imagines the butler roaring about the heat of the master's body, and without explanation or even acknowledgment of his fantasy writes, "What he really said was..." How does one explain this fantasy moment where bodies that appear sweating, kissing, and pressing against one another are replaced with the master's body itself and the arrival of Gatsby? The body leaps out of the text in Nick's exclamation, yet his text would deny it as it moves forward into the next scene of more seemly repression.

The hole, the wound, the lack, the thin red circle in the water, the shit on the page, the gap in the text, the rupture of chronology: each, it would seem, opens up to interpretation, while resisting the violence that interpretation would impose through the very force of its rationality. Nick appears to want it both ways: to be the active and impartial interpreter of Gatsby and the passive participant of his own text's seduction. I have been suggesting that Nick's narration and his ambivalent fascination have demonstrated his desire to have Gatsby, although that desire is always veiled by the luminous image he constructs in Gatsby's place and by the impenetrable surface of prose that covers Gatsby's absent body. Writing, in the novel, is predicated on the breathlessness of the dead body that haunts the narrative as it tries to bring the body to life while at the same time masking its materiality. Nick's desire thus circles around Gatsby, creating those gaps in continuity, logical holes, and textual ruptures in the narrative, even as he works to erase that impression, using his narrative authority as a form of subterfuge. The logical questions, then, that have interested critics about the novel—why, for example, did Gatsby die, who knew what, did Tom Buchanan know that Daisy was driving, and did he send George Wilson nevertheless to murder Gatsby—become moot, themselves insignificant against the novel's glamorous and violent aesthetic. While they may point to wider moral questions, the novel is more interested in those shameful spaces of desire that morality endeavors to legislate and that must be rendered invisible. In the end, we learn that the "huge incoherent failure of a house" where Gatsby once lived is defaced by some boy's "obscene word" (188). As one of his last gestures in West Egg, Nick will erase its stain with his shoe; his final act of denial befits our narrator and is perhaps the most appropriate end to a narrative whose glamour rises out of its excess, the vision of the exceptional, and the effect produced by the object of desire that will appear, a ghostly accident and ghostly burden, only through the image in writing. Glamour, the externalized effect of Gatsby's violent death, is visible only on the surface, its gloss almost impenetrable, its writing wary of the necessary compromise of words themselves.

Glamour depends on illusion, an illusion that is mediated not only by the artifice of language but by the echoes of technology that come to shape our relationship to language in the early twentieth century; glamour signals a new and dehumanized order of desire that will occupy and disturb not simply the writings of modernism but also the critical discourses that insist on interiority as its most significant hallmark. I now turn to Mansfield's story because it revels in its excess and in the giddy possibilities of narrative exteriority. No repression is at work in "Je ne parle pas français"; rather, it celebrates the violence at the heart of its writing. Interiority may be modernism's greatest fiction, or greatest ruse: Mansfield stages an experiment in pure exteriority, conceiving her characters like a collection of sundry articles. Her narrator explains: "People are like portmanteaux—packed with certain things…thrown about, tossed away, dumped down, lost and found…squeezed fatter than ever" (76). Characters are framed by tabloid images, tattered wallet photos, mug shots, and postcard pornography: the narrator will shuffle through these images, pulling one or the other at random to demonstrate not only his own linguistic proficiency and delight in the dehumanized frame that technology provides but also his mastery over the players in the performance he directs.

Mansfield's Fatal Glamour

Mansfield, like Fitzgerald, reflects on the seduction of the gorgeous phrase throughout her story, "Je ne parle pas français,"[31] yet without the wistfulness that characterizes *Gatsby*. Indeed, rather than submerge the tale of erotic fascination and the sordid functions of language, Mansfield exploits them in her parodic tale of writerly narcissism. In this cynical narrative, she plays with a notion of pure exteriority, creating characters who are little more than surfaces, who cannot be plumbed for their depths, but who remain, often exasperatingly, superficial and without any attribute to suggest their humanity. Glamour, in this story, is figured as cold, indifferent, and foreign (and here Mansfield prefigures the Hollywood glamour of such figures as Theda Bara, Marlene Dietrich, and Greta Garbo). Here, the otherness belongs to the French, although we know that the modernist gaze often casts itself farther afield in determining the exotic, primitive, or glamorous object. While Gatsby's glamour depends on a dream, the brash illusions fostered by the promise of "America" in the 1920s, Mansfield will explore a vision far less naive. Her rendering of the French subject will be bolstered less by a promise of the bright and shining future than by a legacy she associates with decadence.

"But Lord! Lord! how I do hate the french," writes Mansfield in one of her notebooks. "With them it is always rutting time. See them come dancing and sniffing round a woman's skirts."[32] She writes, at about the same time as her disgusted notebook exclamation, the story whose title, "Je ne parle pas français," carries not simply an expression of inability but a statement of refusal: I cannot and will not speak French. To speak French, it would seem, would be to enter into a moral and spiritual void, a world of insincerity, superficiality, and unchecked pleasure. Mansfield's story will explore cruelty and its imaginative possibilities, using a native French-speaker, a self-declared "true Parisian"[33] as narrator and villain. The French langue, of course, is also the French tongue, a tongue with a taste for pleasure and a facility with the figure, especially in its metaphorical form. The French tongue is eroticized, made both alien and somewhat dangerous in its capacity to fascinate. The convergence of langue and illusion through fiction will produce a glamour predicated on violence, a glamour that fascinates and repels, attracts yet spells annihilation for all that is soft, pure, and innocent.[34]

Mansfield's story, like many other modernist narratives, functions through ambiguity, evading meaning as part of its narrative strategy, while simultaneously satirizing its own evasions. The story goes like this: Raoul Duquette, the story's narrator, meets an Englishman, a writer with a dreamy half smile, a low, soft voice and, not insignificantly, excellent French. They become inseparable, until Dick suddenly leaves Paris to return to England. Some time later, Raoul receives a letter from Dick asking that he find rooms for him and a female friend. Once they arrive in Paris and are shown the rooms, Dick disappears, leaving only a letter explaining that he could not hurt his mother in this way and has returned to England. Raoul assures the abandoned woman, Mouse, that he will not desert her and that she has in him a reliable friend. Yet he does leave her to fend for herself in the strange city.

The story ends as it begins, with Raoul in his favorite café, musing over the story. From the beginning, he has been congratulating himself on his writing talent. Reaching over to the next table for paper, or some such surface to inscribe, for example, Raoul remarks:

> No paper or envelopes, of course. Only a morsel of pink blotting-paper, incredibly soft and limp and almost moist, like the tongue of a little dead kitten, which I've never felt. I sat...rolling the little dead kitten's tongue round my finger and rolling the soft phrase round my mind while my eyes took in the girls' names and dirty jokes and drawings of bottles and cups that would not sit in the saucers, scattered over the writing pad. (75–76)

Writing produces its victim, inscribing death with lascivious attention in its cold and heartless phrase. Whatever is sweet and guileless cannot survive: the morsel of blotting-paper, designed to stem the excess materiality of writing itself, becomes an image of bodily refuse, the kitten's tongue rolled between the writer's fingers, a necessary death for the production of modern prose. The cat has lost its tongue, and Raoul revels in the excision: nothing sentimental will mar his pages (and here Mansfield seems to predict the clean and athletic prose that will soon be executed by Ernest Hemingway, language shorn of all that superfluous fluff that is so anxiously disavowed by Fitzgerald).

Rolling the phrase around his mind as he might a good wine on his tongue, Raoul continues: "But then, quite suddenly, at the bottom of the page...I fell on to that stupid, stale little phrase: Je ne parle pas français" (76). The French language, it would seem, gets in the way of the kitten's tongue, barring the morbid vitality of one image with the stale obstruction of the other. The combination produces a surprising result:

> There! It had come—the moment—the geste! And although I was so ready, it caught me, it tumbled me over; I was simply overwhelmed. And the physical feeling was so curious, so particular. It was as if all of me, except my head and arms, all of me that was under the table, had simply dissolved, melted, turned into water. Just my head remained and two sticks of arms pressing on to the table. But, ah! the agony of that moment! How can I describe it! I didn't think of anything. I didn't even cry out to myself. Just for one moment I was not. I was Agony, Agony, Agony. (76)

One can hardly forgive this Frenchman, or so the story's logic goes, for the excess of his emotion, the glee with which he describes his pain, the performance that bespeaks only a parodic display of emotion in this passage of masturbatory repetition. The kitten's tongue, a dead phrase, the girls' names, lewd jokes, the exuberant and repeated expression of Agony—all combine with the force of a creative, if sordid, explosion. Whether Raoul at this moment responds to memories produced by the French phrase, or whether his geste reflects the gestation of an idea, a moment of inspiration, is not clear. What is clear is that this is a version of the modernist moment, not the eternal moment we might associate with E. M. Forster, nor the Bergsonian or Woolfian moment where an instant of time contains the fullness of life, the five-act play Clarissa Dalloway, for example, experiences in a fleeting vision, but a trashy and perishable moment that will, nevertheless, circulate throughout the story.

The French phrase, then, in its very staleness, its failure to breathe life, its static repetition by those who would reject comprehension, operates like a charm or a fetish, as Gatsby and the glassy surface of Fitzgerald's novel had, to the writer who takes the obdurate words as a challenge and stimulus. The words on the soiled page operate similarly to that of the fetish, sharing its deathly arrest and impenetrable surface: the narration will simply rest on the surface, reveling in its own production with little pretense to psychic or other exploration. Rather, the phrase, now without meaning, becomes an object of both disgust and fascination that prompts Raoul to further narrative production, and thus further pleasure. Certainly the narrative mode is both autoerotic and antisocial: Raoul, as he sits alone in the café, writes to the image he admires in the mirror before him, his narcissism providing the form, if not substance, of his narration. His style is nothing less than flamboyant, his pose fixed, his narrative composed of digression, his effect notably and openly queer.

Yet sexuality, in this vision, is captured in tawdry poses, cheaply framed and mildly pornographic: Raoul's libido strikes one as indiscriminate, his self-styling aimed at winning admiration and perhaps some quick cash; over the course of the story, he will present himself as a seductive baby, a perfumed terrier, a prostitute, a pimp, a rejected lover, and the celebrated writer of notorious themes. He writes and reads before mirrors, catching the vision of himself and adjusting it for maximum effect and for his own (and our) solitary pleasure: "I confess," he writes, "that without my clothes I am rather charming. Plump, almost like a girl, with smooth shoulders, and I wear a thin gold bracelet above my left elbow." Then he adds, "But wait! Isn't it strange I should have written all that about my body and so on? It's the result of my bad life, my submerged life. I am like a little woman in a café who has to introduce herself with a handful of photographs. 'Me in my chemise, coming out of an eggshell. . . . Me upside down in a swing, with a frilly behind like a cauliflower. . . .' You know the things" (83). Sexuality is both queer and nonrelational in the story: it is a pleasure to be accessed through narrative, a narrative that refuses connection between beings and inserts instead the lens of the camera, the titillation of pornographic poses, and the unlimited possibilities for extended and repeated cruelty, an eroticized cruelty, that Raoul's writing allows him to savor. Mansfield's story is not an erotic one, but it hovers at the borders of that submerged world, enjoying while safely disdaining its pleasures from an English vantage point that is, throughout the story, associated with the authentic.

Modernism might enshrine the notions of depth, interiority, and authenticity—as critical discourse has always claimed—but in so doing, it entombs any notion of authenticity in the captured image, the breathless phrase, hoping, it would seem, to fend off this other knowledge, this vision of a depthless surface reflected in the provoking form of Raoul Duquette. As modernist narrator, Raoul surrenders any idea of authenticity in the face of his own performance, but one senses that Mansfield herself has not given up on the representation of truth and sincerity—a truth that may be sustained as long as one does not enter the French language. The static phrase "je ne parle pas français" thus may be a placeholder of authenticity for Mansfield, if not for Raoul, the uncorrupted site that bars the eroticism and therefore degeneracy of the other language. It is not Raoul, after all, who utters that "stale little phrase" in the story he subsequently narrates, but Mouse, the fragile, exquisite, frightfully English girl who is abandoned by her lover, Dick. Clad in fur, stroking her muff nervously (Raoul refers to her grey fur muff as Mouse II), Mouse certainly is no Venus in Furs, but the sacrificial victim to a cruelty that will be associated not with her lover but Dick's jealous admirer, our narrator.

In the end, however, Raoul will write, "Je ne parle pas français. That was her swan song for me" (114), summing up Mouse's creative role: the phrase, revised now into a tragic gift, Mouse's performance of suffering and beauty, acts as the sharpened instrument for his morbid pleasure. It is never clear whether he has fabricated the tale of the beautiful Dick and the pathetic muff named Mouse, or if he is indeed recounting past events. And, in any case, it does not matter. Raoul—writer, narcissist, libertine—asserts his omnipotence and cruelty in this story, exacting his pleasure from writing, a writing that will be itself a form of violence perpetrated on its characters, its readers, and on the fantasy of meaning. What meaning the story offers is the meanness of narrative, the pleasure in making the dead phrase live, infusing it with blood that it might suffer exquisitely once more. Writing is an ongoing production of fatality for Mansfield, an exhilarating immersion in the seduction of language.

Mansfield's writing offers its own insistent revision with its knowledge of the cruelty on which beauty depends, the pain that feeds art and makes writing luminous. In a letter from wartime France, she describes a scene of domestic bliss:

> And then came our little house in sight. The outer door of our villa was open....When I reached the stone verandah, and looked again upon the almond tree, the little garden, the round stone table, the seat scooped out of stone...and then looked up at our pink house, with the swags of shells painted over the windows and the strange blue grey shutters I thought I had never, in my happiest memories, realized all its beauty....As I came down your beautiful narrow steps—it began to rain. Big soft reluctant drops fell on my hands & face. The light was flashing through the dusk from the light house and a swarm of black soldiers was kicking something about on the sand among the palm trees—a dead dog perhaps or a little tied up kitten.[35]

The shock of cruelty pierces the descriptive veil yet works to intensify the pleasure of the preceding words. Cruelty demands, perhaps, the translucent veil, the fantasy of indifference, a cover for the inescapable pain that modernism relentlessly presents us; here too we recognize Nick Carraway's narrative mode. This, in the end, will be the fatal glamour offered by both Fitzgerald and Mansfield: the cool indifference and rejection of feeling that both characterizes the narrative experience of modernism and provides some compensation for its violence. Mansfield may wish to remain uncorrupted by those pleasures she associates with the French, pleasures that suggest for some a rejection of discipline and morality, yet these pleasures, like writing itself, extend one's reach and allow new narratives, so that the soiled page might no longer read "je ne parle pas," but instead simply, and in Raoul Duquette's lusty accent, "je parle."

Just as modernism looks back while insisting on its progression, like Walter Benjamin's angel of history overlooking the clutter and catastrophe of historical making, or Nick's boat beating endlessly on against the current as it is borne backward, Nick records the collapse of meaning through fascination while attempting to create its substitute image in language. Mansfield, in turn, represents that collapse in the cruelty of Raoul and the ambiguity of his motives. The loss of illusion is the central painful event that befalls many of Mansfield's characters and certainly all of Fitzgerald's—from Amory Blaine, to Anthony Patch, to Nick Carraway, to Dick Diver. As Amory Blaine's world collapses around him toward the end of *This Side of Paradise*, he feels "like a face in a motion-picture,"[36] the aura fade and realizes later that this was a moment of death. Physical death—in Amory's mind signified by the "dynamic shadow" (248) lifted swiftly by a breeze—and death of illusion are equally destabilizing: Nick, like Amory, will find the ability to continue, to live without the pleasures and intoxication of illusion, in the stalwart codes of convention. Glamour may have kept these men going, as it did the young Kurtz-obsessed boy in *Heart of Darkness*, but it is glamour that threatens them too. The question that hangs over these stories of the Jazz Age is "Why go on?" But, of course, they do go on: "As an endless dream it went on; the spirit of the past brooding over a new generation, the chosen youth from the muddled, unchastened world, still fed romantically on the mistakes and half-forgotten dreams of dead statesmen and poets."[37] Glamour, the ongoing appetite for illusion, and the rejection of the base material that might dull its shine, motivates this generation to follow, inevitably, the dream of success and the enchantment of life lived within a gorgeous bubble, or at least within the gorgeous phrase.

3 : PHOTOGRAPHY

Scenes and groupings torn out of the impetuous life of the hour are
suddenly made momentous, given a new glamour and significance.
And that, one likes to believe, is, after all, the special function of this
newborn art of ours.

—DIXON SCOTT, *The Amateur Photographer* (1909)

The Radiance of Form

When Virginia Woolf undertook a contract with *Vogue* in 1924 to write
four articles, some saw it as her selling out to the commercial interests of
the glamour industry. In the rich language of Hermione Lee: "*Vogue,* with
its reports on the parties and the shows and the upper-class beauties, and its
directives on the shorter, straight skirts, the feathers and fringes, the backless
evening dresses in metallic colours, the capes and cloches, the shingled (or
bingled) hair, the jerseys and the elegant underwear, might seem a far cry
from the *Nation* or Hogarth Press."[1] Woolf, along with many of her Blooms-
bury compatriots, contributed to the fashion magazine and were criticized
(Woolf in particular) for "descend[ing] from the heights" to "scatter…pearls
in Mayfair." Woolf, however, did not see it this way and remarked to Vita
Sackville-West, "And what's the objection to whoring after Todd [*Vogue*'s
editor]? Better whore, I think, than honestly and timidly and coolly and re-
spectably copulate with the Times Lit. Sup."[2] Woolf's vexed relationship to
fashion would suggest that this was not, at any rate, where her investments
lay, and indeed, her partnership with *Vogue* didn't last very long. In this
chapter, I suggest that Woolf did not in fact locate glamour in the traditional,
or obvious, arena of couture and the "fashion papers,"[3] yet she was deeply
invested in finding glamour, or producing it, in the language of her novels.

Not that she named it as such. Woolf sought to capture the luminous
effect, the heightened sense of desire focused in an exquisite moment;[4] this
interest would be most readily apparent in *Mrs. Dalloway*. This novel, often
framed by critics as an extended elegy, studies stilled time and produces

an effect of writerly glamour, created through the photographic or deathly moment and circling around the what-might-have-been that the photographic frame allows its viewer to consider. Just as Dixon Scott imagines the photographic moment when a scene, torn out of its sequential narrative, is made glamorous,[5] Woolf will imagine a work that operates according to a grammar shared with photography. Whether it is the violence of the action, the unlikely stasis produced from impetuous life, or the borders provided by the photographic frame, the effect is significant, momentous, and specific to the medium of photography. What is the relationship between glamour and this "newborn art"?[6] Scott's terms are central and in this chapter I consider the effects of stasis, the excision of time, and the role of fantasy in photography. I am most interested in seeing how these effects in turn become visible in modernist writing. While many disparaged the medium of photography (hardly understood in those years as an art form, despite the diversity of approaches by Alfred Stieglitz, Man Ray, Berenice Abbott, Paul Strand, Laszlo Moholy-Nagy, and others), they integrated the medium's visual forms of representation into their own narratives. Modernists may have disapproved of any form of mimetic claim, but their work was often and importantly influenced by the increasing attention to visual media and the experience of a visual culture.[7]

Woolf was interested in the conditional tense—and particularly the past conditional tense—to which the photograph, most particularly, gives access. She thus investigates a relation to time that is not stable or absolute but contingent, the conditional of desire that turns away from the future toward the material gathered from the enchanted and illuminated past, and turns toward the future in the possibilities it offers and the possibilities offered by her new brand of fiction. *Mrs. Dalloway* writes the problem of writing glamour—tracing its luminous envelope, going beyond the complexities of writing the image—and creates an ecstatic stasis as the image of desire. A nostalgic longing for a more beautiful past suffuses Woolf's novel as she works to recover lost enchantment—the "glamour of the past" she refers to in her autobiographical "A Sketch of the Past"[8]—through her prose form that relies on the moment torn as if by the century's "newborn art" from the tyranny of sequential time.

The reader here might find it at the very least peculiar to link *Mrs. Dalloway* with photography, given the novel makes no explicit claim to the visual form. More than a decade later, Woolf would offer an explicit analysis of photography in her antiwar polemic *Three Guineas*. Here she focuses on its representational function in a time of war, the crude "statements of fact addressed to the eye" that triggers a fusion of memory and feeling. And here it is a violent sensation one experiences in response to war photos, their violent content pressing on the viewer.[9] I am not interested in the analysis of war-time photos but rather in the less mimetic possibilities of photography, the grammar it opens up, its influence on modernist prose as a way of framing memory, desire, and the capture of a lingering moment. Indeed, from its opening line, *Mrs. Dalloway* shares something with the formal grammar of photography. When Marjorie Perloff writes: "The very opening sentence of a 'successful' modern novel—say, 'Mrs. Dalloway said she would buy the flowers herself'—would point obliquely but surely to the novel's central theme and structure. *Reading,* under these circumstances, became a riveting experience, culminating in what we had learned to call an epiphany: the underlying *form* of the work became radiant,"[10] she points to the novel's particular light. The novel's succinct opening line does tell a great deal about the narrative that awaits its reader and, as Perloff puts it, the radiant form that Woolf works to produce. Compressed in the novel's first sentence are past, present, and the past conditional reporting of Mrs. Dalloway's future-tense statement "I will buy the flowers." Not that this is a novel about strict grammatical tense: the novel rejects any grammar that insists on indissoluble lines separating the tenses. In essence, it corrupts grammar, the system that maintains the rules of chronology and the firm boundaries between lived and about-to-be-lived time. *Mrs. Dalloway* is most concerned, even fascinated, with the moment, that highly subjective instant of time that is able to stop motion in a flash, suspend time, and allow a vision that might otherwise roar by in the rush of a day's events. This vision, created in a moment of suspension, thus shares many attributes of the photograph and produces glamour—its radiance, glitter, and beauty—in its language. Predicated on absence, loss, and the desire to hold the past in the shimmering light of the present, glamour promises a different narrative, one built on those desires that linger, circling around the scenes, acts, or events that might have been and that exert their influence on the what will be.

Of course, Woolf meditates on the moment in much of her work, and most explicitly in her essay "The Moment: Summer's Night," in which she asks, "Yet what composed the present moment?" and answers, "If you are young, the future lies upon the present, like a piece of glass, making it tremble and quiver. If you are old, the past lies upon the present, like a thick glass, making it waver, distorting it."[11] The medium of memory in Woolf's image is glass, the flat, reflective surface offering a metaphor for the unstable present, always distorted by past and future. The Woolfian moment, as Jane Goldman points out, has "exercised critics" who explain its "elusive qualities" through the Bergsonian notion of "la durée," that is, the spatial rather than sequential experience of time, or, as Goldman herself argues, as a moment implicitly connected to the material world and therefore with implications for feminist politics.[12] Here, rather than seek the material difference that Woolf's moment makes, or the almost mystical experience explained through "la durée," I want to consider the ways that *Mrs. Dalloway* creates a language of glamour through its attention to light, stasis, and the framed image that might produce a momentary, and momentous, terror and ecstasy, a reformulated sublime that I have been calling glamour.

In *Mrs. Dalloway,* this glassy convergence of time marks Clarissa's earliest memories of Bourton narrated on the novel's first page. The passage begins with an exclamation in the present that merges immediately with the past:

> What a lark! What a plunge! For so it had always seemed to her, when, with a little squeak of the hinges, which she could hear now, she had burst open the French windows and plunged at Bourton into the open air. How fresh, how calm, stiller than this of course, the air was in the early morning; like the flap of a wave; the kiss of a wave; chill and sharp and yet (for a girl of eighteen as she then was) solemn, feeling as she did, standing there at the open window, that something awful was about to happen.[13]

The exuberant present-tense cries ("What a lark! What a plunge!") followed by Clarissa's memory of Bourton convey the immediacy of a past that will not remain firmly embedded in history. Clarissa sees herself, bird-like, plunging out the window and through the air at Bourton; moving back in time, she is next framed by the open window, solemn and still, with a premonition that something is about to happen. Memory and the recollection of the future merge in the strange slip of tenses that reminds Clarissa of the anxiety she felt at that moment in the window. Something awful was about to happen she remembers feeling, layering the past over the future. The past, hardly something that has ended and been petrified in memory, remains flexible and prone to emerge at any given moment. The future also lurks in the memory (the future perfect, the what will have been), and throughout the novel we are aware that backing and illuminating every thought Clarissa has is the knowledge of the party she will give that evening. The merging of time and tense in this passage provides the first glimpse of the diffusion and arrest of time that will characterize Woolf's experiment in modernist form.

Like Walter Benjamin, Woolf presents a version of aesthetic experience that is linked to a transformation in subjectivity and perception. Benjamin, of course, argues that these new modes of experiencing the world and its images come via technical advancements in various media. While Woolf offers no explicit commentary—at least in this novel—on mechanical reproduction in the early part of the century, she certainly posits an altered subject, one shaped by the historical events and conditions of the day. Yet Woolf's subject—fragmented, diffuse, and diaphanous—cannot be reduced simply to a question of history or context. Rejecting the conventions of realist fiction—conventions Woolf would tie to historical authority—she creates in Clarissa Dalloway a character who performs her own identity and understands the necessity of putting on a face specific to each occasion she encounters. She is both tremendously connected to the exigencies of society and completely isolated from that same world. While much about Clarissa is in fact conventional (her ties to class distinction, her tastes, her carefully self-monitored behaviors), she is radically fractured, a character who stands outside herself and wills definition on herself: "She pursed her lips when she looked in the glass. It was to give herself point. That was her self—pointed; dart-like; definite. That was her self when some effort, some call on her to be her self, drew the parts together, she alone knew how different, how incompatible and composed so for the world only into one centre, one diamond, one woman who sat in her drawing—room and made a meeting-point, a radiancy."[14] Clarissa's sense of alienation emerges from the knowledge that the disparate and incompatible elements of her character cannot be unified. Nevertheless she is able to perform the appearance of unity and with the metaphor of a diamond—that privileged stone bearing the promise of one's heterosexual value—Clarissa glitters, outshines her expensive setting and appears impregnable. This self-creation as the point, the dart, the diamond center—akin to Judith Butler's concept of the "stylized repetition of acts" that constitutes identity[15] and gives the illusion of unity—provides Clarissa with some sense of invulnerability and impenetrability. Her performance of the multiple facets of identity like the facets of a delicately cut stone will be majestic as she prepares for the evening's grand event. Woolf at one point in her writing of the novel worried that this character might be "too stiff, glittery & tinsely,"[16] yet these attributes give a luminous presence to Clarissa Dalloway.

The Body through the Lens

Clarissa does not share the timeless physical quality of the diamond but wears her recent illness in the pallor of her face. While she must live according to the unforgiving time of the human body, she nevertheless inhabits a perceptual world bound not by an insistent futurity but by the fluid wash of past, present, and future times. Woolf may have initially called her novel "The Hours" but even the changing of the hour, that most arbitrary marking of the passage of chronological time, creates a momentary rent in its workings: "One feels…Clarissa was positive, a particular hush, or solemnity; an indescribable pause; a suspense…before Big Ben strikes. There! Out it boomed, First a warning, musical; then the hour, irrevocable. The leaden circles dissolved in the air."[17] Time is at least momentarily stalled until the boom, the leaden circles fill the air, then dissolve. The mechanics of Big Ben, produced in the name of future-oriented progress, nevertheless inspire a suspended moment, free from the mechanics of movement and the relentless forward motion of time. The leaden circles represent the visually-rendered remainder of the chiming bells but could also figure another figure, or metaphor, for the act of writing (or *ekphrasis,* of writing the image, and here, the verbal representation of a fantasy image). The circular panes of leaded glass through which Woolf observes might be figured as not only the striking bell but also a round window (and this novel has a penchant for windows) or a camera lens. They mark the remains of a movement that has already taken place, a frozen instant of time—one could almost imagine the striking of Big Ben to be the click of a camera—the pause beforehand, the suspended motion, the sustained pose, the suspense before the flash.

The transformation in subjectivity that Woolf depicts is tied to those modes of technical perception that produced, in the nineteenth century, a newly framed face with unprecedented temporal effects. Photography was thus hardly new in 1925 (in fact it would soon near its centenary), but its forms had achieved a cultural ubiquity that would come to define the twentieth rather than the nineteenth century. Like the early photographic sequences of Eadweard Muybridge that would reveal, for the first time, the surprising motion of a horse's legs at full gallop, Woolf provides momentary fragments of time that are illuminated in contrast to the ordinary and numbing experience of mechanical time. Muybridge's photographic series of the racehorse Occident in 1878 were met with shock: the unpredictability of the movement demonstrated the inadequacy of the human eye in appreciating detail, and, in a moment, a centuries-old assumption was corrected by the photographic sequence. Beaumont Newhall writes: "Though the photographs were hardly more than silhouettes, they clearly showed that the feet of the horse were all off the ground at one phase of the gallop—but to the surprise of the world, only when the feet were bunched together under the belly. None of the horses photographed showed the 'hobby-horse attitude'—front legs stretched forward and hind legs backward—so traditional in painting. The photographs looked absurd."[18] While Woolf may have written that she was "galloping" through *Mrs. Dalloway,* her work reveals the unseen motion that photographing the gallop allowed Muybridge to reveal and provides a view of the normally invisible interimplications of past, present, and future. Woolf's method, while not mimicking photography, nevertheless shares attributes with the camera's product: just as the photograph has a relation to the past that is neither stable nor assured, the past without notice swells up throughout the events of the June morning chronicled, or better, framed and captured in *Mrs. Dalloway.*

Woolf was no particular fan of photography, although her knowledge of it was great, as numerous critics have shown. Woolf, writes Maggie Humm, was an "inveterate photographer" herself since childhood and was, of course, aware of the celebrated portrait photography of her great-aunt, Julia Margaret Cameron, which Hogarth Press published with an introduction by Woolf herself.[19] Yet her ambivalent and frequently hostile response to the growing number of photographers also shows itself in much of her work. A photograph, or a Kodak-wielding character, appears in every one of her novels, generally denoting a shallow tourism, a false sense of the past, mere decoration, or the bourgeois attempt to be artistic. Woolf's depiction of Lady Bradshaw's interest in photography in *Mrs. Dalloway* echoes Baudelaire's more aggressive commentary in 1859: "As the photographic industry was the refuge of every would-be painter, every painter too ill-endowed or too lazy to complete his studies, this universal infatuation bore not only the mark of a blindness, an imbecility, but had also the air of vengeance."[20] The photograph provided the material illustration of a superficiality that Woolf abhorred, its mimetic capacity perhaps reminding her of the aesthetic forms she was attempting to renounce in her literary work. The arrested image in her review essays enjoys no more respect than her fictional references. Woolf, in her 1918 book review "The 'Movie' Novel" castigates the author for the shallowness betrayed by the quick pacing of the book: "As in a cinema, one picture must follow another without stopping, for if it stopped and we had to look at it we should be bored." In a review of Joseph Hergesheimer's fiction in 1919, Woolf writes dismissively that his images "seem to recur to the photographic figure, to be arrested in their development."[21]

Woolf's description of the photographic image in her last novel, *The Years,* reveals a more complicated ambivalence toward the photographic image (rather than simple hostility) and demonstrates Woolf's continued return to and fascination with the snapshot image. Toward the end of the novel, North Pargiter returns to England from a long residence in Africa.

As he reflects on the impoverished circumstances of his cousin, a larger consciousness enters his description, as if Woolf herself merges with her character, and both surmise: "These little snapshot pictures of people left much to be desired, these little surface pictures that one made, like a fly crawling over a face, and feeling, here's the nose, here's the brow."[22] The snapshot reduces its subject to a collection of anatomical features that are barely discernible in such fragmented proximity. Woolf gives a sense not only of the parasitic nature of photographers but also of an implicit link to death within the frame of the snapshot. The face that would allow a fly to traverse it from nose to brow without twitching would likely be that of a corpse. The image here is cold in its close-up of an occurrence that would normally be accessible only through the journalistic photograph. There is an abject quality to Woolf's description as the photograph frames the face in such proximity that its viewer identifies with the insect that climbs over its pores. As Benjamin might agree, there is no humanity in the camera image, only the cold remains that entice not the warmth and reciprocation of a human gaze but only the perambulations of a fly. The camera eye in *Mrs. Dalloway* is also not removed from the spectre of death: the reader is made aware of the life-threatening illness that still clings to Clarissa from the earliest pages of the novel and will soon experience the suicidal visions of Septimus Smith. Death hovers over the novel, as it does the photographic image. The focus in *Mrs. Dalloway* will not be on the individual features, the overexposed pores and hollows of the characters' faces, but in the effect of its human remains. Much can, and has, been written about Woolf's various opinions of the photographic medium, but more relevant for my purposes is her own use of the still image and its power to reformulate time.

Woolf, then, while not approving of the snapshot reduction of people to "surface pictures," does indeed focus on the arrested image in *Mrs. Dalloway,* creating her novel as a series of single frames. The camera-like sequencing of the novel has not gone unnoticed by critics. Joseph Allen Boone has, for example, noted the "cameralike gaze" of the novel's field of vision: "For Woolf imaginatively simulates in prose of what is called in cinematic terminology the continuous take—the craning long shot moving in for a close up."[23] While Boone focuses on the seamless movement of the camera as it circumnavigates from outside to inside, I prefer to consider the stopped time of the photographic frame that Woolf's images evoke. Boone writes that the "use of present-tense participial phrases generates forward motion; their litanic repetition creates the sensation of action about to be completed, of meaning about to emerge, if we just keep pushing ahead."[24] He argues that there is no stalling of time but a continual propulsion forward, aided by the grammar of the present-tense participial phrase. Woolf's text, however, is equally as interested in the productive stasis of the moment, that instant of frozen time that causes the eye, and the frame, to pause. For example, in our first view of her, Clarissa Dalloway is "perched" motionlessly on the curb of Bond Street "waiting to cross, very upright."[25] Our frame is provided by the vision of Scrope Purvis, whose name suggests voyeurism in its proximity to "scope" and "pervert." Scrope's name carries the weight of the visual apparatus and its erotic interests, yet he is a character we will never meet. Scrope's vision hardly conveys the typical object of the voyeuristic gaze: Clarissa is pictured here as stiff and in suspended motion. Although it is Scrope who holds the privilege of vision in this moment, he will not be seen or heard from again, as if Woolf chooses in the first pages of her novel to discard, however idealistically, the patriarchal authority of the gaze itself. Clarissa authors her own image for the most part in this narrative and is highly aware of the poses she strikes. She sees herself at moments framed (at the mirror, imagining herself in the gaze of others) and fashions her expression and her posture accordingly. Clarissa looks, is seen through, pauses, and is framed by windows throughout the scenes that make up the novel: Woolf's text hesitates, allows the moment to linger in a heightened form, so that its effect will be most fully realized.

The Moment of Glamour

The moment is of particular consequence for Clarissa Dalloway, whose movements will be pictured, often in exquisitely arrested detail, during "this moment of June" (4). Rendering the moment as distinct and set apart from the ordinary passage of time is Woolf's method of slowing down the frame, turning a glance into a sustained observation. There will be no reckless galloping forward of narrative time but the unsteady interplay of past, present, and future that become layered, almost inseparable from the image of Clarissa: reflecting on her age, Clarissa "(crossing to the dressing-table) plunged into the very heart of the moment, transfixed it, there—the moment of this June morning on which was the pressure of all the other mornings, seeing the glass..., seeing the delicate pink face of the woman who was that very night to give a party; of Clarissa Dalloway; of herself."[26] Clarissa is transfixed here, offered to the reader as if framed in a photograph. She, examines the face that is reflected before her as another person might. She sees herself in a stylized repetition, as if in the infinite reflection of a mirror in a mirror, the layered years, images and frames depict a countless number of Clarissa Dalloways. The passage of time comes to a halt as moment on moment is layered. Although Clarissa reflects on her age, the moment is ageless and outside of time. Even her movement as she crosses to the mirror is given in parenthesis, as if occurring in a shadow outside the range of a camera. The moment is highlighted, removed for an instant from the fluid stream of images that course through Woolf's text.

Leo Charney has commented that "the concept of the moment provided a means to fix an instant of feeling" for those theorists of the late nineteenth and early twentieth centuries (omitting Woolf from his list of thinkers that includes Benjamin, Heidegger, and Pater). In Charney's cultural history of the moment, he writes of the new interest in sensation and the attempt to rescue it from the ephemerality of modernity:

> Experiencing a moment…meant feeling the presence of the moment, fully inhabiting it. The moment exists to the extent that the individual experiences immediate, tangible sensation. This feeling is so intense, so strongly felt, that it tapers off as soon as it is first felt. The experience of strong sensation articulates the possibility of a moment both through an intensity of feeling which communicates immediate presence and through the waning of intensity by which the moment contrasts with the less intense moment that follows it.[27]

The momentary, Charney argues, was the "defining trope of the modern" and illustrated the multiple voices, random images and encounters, sensations and fragmentary meanings of the period.[28] Benjamin defines the quintessential modern experience in his essay "On Some Motifs in Baudelaire": "[Baudelaire] indicated the price for which the sensation of the modern age may be had: the disintegration of the aura in the experience of shock."[29] The aura is lost in the intensity of that fleeting shock which framed, for an instant, the flash, the suspense and the illumination of the moment. The thirst for sensation combined with the immediate loss of that sensation once the moment of shock is felt enacts the repetitive currents of desire. Woolf offers her reading of the moment as "largely composed of visual and of sense impressions," adding that "one becomes aware that we are spectators and also passive participants in a pageant. And as nothing can interfere with the order, we have nothing to do but accept, and watch."[30]

The moment does not follow a sequential logic; rather, "no order is perceptible; there is no sequence in these cries, these movements.…Nothing can be seen. We can only see ourselves as outlines, cadaverous, sculpturesque."[31] The moment provides the deathly awareness of one's own stasis, one's sculpted paralysis in the face of the world's spectacle; yet, paradoxically the moment is alive with feeling, the almost overwhelming sensation of an instant. Woolf's novel is awash with such lyric moments, removed from time and the progressive rush forward; the text of these moments is frequently invested in the immediacy, or past immediacy, that surges into the present of desire. The lyric's suspended moment in time, both infused with and drained of possibility, offers a non-narrative model for modernist fiction that Woolf here develops. The suspended moment made available through the photographic image, then, allows lyricism to become the primary mode here and in much of the writing in the modernist era. The moment, suffused with a desire that is tantalizingly present and *almost* satisfiable, inevitably recedes and is replaced by loss, participating in the endless sequence of desire and loss that is highlighted by the extraordinary sensation of the moment.

Woolf writes more autobiographically about the moment in her essay, "A Sketch of the Past," collected posthumously in a volume titled *Moments of Being*. In this memoir, Woolf looks to her own writing process and those flashes of sensation, those "sledge-hammer"[32] blows that overtake and sometimes terrify her, yet lead to a vision in writing: "Though I still have the peculiarity that I receive these sudden shocks, they are now always welcome; after the first surprise, I always feel instantly that they are particularly valuable. And so I go on to suppose that the shock-receiving capacity is what makes me a writer. I hazard the explanation that a shock is at once in my case followed by the desire to explain it....I make it real by putting it into words."[33] Woolf's comments about the shock-receiving capacity, written in 1939, are strikingly similar to Benjamin's comments on Baudelaire, who, he wrote during the same year (in the German original), "placed the shock experience at the very center of his artistic work."[34] Shocks, the moments of being as opposed to the everyday "cotton wool" of nonbeing, are at the heart of the aesthetic experience for Woolf and are associated with the extremes of terror and rapture:

> Perhaps this is the strongest pleasure known to me. It is the rapture I get when in writing I seem to be discovering what belongs to what; making a scene come right; making a character come together. From this I reach what I might call a philosophy; at any rate it is a constant idea of mine; that behind the cotton wool is hidden a pattern; that we—I mean all human beings— are connected with this; that the whole world is a work of art; that we are parts of the work of art. *Hamlet* or a Beethoven quartet is the truth about this vast mass that we call the world. But there is no Shakespeare, there is no Beethoven; certainly and emphatically there is no God; we are the words; we are the music; we are the thing itself. And I see this when I have a shock."[35]

The shock shatters any illusion of individual agency, instead replacing it with a collective sense of humanity as self-authored. A sense of collapse overwhelms Woolf's sensation of the shock, but it is collapse with immensely productive results. In that moment she recognizes the aesthetic potential of the world and the fictionality of any essentialist understanding of the subject. The shock does not reveal any truth except that there is no truth; nothing is unmediated or outside of representation. Woolf gives no sense of interiority when she writes that we are the words, the music, and the performance of greatness; this understanding is built into the character of Mrs. Dalloway, who inhabits a space that is wholly aesthetic, wholly performed, and wholly caught up in surfaces, even if her character is delivered via the interior narrative of indirect discourse. The shock may bring terror or pleasure (the strongest Woolf knows) in the heightened moment that makes its subject vulnerable to the extremes of sensation. Certainly the rapture Woolf describes, exploding over the course of a moment, is orgasmic in its rawness and creative intensity.

In one of *Mrs. Dalloway*'s most famous passages, and one that has undergone the most thorough scrutiny, Clarissa tries to understand the exhilaration of desire—the desire inspired by women—through a reverie on the orgasmic moment:

> Yet she could not resist sometimes yielding to the charm of a woman, not a girl, of a woman confessing, as to her they often did, some scrape, some folly. And whether it was pity, or their beauty, or that she was older, or some accident—like a violin next door (so strange is the power of sounds at certain moments), she did undoubtedly then feel what men felt. Only for a moment; but it was enough. It was a sudden revelation, a tinge like a blush which one tried to check and then, as it spread, one yielded to its expansion, and rushed to the farthest verge and there quivered and felt the world come closer, swollen with some astonishing significance, some pressure of rapture, which split its thin skin and gushed and poured with an extraordinary alleviation over the cracks and sores! Then, for that moment, she had seen an illumination; a match burning in a crocus; an inner meaning almost expressed. But the close withdrew; the hard softened. It was over—the moment.[36]

Able to access the sexual pleasure of women only through speculating about what men feel (and through the prism of her own sexual experience), Clarissa takes the imagery of heterosexual intercourse and feminizes it.[37] In the illumination of the moment Clarissa perceives the possibility of sexual pleasure once inhibition is overcome and the body gives in to its desire. The burning flame in the flower signifies a luminous female sexual desire that remains fragile and is soon and too easily extinguished. Her meaning here is almost expressed but cannot be revealed explicitly as it remains coded, accessible only through the images associated with male sexuality (expansion, tumescence, gushing, withdrawal, softening). Instead the moment wavers perilously between the failure of male/female intercourse and the description of a transformative nonheterosexual sexuality. As if repeating the snuffing of the match, Clarissa's thoughts return to a blundering Richard (and the banality of socks and water bottles), retreating as she did when she married him to the safe, if unsatisfying, haven of heterosexual normativity. Yet the moment here is (homo)sexualized, made orgasmic and filled with the longing for something that remains just outside of one's grasp and outside the bounds of the world Clarissa inhabits. The desire that this passage narrates becomes synonymous with the moment in Woolf's novel and will continue to bear its erotic pleasure and longing. Encapsulated in the crocus passage, therefore, is desire imagined and just out of reach, a beautiful possibility held in prose, like a bee in amber embedded in a gorgeous, and deadly, frame.

From the threatening precipice of sexual desire, Clarissa's thoughts drift to the safety of domestic life and then move again, in smaller steps, toward the exhilaration of sex, in a domesticated mode, through the question of love: "But this question of love (she thought, putting her coat away), this falling in love with women. Take Sally Seton...Had not that, after all, been love?"[38] The moment has created a vision that Benjamin describes when he writes, "The past can be seized only as an image which flashes up at the instant when it can be recognized and is never seen again."[39] The image of Sally arises in Clarissa's mind as fresh and unpredictable as she once knew Sally to be. Neither stagnant nor unchanging, this image will disappear, only to reappear in a different guise. As she considers Sally and the violent interruption, "Like running one's face against a granite wall in the darkness! It was shocking; it was horrible!,"[40] she feels a renewed hostility for Peter, whose appearance altered the course of that evening at Bourton, and perhaps more. The shock of that remembered wall produces new insight: "All this she saw as one sees a landscape in a flash of lightning."[41] Like the photographic flash that allows vision in the dark, Clarissa's moment of shock renews her desire with an immediacy long-forgotten. Memory and desire combine in the flash of that moment, producing the glamour effect of Woolf's writing. Glamour is bound by the desire-infused moment, suspended here in writing that allows us repeated access to it. In the crocus passage, the sexually charged moment cannot sustain its force and dissolves into a question of love, but Woolf will repeatedly reframe the moment throughout her narrative. In fact, the novel is conceptualized as a moment, even, as I suggest, as *this* moment. Woolf's text pauses, as if to reflect on the still form that transfixes its desiring characters—and its desiring reader.

The Grammar of Photography

Desire thus permeates each instant of stalled time in Woolf's conception of her novel. Like Muybridge's photographic sequences that reveal a motion otherwise inaccessible to the human eye, it also betrays a necessarily invisible, or at least encoded, desire. Because of his invention of the zoogyroscope, or zoopraxiscope, a device that projected illuminated images and gave the illusion of motion, Muybridge is often referred to as the father of motion pictures. While this is an appropriate description, his importance rests equally in the creation of the still frame depicting movement as a different kind of text in stopped frames, separated by gaps on the page, and open to different kinds of interpretations. Unlike his contemporary Etienne Jules Marey, whose photographs depicting motion were superimposed within the same frame, Muybridge's are formally laid out in sequences with black bars separating each image. His 1887 sequence depicting the movements of two men in the act of wrestling, for example, documents the initial embrace as the wrestlers' bodies meet. In stopped motion we see each of the movements framed as one body overtakes the other and finally forces it to the ground. The frames show the victor's arms tightly clasped around the chest of his opponent, who is thrown to the mat, his lower body visible and vulnerable to the camera eye. By filming the wrestlers without clothes, Muybridge attempts to provide unencumbered evidence of their gestures and musculature in motion. He also creates a sequence that cannot be read outside the realm of desire. In real time, perhaps, the action would appear as both quick and brutal. In the stopped frames of Muybridge's sequence, however, the contours of the men's bodies as they press together are the text and not the speed and agility of one wrestler as he throws the other to the floor. By halting the forward motion, a space is opened up in which desire may become visible. The temporal thrust, as it were, of the wrestlers is suspended and the almost visceral quality of their touch takes precedence. By removing the action from the temporality of forward motion, then, an erotic narrative emerges that might otherwise have rushed past with the speed of a moving picture.

One of Muybridge's photographs represents a paradox that Woolf's novel is invested in exploring: both photo and *Mrs. Dalloway* raise questions of

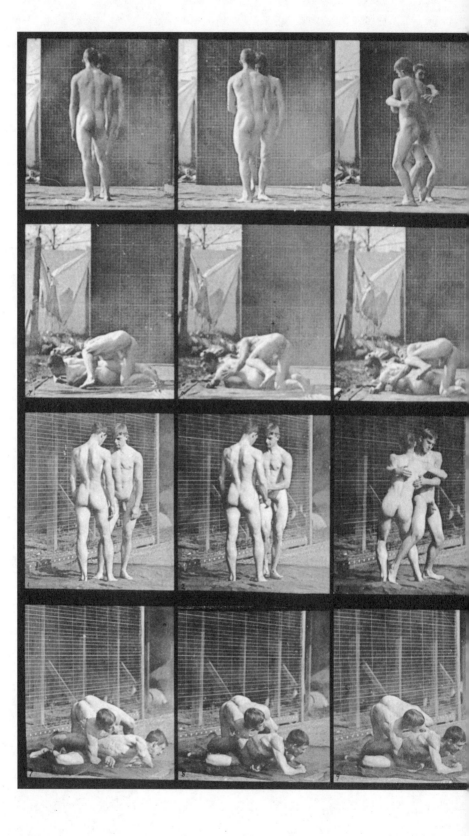

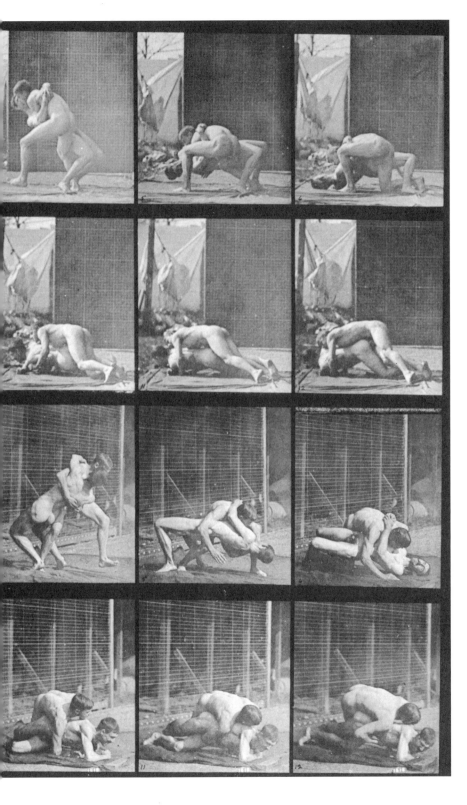

penetrability and the smooth surface. One man, enfolded in the other's arms as he is thrown to the floor, is pictured in a particularly exposed position with his buttocks framed by the camera and vulnerable to penetration. Yet the medium that exposes the buttocks produces an impenetrable surface, one that Barthes has remarked is flat, platitudinous, and resistant to the inquiring eyes of its viewer.[42]

In Woolf's text, both Clarissa Dalloway and Septimus Smith are presented as characters anxious about the possibility or impossibility of their penetration. Is this resistance to penetration a comment on interpretation and the groping eyes of the reader? Clarissa, holding onto a fantasy of her virginal self, retreats in the evening to her tightly-stretched and narrow bed and resolutely maintains a diamond-hard surface that is resistant to penetration. Her sexual desire for men, if ever she felt any, has vanished and only the idea of women wakens in her a momentary, almost frightened, flicker of desire. Even the image long associated with female sexuality, the flower, seems to be removed from the sphere of sexuality: the flowers Clarissa looks over in the shop are described as "exquisitely cool," "dark and prim," pale "as if it were the evening and girls in muslin frocks came out to pick sweet peas and roses."[43] Yet the flowers, delicate like the match in the crocus, bear the promise of an awakening: "it was the moment between six and seven when every flower…glows; white, violet, red, deep orange; every flower seems to burn by itself, softly, purely in the misty beds." The passage moves most subtly from the virginal girl to the red and deep orange flowers burning alone in bed. Sexuality, for Clarissa, is only conceivable as singular, since her desires are unspeakable and only thinkable when translated into the purer language of flowers. Significantly, her thoughts move fluidly from her love of the flowers, her affection for the woman helping her to select them, back to "that monster" Miss Kilman, her daughter's tutor and Clarissa's rival. Hate penetrates Clarissa's fantasy of desire as the parody figure for lesbian sexuality, Miss Kilman, creeps into her thoughts and perverts their flowery eroticism. The text doesn't allow us to linger over this moment of overt sexual anxiety, however, and the "pistol shot," the "violent explosion" of a car interrupts Clarissa's thoughts.

But what of glamour? Desire, Woolf's novel demonstrates, is most suited to memory, the contingent, the past conditional tense, non-absolute, unknowable, the what-could-have-been, what-would-have-been. Surely desire is at its most excruciating in the longing for what-could-have-been but never will be, a desire that glamorizes the past. This is the tense of regret, remorse and mourning. The past conditional frames a desire and marks the impossibility of its fruition: "if only I had." The subject can never know what would have been, and this amplifies the simultaneous pain and plea-sure of lost potential. Desire, rather than rushing forward, rushes back, its subject wishing it had done this, been there, or said that. The conventions of narrative desire are devoted to the pushing forward of plot and the achieve-ment of closure; Woolf, instead, explores the rush backward (and in doing so, revises the continuum of backward/forward since there is no necessary trajectory from one to the other in her work) and the repetitions, interrup-tions, and unresolved narratives that punctuate her text. The desire erupt-ing from Woolf's narrative doesn't seek closure, but returns to alternative possibilities whose endings are open and unknowable. This desire exists, then, in the ever-interrupted, ever-encircling realm of the past conditional. Glamour, the ache for the beautiful thing just out of reach, frames Clarissa's memory and constitutes the radiant veil of the novel's form.

Woolf's novel and her use of images such as the leaden circles emanating from the clock tower anticipate contemporary theoretical questions about the "remains" or "remainder" of desire, the "evidence," as it were, inscribed on the page, in language, and in literary form. If photographs are a visual remainder of the past, subject to the unstable memory of the present and future subject, what relationship do they bear to the written trace of de-sire? Jacques Derrida asks, "What 'remains' when desire has just inscribed something which 'remains' there, like an object at the disposal of others, one that can be repeated?"[44] Woolf avoids the reification of desire through her projection of multiple views in multiple and simultaneous tenses. By creating the image of desire within a frame that one accesses through the past, Woolf uses, I have been arguing, photographic means: the mood of the photograph could best be described in the terms of the past conditional that inscribes a remainder of desire. Photographs provide the would-have-been of memory: they present images from the past of people we would have liked to have been, things we would have liked that person to have done—the smiling member of a happy family, the youthful countenance on a becoming face, the self as sophisticated world traveler, and so on. Photo-graphs are not strictly mimetic and their effect relies as much on fantasy as the realistic forms depicted within the frame—they provide an enchanted vision of the past, one based not on what one remembers, but what one de-sires. Fiction plays a large part in the pleasure taken from the photographic image as one revisits a past image framed as the preferred interpretation of the past (while photographs might represent loss, they generally depict an insistently cheerful presence). In the photograph one can see the remainder of desire, those outlines repeated throughout that historical record of our desires, the photo album.[45]

In a passage that begins, "She would have been," Clarissa considers how her life might have been if she "could have looked even differently,"[46] and imagines herself with the superficial attributes of Lady Bexborough. The surface captivates Clarissa, who understands the power of the aesthetic. Even though her body has nice features, it has not yielded all she would desire. "But often now this body she wore (she stopped to look at a Dutch picture), this body, with all its capacities, seemed nothing—nothing at all." Making her way up Bond Street, stopping momentarily to view a painting (and this parenthetical insertion underscores the novel's pervasive attention to the aesthetic), she assumes her body as she might assume a pose and sees its possibilities as lying only in the past tense now that she was "not even Clarissa any more" but Mrs. Dalloway. Heterosexuality and the marrying, the having of children it implies, is over for Clarissa, whose body and its desires now give her the "oddest sense of being herself invisible, unseen; unknown."[47] Another body she could have worn, perhaps, would have allowed her desires to grow and not die with the necessary, or at least expected, achievement of marriage and children. Clarissa Dalloway renders her desire in the confines of the simple past ("It was all over for her. The sheet was stretched and the bed narrow"),[48] which she blends into the future with her prophetic coffin-like image of narrow confinement. Indeed, the future itself seems over and finished for Clarissa as well. Sitting down to repair her dress for the party, her thoughts turn toward its seamstress, who has since retired and moved to another town: "and if ever I have a moment, thought Clarissa (but never would she have a moment any more), I shall go and see her at Ealing."[49] It is unclear whether the prophecy added in ambiguous parentheses is the sudden addition of an as-yet-unheard omniscient voice or is simply the pessimism of a busy woman's mind. The parenthetical comment, with its overt suggestions of death, operates to foreclose the future and any desire Clarissa might project there. Instead the novel sets desire in the past tense and in the past conditional of what might have been.

The past and its possibilities will continue to move Clarissa and make her question at times the reality of the present. While she is sewing her dress for that evening, Peter Walsh arrives and their conversation throws her anew into a fantasy space removed from time: "Peter Walsh had got up and crossed to the window and stood with his back to her.... Take me with you, Clarissa thought impulsively, as if he were starting directly upon some great voyage; and then, next moment, it was as if the five acts of a play that had been very exciting and moving were now over and she had lived a lifetime in them and had run away, had lived with Peter, and it was now over."[50]

Fantasy and the power of fiction combine to create a lifetime lived in the course of a moment. Clarissa's desire makes her audience to this drama and when its five acts come to a close, she is, for the moment, satiated by the fantasy. Just as Clarissa wonders what life would have been like if she had married Peter or if she had been dark like Lady Bexborough, her thoughts meander around the unspeakable potential of Sally's kiss if Peter had not interrupted it. The would-have-been affair, which might have turned the world upside down, must remain behind the thick veils of fantasy for Clarissa. For there she would have been—if she had not been interrupted by Peter, if she had not become Mrs. Dalloway—there she would have been in the arms of Sally Seton.

One senses that, if possible, Woolf would have written this book so that it took place in the course of a moment—a brilliant and illuminated moment—rather than a day. Such a novel might have traced the swirling desire of that moment in Sally Seton's arms, might have held onto the glamour of the past. Of course, it is impossible to recuperate what Woolf would have wanted, to know what Clarissa would have done for that fluid and eddying moment, yet still I propose that Woolf did indeed write the history of a moment in Mrs. Dalloway, and it is that moment in which Mrs. Dalloway would have been if not interrupted by the multiple systems of enforcement that ensure the "proper" direction (and forward trajectory) of desire. The moment Woolf writes into narrative form as Mrs. Dalloway is the moment of desire with the power to invert the world. This is the possibility of modernity for Woolf, the sensation of the moment inscribed on the page. Yet this is a belated moment, viewed as a possibility that is irrevocably past. While Woolf may have had no great love for the photograph, her novel achieves something in language similar to the effect of a photograph, that light written into form, the image on the page. Like the diapositive, Woolf's characters are projected through light, their images achieving a form that shimmers as if cast onto a screen through a slide transparency. Indeed, Woolf imagined the novel as suffused with light: "For my own part I am laboriously dredging my mind for Mrs. Dalloway & bringing up light buckets."[51] To consider the past conditional tense—what Woolf would have liked to achieve, for example, or what Clarissa Dalloway would have liked to have been—is particularly relevant to the photograph, the material remainder of what has been, of a movement already taken place through light. It shares the same temporal logic, a relation to the past that is not stable or absolute but contingent, the would-have-been of desire that turns away from the future toward the material gathered from the enchanted and illuminated past.

Woolf is interested in the aesthetics of desire here, in taking the shock of modern experience and writing it as the shock of desire. Woolf, aware of the possibilities of a new aesthetic and literary form, confided in the pages of her diary: "I foresee, to return to The Hours, that this is going to be the devil of a struggle. The design is so queer & so masterful. I'm always having to wrench my substance to fit it. The design is certainly original, & interests me hugely."[52] Substance is subordinate to design, or "radiant" form in Perloff's words, in this conception of the novel. Woolf's method is not to be confused, then, with the operations of an amateur who produces an image with the flurry of the snapshot-intent to capture content at the expense of form. Woolf is formal, controlled, aware (perhaps above all) of the aesthetic. When Derrida is questioned about the work of an author he greatly esteems, he answers: "The composition, the rhetoric, the construction and the rhythm of the works, even the ones that seem the most 'decomposed,' that's what 'remains' finally the most 'interesting,' that's the work, that's the signature, this remainder which remains when the thematics is exhausted (and also exhausted, by others, for a long time now, in other modes)."[53] Form, signature, that remainder of an author's presence in the text, are what "finally" is most interesting about a work. The question becomes one of aesthetic remainder, then. Could we push this supposition, this authorial signature farther, to incorporate an aesthetics of glamour as the remainder of desire as it appears on the page and in literature? How visible is Woolf's signature? Her desire in form? Woolf rejects mimesis (interestingly, mimesis is the photograph's most overt and thus most misleading feature) for the more compelling shape of abstract form: she does not entirely remove the aesthetic from other experience, but makes it integral to experience, uniting—perhaps perilously—the realms of politics and aesthetics: "In this book I have almost too many ideas. I want to give life & death, sanity & insanity; I want to criticise the social system, & to show it at work, at its most intense—But here I may be posing."[54]

Fashioning the Pose

The pose, of course, is the essence of form, assumed or predetermined by the subject and held to achieve a desired effect. Woolf does not refer to herself as positioned in front of a camera lens, yet the pose she strikes has the elements of that suspension before the flash or that stillness required of the photographic portrait or representation. Her remark is, presumably, ironic and concerns the posture of being a political writer whose concerns should be taken more seriously than the mere architect of form. Woolf's comment about the pose also suggests her awareness of her own image as construct, as posture, and a self-representation as author.[55] In other writing, Woolf pokes fun at the celebrity autograph, the self-writing, when she imagines the literary icon, emptied of meaning, who she is destined to become: "a lady in a rose coloured tea gown, with a lap dog, a fountain pen, and a habit of writing her name with a flourish across what she calls photos of a celebrated authoress."[56] The pose may be a matter of caricature, but it also carries some significance for Woolf, who understands its implications and its relationship to the iconographic, even photographic, world. The pose, as Kaja Silverman has noted, carries significant transformative power: "The representational force which the pose exerts is so great that it radiates outward, and transforms the space around the body and everything which comes into contact with it into an imaginary photograph. Indeed, the pose includes in itself every other feature of the photographic image which is relevant within the domain of subjectivity."[57]

Woolf advances her ironic understanding of the pose in the narrative depiction of Clarissa, whose pauses at moments achieve a heightened dramatic effect. Early in the day, what she perceives as her social failure leads Clarissa to project the what-will-have-been of her evening, ending with her solitary pose: "She began to go slowly upstairs, with her hand on the banisters, as if she had left a party, where now this friend now that had flashed back her face, her voice; had shut the door and gone out and stood alone, a single figure against the appalling night."[58] Clarissa pauses at the top of the stairs, beside an open window, which frames her despondency and gives her a sad majesty that Woolf undercuts as she ends the passage: "As she paused by the open staircase window which let in blinds flapping, dogs barking, let in, she thought, feeling her self suddenly shrivelled, aged, breastless, the grinding, blowing, flowering of the day, out of doors, out of the window, out of her body and brain which now failed, since Lady Bruton, whose lunch parties were said to be extraordinarily amusing, had not asked her."[59] The pose with its rather tragic proportions becomes something of an ironic comment on its own ability to achieve an image once we reach the source of Clarissa's sadness, that she had not been invited to a lunch party that promised to be extraordinarily amusing and a mark of social success. Of course, for Clarissa, the party is the supreme aesthetic event, a triumph of form and an expression of talent for the arrangement and effect of surfaces.

Clarissa's failure to succeed at, or even be included in, Lady Bruton's luncheon reflects the anxiety she feels about her own event that evening and the possibility that her carefully arranged pose will not be fully apprehended by an admiring audience. This is Clarissa's moment to display herself in her diamond-hard brilliance, and her anxiety will continue until the party proves itself a success. As the party begins, she has not yet quite achieved the pose she will assume, although her performance is likely seamless:

> It was too much like being—just anybody, standing there; anybody could do it; yet this anybody she did a little admire, couldn't help feeling that she had, anyhow, made this happen, that it marked a stage, this post that she felt herself to have become, for oddly enough she had quite forgotten what she looked like, but felt herself a stake driven in at the top of her stairs. Every time she gave a party she had this feeling of being something not herself, and that every one was unreal in one way; much more real in another. It was, she thought, partly their clothes, partly being taken out of their ordinary ways, partly the background.[60]

Woolf seems to investigate the posture, the performance one gives in the social setting of a party. Two weeks before Mrs. Dalloway was published, she wrote in her diary: "I should like to investigate the party consciousness, the frock consciousness &c…where people secrete an envelope which connects them & protects them from others, like myself, who am outside the envelope, foreign bodies. These states are very difficult (obviously I grope for words) but I'm always coming back to it."[61] Woolf's comments suggest something of the pose, yet she adds a diaphanous sort of veil that she chooses to call an envelope—that repository of words sent in communication to another. Both word and image meet in Woolf's imagining of a transparent force that connects and protects the individual in a social interaction, or at least the specific social interaction one encounters at a party. The "envelope" is ineffable— even the prodigious Woolf must grope for words to explain its effect. Could the envelope be a remainder, the inscription of the trace of desire? This envelope bears or contains Woolf's authorial signature, a signature that produces the diffusive effect of glamour.

There is a quality to Clarissa Dalloway that is suffused with light and that propels her into the frame. Scarcely embodied, Clarissa concerns herself with the effect of the illusion she projects (since she claims some agency in her propulsion into the frame). The illusion of light, projected by Woolf through words, is like that filmy envelope, the vehicle of written communication that remains *almost* ineffable, described only through the coarse groping for words that contrive to give some sort of definition to something with less shape than a vague luminosity. In this way, *Mrs. Dalloway* writes the problem of writing glamour. This difficulty goes beyond the complexities of ekphrasis to capturing its remainder, a sort of ecstatic stasis constituted by desire and the impossibility of attaining it. Glamour, interpreted here as a kind of literary trope, yields to the necessity of embodiment, yet creates the subject as constituted by light. There is human form, but one encased as if by an envelope bearing a signature, communicating or radiating light, protected against the darkness that confers its shape. Writing the remainder is both inside and outside of time: the text may always be historically located, yet nevertheless exists, timelessly and conditionally, through its remainder. Mrs. Dalloway is, of course, historically embodied in the social structures of the novel. She suffers the constraints of gender and enjoys the privileges of wealth and race; she suppresses her unspeakable desire for Sally and other women, has survived illness and a world at war. Clarissa Dalloway is both *of* a world and exists beyond it. Woolf, highly aware of the political nature of all experience, is also fascinated by that gauzier realm of light existing at the edges of vision and constituted by vision. She is perhaps most fascinated by the process of putting this light into writing, shaping a grammar to fit its misty contours, and creating an image composed of shadow and light.

The Terror and the Ecstasy

The darkness that gives light definition encroaches on Mrs. Dalloway's party. The much-anticipated event, a success she at last recognizes, is interrupted by death when Sir William Bradshaw brings news of Septimus Smith's suicide. Paralyzed by his horrible visions throughout the narrative, Septimus finally leaps through the frame where his body will at last be impaled, penetrated, by the railings below. We learn of this penetration through Clarissa's consciousness. It is her inquiry that produces Smith's gruesome method of suicide: "He had killed himself—but how? Always her body went through it first, when she was told, suddenly, of an accident; her dress flamed, her body burnt. He had thrown himself from a window. Up had flashed the ground; through him, blundering, bruising, went the rusty spikes."[62] Clarissa feels the frame, the frame that normally offers protection, then the penetrating spikes as her question is answered by her guest. Septimus has leapt through the frame and achieved some sort of narrative closure. She first sees only horror, then recognizes the defiance in his leap: "Death was an attempt to communicate; people feeling the impossibility of reaching the centre which, mystically, evaded them; closeness drew apart; rapture faded, one was alone. There was an embrace in death."[63] The penetration of Septimus's death—of his body, of her party—is the embrace of the moment and Clarissa feels his renewed rapture and the unspeakable moment of her desire. Yet she continues to fear the desire that this un-known man has so recently embraced and her fear leads her back to the performance at hand: "Somehow it was her disaster—her disgrace. It was her punishment to see sink and disappear here a man, there a woman, in this profound darkness, and she forced to stand here in her evening dress."[64] The pose itself is her disgrace as if Clarissa were forced to assume a costume that was suddenly in bad taste and that another self-representation, one perhaps that equaled the heroism of the young man, would have been far preferable. Septimus has sunk into darkness, while Clarissa stands resplen-dent in the brilliant light of her party and the purity of his act seems to make tawdry the success of hers. His act was an attempt to communicate, to make contact, to share something with others. It also, in some sense, pro-tected his moments of vision and of desire that were in peril (those which Sir William's institution would ostensibly cure).

Clarissa retreats from the party she now sees as her own private catastro-phe into an empty upstairs room. "She walked to the window....She parted the curtains; she looked. Oh, but how surprising!—in the room opposite the old lady stared straight at her!" Like the moment when Clarissa looked transfixed at her mirror image as if it were a stranger's, she looks into the face of another woman. Not knowing whether she has been seen or not, Clarissa watches with fascination as the older woman prepares for bed:

> The clock began striking. The young man had killed himself; but she did not pity him; with the clock striking the hour, one, two, three, she did not pity him, with all this going on. There! The old lady had put out her light!...But what an extraordinary night! She felt somehow very like him—the young man who had killed himself. She felt glad that he had done it; thrown it away. The clock was striking. The leaden circles dissolved in the air. He made her feel the beauty; made her feel the fun. But she must go back. She must assemble.[65]

After her initial shock, she views the woman as she might privately view a photograph. When the light is extinguished and the house opposite dark-ens, Clarissa's thoughts turn to death once more, yet this time with an ap-preciation of the catastrophe. The old lady, a figure whose own waning life is visible in her quiet preparations for bed, is a figure for death. Like the photograph which, writes Barthes, "always contains this imperious sign of my future death,"[66] Clarissa recognizes her own mortality, bound up with the private, even intimate, image in the illuminated window. Both Septimus and Clarissa eventually become aware of the frames that contain and bind them. Septimus chooses to leave the confines of the frame, to jump out of it in the form of a window, to be penetrated by the railings below. He can no longer live within the logic of the image and thus removes himself, violently, from it. Clarissa instead chooses the frame, its appearance of safety, its impermeable surface, and finds beauty there.

Septimus's leap to his death becomes aestheticized in Clarissa's vision. As the image of the leaden circles returns and they once again dissolve, she sees the beauty of his act and the harmony of its performance. The penetration of the man on the iron railings may be horrible, but beauty exists in horror, in the ridding of a body no longer fit to be worn. Clarissa cannot pity Septimus because she too closely identifies with the harmonious close to his life. Like the work of art and the communication she hopes to offer through her party, Septimus's death is the perfect expression of self and adds something heroic, something extreme in its sensation, to the evening. Without the interruption of this death, her life would remain unremarkable, shapeless, without heroism. Nothing is left of Septimus but his image, a representation, the leaden circles that suspend the perfect moment, then dissolve irrevocably. Septimus experienced the moment in perhaps its purest form, hovering between life and death, and Clarissa felt the fun. Having identified herself in the image of the older woman, finding new definition in the contrast offered by death, Clarissa consigns the suicide, like Peter's tears in an earlier scene, to the realm of fun, or the pleasure she feels in its aesthetic rightness and its bestowal of life on her. Just as the party is an offering (an offering that is eroticized by the desire that saturates it), so is his death, and she recognizes the beauty of the gift.

In death, Septimus most clearly represents an alterity that Clarissa comes to appreciate. As Clarissa's double, Septimus enacts the abjection of self, the loss constitutive of subjectivity, and the unstable boundaries inherent in the notion of difference itself. As Clarissa gazes out that window onto a vision of herself, she comes to understand the balance that Septimus's death has bestowed. His abjection lays the foundation for her brilliance. The beauty she creates through her attention to surfaces masks the world of filth and misery. With this revelation, Clarissa is prepared to "assemble" and return to the redefined ground of her party.

In her absence, Sally and Peter have been reminiscing and anxiously awaiting Clarissa's reappearance. The last lines of the novel return to the layers of past, present, and future. Sally, tired of waiting, rises to say good night to her host:

> "I will come," said Peter, but he sat on for a moment. What is this terror? What is this ecstasy? He thought to himself. What is it that fills me with extraordinary excitement?
>
> It is Clarissa, he said.
>
> For there she was.[67]

The last lines repeat the movement of the novel: Peter makes a future-tense statement, that he will come, yet sits transfixed in the present moment suffused with past desire. The moment brims with the anticipation he had known years earlier at Bourton, an anticipation we know will be inevitably disappointed. The sensations of terror and ecstasy fill the moment as Peter states, "It is Clarissa," and the narrative resumes, abandoning the present declarative for the more evocative surge backwards of desire, to the hopeful delusion that it will be different this time. Like the anticipation of the past conditional itself with a grammar based in illusion, the passage stands like a photographic gesture, grasping backward at the fictions created within its frame. There Clarissa was—at Bourton, in her youth, in the doorway—the final sentence introduces ambiguity by reverting to the indirection of the past tense narrative voice. With a passive statement, beautiful in its simplicity, the novel concludes.

Woolf was pleased, we know, with the "last words of the last page of Mrs. Dalloway."[68] She would write a couple of months later, anticipating some negative reviews, "And I suppose there is some superficial glittery writing. But is it 'unreal'? Is it mere accomplishment? I think not."[69] What is the writing of the novel? Woolf concedes that it may contain some glittering surfaces, but does this annul reality, as she suspects may be the charge? She raises, ultimately, the question of reading, that process by which we encounter the diamond facets of the literary work. Woolf asks whether the mode of representation, her language, will deflect the eyes of the reader to the text's superficial accomplishment—its talent in making phrases—and not to its emotion, insight, or vision. Yet, are they not the same thing? What the reader will encounter in Woolf's novel is the glittering surface of language and the certain knowledge of death—Septimus's, Clarissa's, Woolf's, the reader's own. What the reading will produce is a glamour that clings—like death and like the luminous envelope that contains and transmits desire—to its central character and to the novel in the traces of desire it records. Pleasure, as Freud tells us in *Beyond the Pleasure Principle*, is indistinguishable from the drive toward death. Certainly Septimus, and through him Clarissa, found pleasure as he hurtled toward death, the ultimate sublimation of his desire for Evans. Terror and ecstasy are made available to Septimus, Peter, and Clarissa: each produces a singular reading, multiply motivated yet pushing each toward a sort of precipice. It is that precipice that Woolf wished to exploit, the daring peek over its edge in the reading of her novel: this is what Clarissa admires in Septimus, his endless leap of desire, his movement, simultaneously, into the enchanted past and future.

4 : CELEBRITY

They [film stars] are so glamorized and vaporized and made to appear
in print as somebody they aren't at all.
—*Silver Screen*, December 5, 1936

[Garbo] seems not so much the artist as the medium through which
forgotten things of a far past find expression.
—JULIA SHAWELL, "Garbo or Dietrich?" *Pictorial Review*, July 1933

The Birth of Personality

"In or about December, 1910, human character changed," Virginia Woolf
famously noted in her essay "Mr. Bennett and Mrs. Brown."[1] The date has
been chewed over by critics ever since—was Woolf referring to the deaths
of Edward VII or Leo Tolstoy, the effect of industrial and civil unrest that
reached new heights in 1910, or the impact of Roger Fry's postimpres-
sionist exhibition, which transformed art practices and inaugurated, some
claim, British modernism? Human nature—whatever Woolf's referent—
was changing and to this effort she lent her formidable and revolutionary
literary skills. Character, as Woolf deftly explains in this and other essays,
required renovation for the twentieth century and a move away from the
"materialists,"[2] or the likes of John Galsworthy, H. G. Wells, and Arnold
Bennett, who dominated the best-seller lists of the day. Woolf was looking
for a character appropriate to the new century, a character who was not
created through the dulling effects of material details (the "clod[s] of clay"[3]
these men offered in abundance) but through an attention to those qualities that made a character recognizably human. Paradoxically, this required
an evacuation of the hard facts, a letting go of firm boundaries, to reach and
represent the ephemeral qualities of the human subject. Woolf thus aimed to
achieve character that did not suffer the muffling effects of literary convention; indeed, she insisted on character created through attention to the insubstantial and the vaporous.

Woolf advocated this revolution in character, the reaching out into the
unknown, even if the literary experiments might end in failure. "Tolerate

the spasmodic, the obscure, the fragmentary, the failure,"[4] she exhorted her readers, to achieve a new and greater order of literature. The old forms of character were outworn and offered nothing to the aesthetics of a new age. Is it mere coincidence, then, that across the Atlantic Ocean, another revolution in character was taking place in 1910, though for less vaunted objectives than those of high literary modernism? The year 1910 marked not only the threshold of a great era for literature, it also brought in the crass new machinery of popular culture (something Woolf would surely decry) and its product, the media personality. The precise moment of this birth in 1910 has been frequently recounted in histories of the screen: Florence Lawrence, a.k.a. the "Biograph girl," was an actress working in the developing studio industry of Hollywood (Biograph was one of those studios) when a studio executive devised a plan to bring her to public attention. He leaked a fictional report that she had been killed in a trolley car accident, which created an instant response in the media. The public poured out its grief and sympathy in reaction to the news of the "accident," which we now may view as an unprecedented experiment in sensationalism. Lawrence would make her startling reappearance on stage in St. Louis in a carefully contrived media event that assured her the status of celebrity (at least we now recognize it as such). While Florence Lawrence may have enjoyed some public recognition before the "accident," it was nothing compared to the public outpouring of love, once she "died" and then appeared on stage miraculously alive. The moment marked both a new era in publicity and a new mode of representation: celebrity was on the rise.

Warren Susman places this anecdote in a broader popular context, arguing that human character (not to be confused with Woolf's literary character) was undergoing revision during the first decade of the century: character, the old ideal of a former age, was transforming into something flashier and more engaging.[5] Personality, with its emphasis on charm, poise, and likeability, became the watchword of the modern age, bolstered by the publication of self-improvement manuals, the emergence of fan magazines such as *Photoplay* (first published in 1911), and the new industry of motion pictures: "Up to 1910, motion picture studios generally concealed the identity of most screen players. In 1910, however, the idea of the movie star was born. The creation of the star changed the nature of the role of motion pictures in our society. It brought into even more prominent use the press agent and modern advertising."[6] Lawrence's reported fall in the fictional trolley car accident created public fascination for her as a newly emergent star. Charm, magnetism, and fascination quickly emerged as the desirable traits of the twentieth century, replacing such fogyish terms as virtue and strength of character. Character, in the old morally-freighted sense, was practically declared outmoded: "The older vision no longer suited personal or social needs; the newer vision seemed particularly suited for the problems of the self in a changed social order, the developing consumer mass society."[7] "Thus 'personality,'" writes Susman, "like 'character,' is an effort to solve the problem of self in a changed social structure that imposes its own special demands on the self."[8] The self, beaten from without by the shifts in social, economic, and political organization and from within, as psychoanalysis was revealing, by its own irrational impulses, found new lines of demarcation through "personality" that might repair, at least superficially, its wounded sense of coherence. If virtue offered nothing to the modern fragmented subject, the pleasures and pretense of social success acted as some sort of analgesic salve, particularly in the postwar years of the 1920s.

Personality was also on T. S. Eliot's mind in the second decade of the century—in fact, he declared it extinct in his 1919 essay "Tradition and the Individual Talent." His was a plea, or a program, to expel personality from the ranks of literature. Eliot's influential theory of impersonality seemed to fly in the face of the movement in popular culture. Or did it? Eliot wanted to shed the fussy exterior, the biographical detail, the distracting personality behind the pure experience of literature (figured as a chemical reaction in his essay, as I discuss in chapter 1). The authorial shell only muffled the purity of feeling that the best poetry offered. The author threatened the writing with his or her messy humanity—the ego, the wounds, the needs and demands, the mental habits—that were best left outside the poem. Extinguishing the personality for Eliot thus meant an evacuation of the narrowly human from poetic form, an emptying out of realistic or personal detail for the sake of the perfection of form and its expression of feeling. Sharon Cameron offers a reading of the nuances of personality when she writes: "One way of approaching impersonality is to say it is not the negation of the person, but rather a penetration through or a falling outside of the boundary of the human particular."[9] Eliot's theory, produced only in the scant comments he makes in his essay, may not negate the person altogether (which would lead us more properly into the realm of the postmodern) but shows rather the possibilities for loosening the hold of subjective boundaries and stepping aside from the narrow perception of personality, in all its idiosyncratic particulars. Cameron continues: "Representations of impersonality suspend, eclipse, and even destroy the idea of the person as such, who is not treated as a social, political, or individual entity" (ix). Indeed, impersonality leads us away from the "clods of clay" and the dulling detail into the more spectacular possibilities of form. And this sounds a lot like the requirements, and effect, of modern celebrity.

Celebrity: those combined attributes of fame, wealth, public recognition, adulation, and the remove from the prosaic routine of everyday life that together produced an intoxicating distance across which the ordinary mortal could not reach. Here, then, is glamour in its most obvious habitat. The celebrity emerged from the masses through the new attention to personality, the site of rich audience identification based on the limited information made available by the media: the way the hair fell across the brow, perhaps, or a penchant for hats. The celebrity was thus endowed with personality, yet personality, despite its claims to warm humanity and individual charm, emerged as a screen effect, strangely devoid of human substance. One explanation might be the new standards for beauty—a requirement for at least most celebrities—that depended on a mechanical principle: "Photogenic beauty rests its definition of perfection on a smooth, standardized, and lifeless modernism, a machine aesthetic in the guise of a human. Caught in time, it is a perfection that never ages, and experiences no mood swings. The idiosyncrasies of character are forged into the market-tested gleam of personality."[10] Personality, with all its pretense to the unique and individual, was predicated, paradoxically, on lifelessness, on the smooth malleability of the inert form. My interest here is in the glamour that accrues to the celebrity, forged on the popular personality and delivering an effect that takes personality to an impersonal extreme. Indeed, glamour—the effect of the merging of human object, market, and machine aesthetic—depended on an evacuation of the recognizable limits of human life that enmeshed the "ordinary" citizen. Glamour did not emerge from human warmth, morals, and the messy emotions that define the everyday; rather, in their place was the coolly aloof and beautifully coiffed personality, hovering over the multiple indignities of life on the ground.

What connects Woolf's manifesto for reformulated character in fiction, Eliot's call for the extinction of personality in poetry, and the sensational stunt orchestrated to throw the spotlight on an emergent Hollywood star and increase her box office attraction? Certainly all point to a shift in the presentation of the individual, a shift that is linked to the changing climate and changing needs of the twentieth-century subject. While the sharply divergent objectives of great art and box office profit should not be overlooked, Woolf's view of character, Eliot's call for impersonality, and the birth of the media-age personality share some fundamental features, including the evacuation of detail in order to convey luminous (or radiant) form. The celebrity would not provide access to the lumpen details that might mar the effect of her gorgeous surface; rather, she would fascinate through the very absence of those details. Woolf, for example, though she creates an old woman without superficial beauty, provides her as a luminous example of the century's new character: "[Mrs. Brown] is an old lady of unlimited capacity and infinite variety; capable of appearing in any place; wearing any dress; saying anything and doing heaven knows what. But the things she says and the things she does and her eyes and her nose and her speech and her silence have an overwhelming fascination, for she is, of course, the spirit we live by, life itself." Could Hollywood achieve such an effect?

Yes and no. In this chapter, I look at the figure who comes closest to bridging the gap between modernist character and media-age personality, Greta Garbo, who was all personality and, at the same time, none: Garbo, who fascinated millions, remained a resolute mystery to her public, allowing no interviews, no publicity shots, offering no details about her life, instead choosing silence and, most famously, solitude (her most quoted line: "I want to be let alone"). Nevertheless, she achieved a stature unsurpassed even in the contemporary world of the blockbuster and red carpet awards ceremonies watched around the world: "Those of us who were not present at the creation of her screen image have to reimagine the singular hold, both unprecedented and unduplicated, she exercised on audiences of the 1920s and 1930s," comments film historian Richard Schickel.[11] Garbo's sometimes puzzling celebrity tells us something about the desiring structure through which we produce the category of star: her ambition for celebrity was countered always by her resistance to it, her on-screen persona resolutely negated the qualities that suggest personality. Garbo, Schickel agrees, "was always a creature of withdrawal, of silence—thus, ideally, of the silents—an actress who from the first moments she appeared on the screen defined herself by her refusals."[12] She was pure magnetism, but a magnetism forged in negativity, as if the pull of the negative was what most profoundly encouraged the public worship she inspired. Rather than appeal to biography (the details of which Garbo mercifully denied us), or the system of capitalist relations that produced her celebrity, I wish to theorize the allure of Garbo's refusals—those withdrawals, silences, and exhausted performances that, according to critics then and now, defined her celebrity and made the image of Garbo so strangely compelling, so resolutely modern (even Woolfian), and so glamorous.

Just as Woolf dredged up light buckets to create the special luminosity of Mrs. Dalloway or Mrs. Brown, the photographer's art was one primarily constituted by light. Garbo's power rested, at least partially, in the lunar quality of her skin, the glow that erased the human detail and staged the tremendous and ethereal vitality of her eyes. No one better understood this than the generation of glamour photographers who worked in the studio system of Hollywood. Glamour photography, emerging in the 1920s and reaching its apex in the 1930s, was explicitly designed to produce the celebrity as beyond human, as intangible as light. The style of Hollywood portraiture would develop from the pictorialism of the early century, which featured painterly lines in soft focus that were self-consciously artistic (called "fuzzygraphs" by detractors) to highly stylized photographs influenced by modernism.[13] These latter photographs featured high contrast lighting (referred to as Rembrandt lighting) that sculpted its object, redefining facial features for maximum effect. The photographer was enlisted to take the ordinary mortal and transform her into something extraordinary and barely human. Glamour photography emerged as a powerful way to disseminate the star's image and was often acknowledged to be of more importance in creating a public image than the films themselves (Dietrich, among other stars, would make this claim). Celebrities were fashioned with brilliant illumination, floating out from black backgrounds, shining, hard, and hardly human. As the 1920s moved into the 30s, the stars became ever more ethereal, more starkly lit, and more self-consciously glamorous, as retouchers went to work on their images after the studio session was over. Garbo worked at MGM with a number of Hollywood's best photographers, including Harriet Louise, George Hurrell, and Clarence Sinclair Brown. One notes in these photos and in many of her films that Garbo's face is best when sharply defined, when the frame is most severe, her hair pulled tightly back, the background dark, emphasizing the lines and contours that made her of this world and beyond it.

Garbo's celebrity thus depended on competing visions of character and personality, as well as the developing technologies that lay at the definitional center of literary modernism; her extraordinary sixteen-year career in Hollywood fed an increasing appetite for the perfect, mediated image without the messy implications of human subjectivity. The celebrity did not offer life, in the sense of Woolf's Mrs. Brown; rather her superhuman image conveyed something more closely associated with static perfection and therefore death. Yet the power of her image, like that of Woolf's ideal character, lifted her away from the dulling aspects of everyday life and produced an intoxicating image that would enthrall those who encountered it. I want to begin here, then, to articulate the remarkable power of Garbo in the modern psyche and the ways that she came to signify a kind of glamour in the early century that has not been surpassed—indeed *cannot* be surpassed—in our contemporary digital age.

In recent years, the study of celebrity has emerged as a disciplinary field encompassing both biographical and discursive modes of criticism. One of the field's earliest formulations came in Daniel Boorstin's 1962 polemic, *The Image: A Guide to Pseudo-Events in America,* in which the writer decries our contemporary age of self-deception, in which we eagerly enter the "thicket of unreality." Boorstin chalks this up to "national self-hypnosis" and an ever increasing addiction for illusion.[14] The critic has no small task ahead of him, as he acknowledges when he winds up his introduction: "To dispel the ghosts which populate the world of our making will not give us the power to conquer the real enemies of the real world or to remake the real world. But it may help us discover that we cannot make the world in our image. It will liberate us and sharpen our vision. It will clear away the fog so we can face the world we share with mankind."[15] The terms Boorstin uses suggest a fog-free and unmediated world, which mark it historically, at least, as belonging to a world avant postmodernism where the authentic as a category still held meaning. We might agree with some of Boorstin's conclusions—the emptiness of the image, for example, and our demand for a daily flood of illusions—but today the study of celebrity proceeds without the moral outrage that defines his tract and instead offers a reading of contemporary culture as necessarily mediated by the lens of consumerist ideology and media conglomerates. Richard Dyer argues that celebrity constitutes more than empty mirage and sees instead an "elaborate machinery of image-building" with economic, cultural, and historical importance. Others, including David Marshall, look to celebrity structures as telling us something about the ideologies under and through which we live and which provide us some sense of a shared culture.[16]

I am interested, though, in preserving the idea of the celebrity as a ghostly and empty space, a tautology in Boorstin's terms, that frames an impossible desire for us, makes it almost close enough to touch, but resistant to the real world demands of its fans. If the celebrity may be understood as a negative space, a space that absorbs but does not produce meaning, how do we account for its singular power to provoke mass adoration? Cultural studies takes us a long way toward understanding the institutional foundations, mass deception, and ideological underpinnings of celebrity, and recent work has included the interimplications of celebrity and literary modernism, as Aaron Jaffe's work ably demonstrates; yet these studies do not address the strange impersonality of personality, the modernist inflections of the media-produced star. The aesthetic power of the celebrity over the modern subject who invests everything—and nothing, as I will show—in the image becomes crucial in interpreting glamour, particularly (though not exclusively) in the form of Garbo.

From Aura to Glamour

Of course, 1910 also loosely corresponds to the era of the declining aura, in Walter Benjamin's terms, with the rise of technologies that substituted the reproduced copy for the original work of art.[17] The aura described that mystifying or magical effect of art that connected viewer and artist, thus creating a relationship that was unique and authentic. The aura, like glamour, refers to a subjective experience, an effect of perception that draws from a historical and technological context. First appearing in his essay "A Small History of Photography," Benjamin's aura was initially conceived of as an atmospheric trait, arising from the technical challenges of early photography. Already, however, the definition included the binary poles of distance and proximity: "What is aura, actually? A strange weave of space and time: the unique appearance of semblance or distance, no matter how close the object may be." The aura is produced in this fantasy of having, while its object remains unavailable. Benjamin makes clear the movement of contemporary society and its desire to possess the image: "Every day the urge goes stronger to get hold of an object at very close range by way of its likeness, it reproduction."[18] To behold an image in close-up is to possess it, to boast the sort of access that suggests intimacy with the object, even if the close-up represents only a fragment of the original. Details emerge that would otherwise go unnoticed, creating new and spectacular forms of previously familiar objects. A fresh understanding is, presumably, the result, yet the detachment of one moment from any other, its freezing in time, bears critical—even mortal—consequences. Paradoxically, then, the "form" that permits intimacy with the image also dislocates the image from time, making it unattainable.

Benjamin imagined the aura to be a vestige of ancient experience still enmeshed in the enchantments of magic and cultic religion, yet also tied to the hierarchies of power. Mass experience was thus antithetical to the aura, indeed stripped the veil from the object itself: the experience of modern life, according to Benjamin, was defined by the shocks of the city, the experience of the crowd, and public demand for immediate gratification—all operating against the interests of the unique experience of aura. The nature of film worked to destroy aura due to the violence of editing, the relentless changing of the image, and the visual spectacle unrolling before the spectators' eyes, yet never reciprocating the gaze. Yet if, as Benjamin suggests, there can be no copy of the aura, how does one explain the effect of Garbo, the screen icon adored by millions who rivaled religion in the fervor of her fan base? I make the case here that Garbo's glamour—and glamour more generally—comes to stand in the place of the aura, signaling its death yet bearing its enchanted trace; glamour indeed becomes a twentieth-century response to the loss of both authenticity and spiritual belief. Glamour, emerging from the new possibilities of mass reproduction, maintains the qualities of ecstatic illumination while, at the same time, forgoes any possibility of depth or meaning. The movement from the sacred to the profane, from aura to glamour, thus comes amid the multiple pressures of the early century, its shifting subjectivities, technologies, and social relationships that both destabilized *and* energized modern cultural production.

The American poet, novelist, and essayist H. D. voiced her awareness of the complications presented by glamour in the columns she wrote for the film journal *Close Up*. Fascinated by the fantasy of proximity and distance, as well as by the merging of sacred and secular that characterized Garbo, H. D. wrote impassioned reflections that stage the struggle between the magic of the early silent screen star and the commercial impulses of Hollywood that, H. D. believed, destroyed Garbo's glamour through, paradoxically, its manufactured and self-conscious production. Glamour emerges in H. D.'s prose as enchanting and deathly, pure and impure, and tellingly combines the qualities associated with character in the Woolfian sense and the empty structures of personality. Introduced to the Swedish actress in her third feature film, G. W. Pabst's *Joyless Street*, H. D. became a rapturous fan of the young Garbo, seeing in her a kind of "mystical purity," her "first real revelation of the real art of the cinema": "Greta Garbo, as I first saw her, gave me a clue, a new angle, and a new sense of elation. This is beauty.[19] Garbo stands in the pantheon of H. D.'s goddesses and is clearly aligned with what we might call aura. Writing about the screen star's effect in her earliest films, H. D. claims that one could detect "a trace of glamour, the chiselled purity, the dazzling, almost unearthly beauty that one recognised so acutely"[20] but that, she claims, was lost in Hollywood. Film, when created as art, could offer access to the gods, as becomes clear in H. D.'s late 1920s novel, *Bid Me to Live,* when the protagonist, Julia Ashton, goes to the movies: "This was the answer to everything, then, Beauty, for surprisingly, a goddess-woman stepped forward. She released from the screen the first (to Julia) intimation of screen beauty. Screen? This was a veil, curiously embroidered, the veil before the temple."[21] Film could open the doors to the temple, then, and produce a mystical experience. Garbo, for H. D., entered into a sacred relationship with a mythological female past, in line with such creatures as Helen of Troy (to whom H. D. would dedicate much of her literary energies).

Contemporary Hollywood, in H. D.'s account, corrupted the star's transcendent status both in its effort to sell Garbo to the American public and in its embrace of the new sound film that cheapened film as an art. In the late 1920s, the shift from silent to sound technology occupied H. D., whose many defenses of silent film in *Close Up* articulate a sense of loss, a recognition that one experiential era was over (as Benjamin concurred), and that another, dominated by the perfection of the machine, had arrived. In a 1927 column called "Cinema and the Classics", H. D. worried over the auratic world now threatened by the newly emerging mode of the future: "We feel fearful that our world may be taken from us, that half-world of lights and music and blurred perception into which...the being floats as a moth into summer darkness. Like a moth really we are paralysed before too much reality, too much glamour."[22] The silent cinema had offered a dreamy narcotic effect, one H. D. associates with soft focus and hot summer nights. The moth that floats pleasantly becomes, in the era of sound technology, the moth paralyzed by the light, drawn toward the thing that would kill it. H. D. names this deathly effect both reality *and* glamour.

It is a surprising combination—the documentary realism that, in her estimation, sound brings to film and the glamour that H. D. here aligns solely with the "intricate machinery" or the "mechanical perfection"[23] of the newly sophisticated sound film. Her complaint is about the industrialization of art, the loss of the mask that she associates with presound film, and the bald representation of personality that voice and image welded together bring to the screen.

Personality, H. D. recognizes, is part of a twentieth-century vocabulary of industrial production and newly realized consumer relations and signifies the passing of a more noble age. Glamour then indeed does kill the aura in which "this layer of self, blurred over by hypnotic darkness or cross-beams of light, emotion and idea entered fresh as from the primitive beginning."[24] Glamour is starkly aligned with the coldness of technology, the rush into the future (rather than Woolf's linking of glamour with the past), and therefore bears a relationship to reality, although its reality is nevertheless one of masks and illusion. Glamour spells the death of Garbo's aura as it "devitalizes" the "Nordic flower"[25] and presents her, as far as H. D. is concerned, in a less pure form.

H. D.'s comments thus reflect not only H. D.'s ambivalence about glamour (a welcome relief, by the way, from those who simply dismiss its effects as mass deception—it is this, as the early and important interventions of Frankfurt School thinkers made clear, but also much more), but also the ambivalence on which the effect of glamour depends. Paralysis and glamour coexist in the darkened room of the theater, either throwing the viewer into an awe-filled state of rapture or threatening her with a kind of insistent reality made available through contemporary technology. H. D. was prescient in recognizing that the deathliness of glamour could not be sustained for very long. In fact, the era of Hollywood glamour would come to a close during the 1940s and we see this most obviously in the demise of glamour photography. Beginning in 1936, with the first publication of *Life* magazine and its new casual aesthetic, a demand emerged for more natural images of celebrity (in the home, with family, and so on) that worked against the stark artificiality of George Hurrell's or Clarence Bull's carefully staged glamour. With the closing of the studio system soon after the war, stars were no longer viewed as immortal beings but rather were now as human as anyone else (though with more wealth at their disposal). Candid photography, outdoor photography, and color photography reflected the evolving tastes of film fans and a new vibrant aesthetic (of *Life*, one might argue, over death), and eliminated even the trace of Benjaminian aura.

Perhaps the best-known of Garbo encomia, at least among academics, reinforces this point. Roland Barthes' exhilarated two-page essay is likely the most quoted piece on Garbo since its 1972 translation into English. The essay thus famously begins:

> Garbo still belongs to that moment in cinema when capturing the human face still plunged audiences into the deepest ecstasy, when one literally lost oneself in a human image as one would in a philtre, when the face represented a kind of absolute state of the flesh, which could be neither reached nor renounced. A few years earlier the face of Valentino was causing suicides; that of Garbo still partakes of the same rule of Courtly Love, where the flesh gives rise to mystical feelings of perdition.[26]

One is first struck by the hyperbole of Barthes' language, its gushiness in the face of Garbo, the face that hovers silently, supremely, and indifferently over the text. The divine face "is not in the least expressive," lacking the emotion that characterizes Barthes' response to it. If Garbo is pure concept, as Barthes asserts—logical, cold, abstract—her remove is absolute, in the absolute language of mathematics or analytic philosophy. Barthes' rapture is in direct opposition to the coolness of the image he describes. This, perhaps, is where the pleasure resides, in the stark contrast between the absolute on the one hand and the entirely contingent or subjective on the other, or at least in the *imagined* absolute against the reality of one's feelings. One loses oneself in Garbo's image, Barthes writes, as one would in a philtre, that aphrodesiac drink from *phileo* or love. The homonym philtre/filter—or sex and lens—brings together two crucial explanations for Garbo's glamour: her sexuality emerges from the lens that captures her face in close-up, allowing a reading of her magnetism as it emanates from the photographic frame. A filter might also refer to the screen over the lens that produces its effects, reduces flaws, and makes the image even more alluring.[27] Whatever the definition of filter here, the ecstasy that Garbo inspires is sexual as if drunk from a potion, yet available only to the adoring eye.

The "face-object"[28] of Garbo transcends the flesh yet cannot escape its reality (as Garbo the woman most famously knew when she retired at thirty-six into the shadow of veils, large sunglasses, and cloistered celebrity). Yet Barthes deifies Garbo only as celebrity image rather than as actress or as woman. He refers to only one aspect of her image, the face, and in so doing, invokes something mystical: "And yet, in this deified face, something sharper than a mask is looming: a kind of volunteer and therefore human relation between the curve of the nostrils and the arch of the eyebrows" (57). Just as Garbo *almost* transcends flesh, she *almost* transcends gender. Hardly confined to the representation of one gender, her face eludes definition: "Garbo offered to one's gaze a sort of Platonic Idea of the human creature, which explains why her face is almost sexually undefined, without however leaving one in doubt" (56). The face, its smooth lines and clear expression, expresses nothing, will not be subject to the overdetermination of later screen stars. Even ideologies of gender fail to limit its scope. Garbo eludes the "lyricism of Woman" (57) that would confine many later faces yet exudes a sexuality that is undifferentiated, Platonic, secret, and intellectual. There is arguably no lyricism of Woman in Barthes' description, one notes, but a lyricism that rejects heterosexual models and the ideology they answer to (which explains, more than her occasional cross-dressing, her status as gay icon).[29] Garbo's lyricism may not attain to gender categories, but she will produce a lyric suspension that is, at the same time, subtlety *and* excess, sexual *and* sexless, mortal *and* divine.

Barthes refers to Garbo's performance as Queen Christina, the sovereign in slacks who challenged gender norms (she falls in love with a man, for example, while cross-dressed as a man). The face-object of his account is that famous choker close-up that tightly framed Garbo's face from forehead

to chin and concludes the film. Queen Christina has abdicated the throne, choosing love for a man over that of country (the individual over the collective, pleasure over duty). Antonio, her lover, however, will die on board the ship that was to sail them into a romantic future. Alone in the closing shots of the film, Christina walks to the bow of the ship, taking her place as its figurehead, and looks out to sea. The final and famous close-up would fill the screen for almost a minute, as Christina stares into seemingly infinite space. Garbo had received the direction from Rouben Mamoulian to think of nothing, to empty her face of any emotion, to reduce it to its most fundamental features (Garbo asked, "What do I express in this last shot?" and was answered, "Nothing. Absolutely nothing. You must make your mind and your heart a complete blank. Make your face into a mask").[30] In the face of this nothing audiences might recognize the queen's vast powers, her impulse to rule, her refusal to be ruled, reaching into the ineffable; here the face is not reducible to trivial emotion but instead remains mysterious, ultimately unreadable, yet entrancing to its viewer. The shot echoes an earlier close-up, before Christina met Antonio, when she, resisting the pressure to marry and produce heirs, is told: Your father would want it. The camera moves in, framing her face in the cold light of a window, and Christina responds: "Must we live for the dead?" Yes, comes the answer. Christina replies poetically, her face framed in profile, though she seems to speak to no one: "Snow is like a wide sea. One could go out and be lost in it, and forget the world and oneself." In this earlier close-up with its expanse of snowy white cheek, and in the final choker frame, there is knowledge of death and the desire for blankness or for obliteration. In the last shot, she faces that wide open sea and, perhaps momentarily, is lost in it, forgetting all. Deathliness is thus inscribed in this face, emptied of all emotion, as it seeks a forgetting that is absolute and nullifying.

There is something about Garbo's effect that is, as Barthes' essay demonstrates, hyperbolic in its intensity, in its extension beyond the boundaries of human capacity (the handbook of hyperbole, *The Guinness Book of World Records*, in fact bestowed the honor of "most beautiful woman who ever lived" on Garbo in 1954). Perhaps this is the rhetorical, even literary, power of her face to which Barthes responds. What does this mean, a face with rhetorical power? Audiences seemed to insist on Garbo's authority over them, to exaggerate her power, to bow down, at least metaphorically, before her image. And Barthes does not hold himself apart from the mass here but seems rather to perform his rapture in an effort to understand it (although he does not offer any self-critique). Thomas Weiskel claims that hyperbole itself is a trope, an "overthrowing, overtaking, overreaching that is closer to simplification through intensity than it is to exaggeration";[31] this may well be, then, the appropriate trope through which to read Garbo's face, a radical simplification of an extreme power. Weiskel places hyperbole in relation to the sublime, but here it works to describe the kind of ecstasy evoked by Garbo's close-up in early-century film audiences. Most of the critical writing on Garbo remains even today within the realm of the hyperbolic, now as part of a literary tradition that sees Garbo as a magnificent effect of the early century. More specifically, Garbo's face provides a link to an earlier era of enchantment, when the face itself was known without mechanical contrivance.

The qualities Barthes describes—the all-absorbing power of the image, its ability to transcend gender, its erotic charge—also characterize the rule of courtly love to which Barthes refers, as he knowingly pays tribute to and places himself within a tradition of adoration. Does celebrity simply enact this earlier version of iconic worship? The rule of courtly love, as Jacques Lacan has influentially argued, leaves open a vacuole, an empty space where Woman is situated.[32] This is not just any woman but a powerful, even cruel, force who punishes and exhilarates via her indifference. She is a manufactured mythology, like the screen star, and exists within a mediated relation into which her supplicant eagerly enters. Celebrity, like the position of the courtly lady, presents a space of desire that one hopes, hopelessly, to fill. Garbo, like the courtly lady, occupies the vacant central space in the web of representation, yet she takes it a step farther as she undoes even the category of "lady" itself: she is Art, the Thing, and within the web of Hollywood-produced consumer relations, she holds a similar (if degraded) power as the Celebrity. Here then we come to the nexus of abstract terms: character is here degraded, made to conform to the requirements of the mass market in the form of personality. In this relation—the shared sign of best and worst, art and commodity culture—emerges the glamour of celebrity, and particularly the hyperbolic celebrity of Garbo.

The Divine

Gilbert Seldes, a pioneer in the genre of cultural criticism that emerged in the twenties, recognized what equaled religious adoration by film fans: "For a long time after 1920, or at any rate since the beginning of the reign of Greta Garbo, women on the screen were idealized in form and feature like the Madonnas of the Renaissance painters. If you look at a Madonna and Child by Leonardo da Vinci, you will see the strong resemblance she bears to the Garbo types that dominated the screen for over a decade."[33] In a world recently vacated by spiritual meaning, the screen star offered a new figure radiating light, an illuminated image before which the public could bow. This is the subtext in Garbo's 1932 vehicle, *Mata Hari*, the tale of the notorious World War I German spy ("Temptress of the Secret Service" ran the advertising copy) who seduced men to obtain their state secrets. Garbo was at the height of her career, and the role seemed perfectly suited to her on-screen powers of seduction. Mata Hari's love for a young Russian officer will lead her, eventually, to death by firing squad, yet the film, as it plots her final act of espionage, seems most interested in investigating the work of glamour itself. In fact, the film is framed by death—beginning with the execution of three spies and ending as Mata Hari herself is led off to her death. Yet the gray opening frames are quickly forgotten as the film's lavish sets and stunning costumes take up the viewer's attention.

Mata Hari is introduced as a celebrity, a sacred dancer to whom Lieutenant Rosanoff is powerfully drawn and before whom he will soon genuflect. She goes to his flat and, in the critical seduction scene, the young man darkens his future considerably when he pledges to put her before god, country, and honor, proclaiming, "I love you as one adores sacred things." Mata Hari, having achieved her desired effect on the man and not yet caring for anything but his state secrets, will demand that her lover put out the flame burning in front of an image of the Madonna. We know, as Mata Hari does, that the flame burns to guard the man from evil and stays burning in honor of the promise he made to his mother on her deathbed. We also know that the extinguished light will signal to a man who waits below for a sign from Mata Hari: the seduction has begun and he may now enter the apartment to steal the military secrets in Lieutenant Rosanoff's possession. The documents will be spirited away, photographed, and returned to the darkened apartment. The secret agent, meanwhile, will do her work, plunged in figurative and literal darkness (the theme of darkness will be literalized later in the film when Rosanoff is blinded).

Garbo, it is true, is hard to resist in the seduction scene, gowned extravagantly as she is by Adrian, MGM's master costume designer, in draping velvet that falls from her shoulder, generously trimmed in flashing sequins. In earlier scenes, she is literally encased in lamé and jewels, armored against human warmth by the profusion of exquisite gems that adorn her long, lean body (Adrian's costume was extravagant in every way, costing about $2,000 and weighing 50 pounds). In this scene, she wears a glittering cap that frames her face, much like the shining halo that surrounds the face of the Virgin. Here we are not meant to overlook the significance: this is the old world of faith, religion, and filial loyalty facing off against the new world of flashy surface, desire, and glamour. The Madonna doesn't stand a chance and the scene marks a critical shift as the naive soldier is drawn into the darkness whispering, "Forgive me."

Garbo, cast as a rival to the sacred, was playing a familiar role, as Seldes's comments indicate. Her celebrity transcended that of most stars, propelled her to a sphere not only outside of ordinary human experience, but beyond that of most of Hollywood as well, just as her nickname, "The Divine," suggests. Critics in the years since Seldes's remarks have ecstatically, and routinely, claimed that Garbo's beauty resides in the ineffable, outside the lowly constraints of common life and the common word. Cloaked in carefully managed mystery, Garbo encouraged adoration that equaled or surpassed religious faith. *Mata Hari,* though a film of little consequence in film history, offered an interrogation of the role of celebrity, and particularly the celebrity of Garbo. The scene that pits one Madonna against another, then, operates as a paradigm for the shifting allegiances of the period, as well as a site of the complicated desires that motivate celebrity worship. Lieutenant Rosanoff's Madonna stands for one version of truth, enduring as the flame that burns before her and that is snuffed out at the behest of the glamorous woman who rests languidly on a divan stacked with pillows below the sacred image. The pose is of course significant. Garbo's seduction rests on a horizontal plane, without any vertical display of energy that might detract from its air of exhaustion and ennui. Reclining on the divan, Garbo/Mata Hari imposes her will and demands the faith of those—her lover, the audience—who gaze on her in the darkness.

The horizontal pose, apparently, was routine for Garbo, or so argues Charles Affron in *Star-Acting:* "Garbo has been photographed supine in erotic scenes with all her leading men....It is something of a trademark."[34] The 1926 image from *Flesh and the Devil* presents us with this supine Garbo, her face brightly illuminated against the swarthy John Gilbert, who bends over her to deliver "the kiss" (the photograph accompanied a 1927 article in *Photoplay* called "The Evolution of a Kiss").[35] Garbo's face registers cool indifference, perhaps bored pleasure, to its viewer and to Gilbert. Her features—brows, lashes, lips—are starkly outlined against the white mask of her face. Gilbert, bowed down, wearing a high-collared officer's jacket, his eyes closed, his lips pressed against her cheekbone, is the picture of formal worship, while Garbo is more casual, less caring, there and not-there, her luminous face ghostly.

With their insistence on her static perfection, Garbo's films—posing the actress against statues, on beds, and so on—underscore repeatedly her air

of passive, even monumental, calm: "Her greatest moments are those non-verbal and nonverbalizable ones, when she somehow seizes the most transitory states and is able to pass them on to us in their purity, avoiding the words, gestures, and expressions of explicit translation."[36] Garbo, in fact, seems to specialize in doing, expressing, emoting *nothing,* as the celebrated final shot of *Queen Christina* attests. One critic, writing in 1950, recounts an anecdote: "A folk tale of the days when Greta Garbo was becoming a star illustrates some of the difficulties of this early period. Her director was accustomed to working with untalented actors and depending on tricks and contrivances of the camera for his effects. Garbo, however, showed him how she could create a certain feeling by merely lifting an eyebrow. The director was not pleased."[37] Garbo was untouchable in her disdain for gesture, expression, movement, even direction; she somehow managed to position herself outside even the requirements of language as Clarence Sinclair Bull's famous photomontage of Garbo as the ancient Sphinx (knowing and refusing knowledge) ironically illustrates.

Strangely, then, the unlikely combination of inertia (what one reviewer called Garbo's "somnambulistic power")[38] and indifferent sexual appetite produced her remarkable appeal: "On the screen, Miss Garbo typifies the languor of passion. She is the only woman in the world who has capitalized anaemia. When she glides, or 'slouches' through a scene, with mouth partly open, and eyelids drooping, it registers as exotic passion."[39] Garbo, then, is both "the epitome of pulchritude, the personification of passion," *and* the phlegmatic sign of exhaustion ("Those who spend days at the studio often say that 'I'm tired' is almost her only expression").[40] A film viewer published a letter to Garbo in 1937 that stepped out of the mainstream and suggested some frustration with the pose of lassitude: "Your fascination and your finesse, in short your glamour, although it exercised an almost hypnotic influence on your public, could not quite hide the fact that, for some years, your acting was curiously uneven. And that in such films as Anna Christie, Mata Hari, and Grand Hotel, your playing was, more often than not, a highly finished piece of somnambulism. You were clever and sophisticated; but emotionally, Miss Garbo, you were walking in your sleep."[41] Perhaps, Miss Canfield, the letter's writer, underestimates the power of ennui to fan the flames of public ardor. What could be so compelling about the display of exhaustion, what was repeatedly referred to as Garbo's "somnambulism"? Garbo worked on the premise of denial, leaving the audience alone with its fantasies and providing no extraneous clue to her interior state. As a blank, though beautiful, screen, Garbo enlisted the erotic energies of her audience to fill in the emotional absence of her performance while she maintained the aloof distance that defined her.[42]

Garbo thus enacts on screen one of literary modernism's central princi-ples, the extinction of personality. The creation of celebrity, in other words, becomes visible as an invention of form, and bears strong affinities with modernist literature. The most obvious literary analogue to Garbo's sleepy power was created by Djuna Barnes in her 1937 novel *Nightwood* (in fact, Barnes reportedly hoped to have Garbo star in the proposed film version of the novel). Robin Vote, the novel's wayward lover, appears as a kind of vacant space, a lost paradise, onto which the other characters project their desires; introduced as "la somnambule" while sleeping, Robin, however, is aligned with nature, humid and tropical, unlike the cold technology that constitutes Garbo's medium: "On a bed, surrounded by a confusion of pot-ted plants, exotic palms and cut flowers...lay the young woman, heavy and dishevelled. Her legs, in white flannel trousers, were spread as in a dance, the thick-lacquered pumps looking too lively for the arrested step. Her hands, long and beautiful, lay on either side of her face."[43] It is important that we first meet the irresistible Robin in an arrested state as she sleeps, immobile, androgynous, her long hands framing her face (and one thinks of the many Garbo photos where her hands frame her face) for the viewer/reader, as if Barnes is reflecting on the static power of the photographic. Robin hovers like an image over the lives of those characters who are drawn obsessively to her; she is a blank to be inscribed, an "uninhabited angel."[44] Robin, who like Garbo resists all attempts to shape her into any predefined role, including that of wife or mother or lover, will wander, at last, onto the altar of a church: here nothing sacred will endure. Robin is a blank that even culture cannot script as she falls outside the sphere of human language; un-like Garbo, however, Robin falls into the animal realm, on all fours, while Garbo transcends the world of consequences and other sordid realities, by remaining remote and far away.

But perhaps there is more to indifference, to the sleepy performance of a star known for the subtlety of her technique, her closed sets, and per-fectionism. Indifference is defined by absence, the absence of interest or attention or feeling: is there something more in Garbo's multilayered ab-sences that drive her celebrity appeal? Glamour, as I have been arguing, is backed by absence, suffused with longing, and defined by the fantasy of distance. Garbo's stylized image, her indifferent gaze, perhaps reminded audiences—the consumers of and supplicants to her glamour—of their own precarious subjectivity that seemed tied to the relentless momentum of modernization. Indifference, or the "blasé attitude," according to Georg Simmel, necessarily characterizes the inhabitants of the modern city and is the sign of renunciation where "the nerves reveal their final possibility of adjusting themselves to the content and the form of metropolitan life by renouncing the response to them." The "entire objective world" is devalued in this stance, and is met with "a slight aversion, a mutual strangeness and repulsion."[45] Garbo's repeated desire to be alone, to sequester herself away from a public that numbered many metropolises crowding in on her, shares some elements, we might imagine, with the aversion of Simmel's theory. Citing the reified urban subject, Simmel writes that "this type of culture...has outgrown every personal element. Here in buildings and in educational institutions, in the wonders and comforts of space-conquering technique, in the formations of social life and in the concrete institutions of the State is to be found such a tremendous richness of crystalizing, de-personalized cultural accomplishments that the personality can, so to speak, scarcely maintain itself in the fact of it." Personality, in the face of the crystallized impersonality of modernism, suffers an eclipse: impersonality is both the cause and response, then, in Simmel's reading of the sociological effects of the urban. Audiences seemed to recognize in Garbo's indifference a shared experience of modern urban life, an aversion to its press of bodies, and a recognition of the lost-ness of personality, and so they responded with rapture to the personality of the screen star, which would, in the end, signify the death of personality itself. Garbo's magnificent face projected onto the big screen (no one could begin to surmise the mental life going on behind her impassive expression) is thus a corollary to the mental states of her audience, each member in isolation—despite the collective or mimetic activity of the theater experience—feeding on the expression of alienation they felt in modern urban life.

From Garbo's Face to Monroe's Figure

I conclude by considering a more recent advertisement that features the celebrity image and the word "glamour." This ad, its bright red background demanding attention, appeared on billboards and in magazines in the late-1990s. While the ad tries to revive the image of glamour, it reflects more the needs of the product for sale than a modern aesthetics of glamour. Marilyn Monroe looms in full color against the vital red of the ad's background; one word of copy, "Glamour," is suspended in a bar of black below.[46] The word, paired with Monroe's image (altered, with a tiny Mercedes Benz symbol on her cheek in place of her legendary beauty mark), works—at least in the advertising strategy—to sell the product with no further information. Monroe and the Benz are known quantities in the logic of this

Glamour

advertisement and their combination signals everything most desirable to the Benz customer—wealth, prestige, and an abundant sexual appetite.

"Glamour," that one word of text, provides the bond that connects product and image and suggests a kind of sexual satiation in their fusion. The word, emptied of the enchantment associated with the aura, signals only the erotics of consumption, allusively signifying desire and the fantasy of its fulfillment. Presence and absence work together in the ad, with the tight close-up of Monroe's face as seemingly present—bearing sexual promise with parted teeth, a little tongue, and beckoning, half-shut eyes—as the car is absent. One can see that Garbo's image would fail to sell the sedan, her long, hard lines would not signal sensual comfort, her gaze is far too penetrating, even ironic. Monroe's image, rather, is all Woman as she suggests the genuine, the authentic, and the vulnerable. Her face, digitally altered with the insignia of the high-end car, cannot be read without a knowledge of tragedy, a truncated lifetime, the embrace of gendered ideology, and without a vulnerability and openness that makes her the object of rapturous desire. Unlike Garbo, there is nothing subtle, transcendent, or ambiguous about Monroe: she is the flesh made familiar, available, and present. Monroe suggests an immediacy of sensation, the smooth ride enveloped in the warmth, if not flesh, of newly tanned leather. Her parted lips remind one of the breath in her voice, her brand of appeal to a generation now able to purchase its fantasy. Monroe invites one to feast without stepping outside the clear lines of cultural expectation, without ambiguity, and without interpretation. Instead she reflects the satisfied retreat into a domestic ideology where Woman is flesh and productive mother without ambiguity or the complicated redrawing of norms governing gender.

Monroe may whet the sexual appetites of a generation, but her image offers less to the literary appetite. Garbo's face—ambiguous, intellectual, undefined—offers more. Garbo's face, as Barthes would have it, gives us passage from an era of ritualized rapture to that of a less noble fascination. From aura to charm: in that transition is glamour, entangled in melancholic loss and desire, whose magnitude is unspeakable, and continually spoken through our engagement with the image and all it seems to promise. The images of Garbo and Monroe, one emerging from the studio era of the 1920s and 30s, the other from the postwar atmosphere of buoyancy and domestic possibility, hinge then on a competing aesthetic: Monroe's image offers sexual promise with the immediacy of purchase, while the figure of Garbo is less emphatically embodied, more abstract, impersonal, modern, and unambiguously glamorous.

5 : PRIMITIVISM

THE COLORED CABARET: "Swift as the pelting rain, the dusky revue, the clang of song and dance, of beauty and color whirl madly by—figures glide on floor of marble, floor of gold."

    Vanity Fair, March 1925

Glamour and Alterity

In the mid-twenties, *Vanity Fair*, that engine of celebrity glamour and upper-crust luxury, showed within its glossy pages a marked interest in Harlem. The "all-Negro reviews,"[1] such as *Shuffle Along* and *Dixie to Broadway*, had been wildly successful in New York's theater district, and the magazine was eager to exploit the new vogue for African American culture north of Manhattan. The editor Frank Crowninshield contracted Eric Walrond, a West Indian fiction writer, to write lively articles on Harlem culture, including one written in black dialect subtitled "An All-Negro Evening in the Coloured Cabarets of New York" and another on the African American roots of "America's Newest Dance Madness," the Charleston.[2] Crowninshield also encouraged the young Mexican artist Miguel Covarrubias, newly arrived in New York, to illustrate Walrond's articles (and many others) with "Negro cabaret types."[3] Both Walrond and Covarrubias became part of the tightly knit fabric of Harlem artists, made their impressions of Harlem's nightlife known to *Vanity Fair*'s huge national audience, and whetted the appetites of the public for glamorized images of the African American.

The fascination with African American life extended beyond national boundaries, and in 1925 Josephine Baker joined La Revue Negre (with sets designed by Covarrubias), created her infamous *Danse Sauvage*, and stunned Parisian audiences with her jungle-inspired gyrations. Baker understood the potential in exploiting any connection—no matter how phantasmic—between the African American and the tribal African. Viewed as both ebony statue and frenetic savage, Baker epitomized primitive glamour as she forged an alliance between outrageous jungle-inspired performance and the opulence that her celebrity afforded (and which would steadily increase through the end of the twenties and the early thirties, when Baker took to walking her diamond-collared leopard, Chiquita, through the streets of Paris). Primitivism, whether onstage, on newsstands, in fashion, or in literature, emerged as cutting-edge style that returned the modern subject to a hazy past of tribal rite, and unleashed desire. Baker's physical movement almost defied description as many reviewers claimed and marked the distance between the disciplined social body of the early twentieth century and the dream of its return to an earlier, less bounded state. "These blacks feed our double taste for exoticism and mystery" one columnist writes. "We are charmed and upset by them, and most satisfied when they mix something upsetting in with their enchantments."[4] The fascination with the primitive depended on the "upset" of civilized tastes, according to this writer; the danger of the unknown, in combination with the pleasure of its performance, produced a powerful appeal to contemporary audiences.

Baker's style, melding African American dance vernacular with dance traditions rooted in West Africa, thus presented to Parisian audiences a hybrid glamour. The final number, the scandalous *Danse Sauvage,* was intended to diminish the show's obvious American roots, betrayed by its predilection for tap dancing and chorus lines, and to emphasize the naturalness of Africa (represented by Baker's bare breasts):

> Wearing her now-infamous banana skirt, she appeared as the young savage Fatou in an African jungle setting replete with palm trees, a sleeping white explorer, and several semi-nude black male drummers. Though her dancing in this and later performances continued to include steps like the Charleston, her Americanness had so faded by 1931 that she was nominated Queen of the Colonial Exposition—until protesters reminded organizers that she was neither from France nor any French colony.... In early twentieth-century France, then, colonialism buoyed the free associative links between Baker's African American dance practice and a surfeit of allegedly primitive cultures even as it collapsed the distinctions between them.[5]

Building on a foundation of American popular dance—notably the Charleston with its exuberant claims to youth and sexual liberation—Baker added the obvious markers of Africa, from bananas to near nudity. French audiences sought something more distant than the jazz rhythms of American dance; instead they paid to see the spoils of colonialism brought home to the Parisian stage and to be charmed by this new representation of human movement. Baker seemed more than willing to give them their fantasy.

The interest in the primitive, then, was not only a scholarly venture into prehistory; rather, the primitivism of the 1920s emerged as a style that joined primitive arts with Western subjectivity, reshaped the modern body, and attempted to reinvigorate its movements. Hannah Höch's 1926 collage, *Die Süße* (*The Sweet One*), graphically illustrates the combination of archaeological object and identifiably modern subject: the sultry eye, pouty lips, and dancing legs of the flapper are cut out and arranged against pieces of an ancient artifact, including a mask whose broad forehead and striations suggest tribal scarification. The body appears hewn from bone, solid and enduring against the fleeting style of its fair legs and feet, fashionably shoed and crossed as if in mid-dance step and lifted out of the chorus line. A smoky red background calls forth ancient and fiery ritual, as well as the red-light, licentious, and cigarette smoke–filled cabaret space. Popular culture meets ancient form in the Höch image that draws from modernist modes of fragmentation and experimental media to represent a newly imagined contemporary primitive form. Primitive style both incorporated and exploited the stylized lines and artistic forms emerging from the Asian, Oceanic, and African cultures that would all be grouped under the same sweeping term "primitive"[6] and relied on those circuits of capitalism that led from colonialism and included the exportation of artifacts and other goods from the colonies. Höch, like Baker, nods to that circuit of capital as she places the ancient artifact on the contemporary stage, made-up, manicured, outfitted across the boundaries of time, though ready for modern consumption.

Thus, as a movement, primitivism was positioned at the complicated intersection of colonialism, European modernism, and the emergent African American artistic presence that would be known as the Harlem Renaissance. In the United States, Harlem became a focal point for glamorized otherness through its late-night cabarets, jazz performances, and the easily exploited fantasy of tropical sensuality and savage release that magazines such as *Vanity Fair* and performers such as Josephine Baker took up and celebrated. Cabaret shows worked the jungle theme, producing entertainments meant to invoke the idea of Africa, and appeared in many—even most—of the Harlem novels published during the period.[7] The cabaret allowed and encouraged a wild and animal release that was openly sexual, unrestrained, and ferociously instinctual. But primitive representation was only primitive in name: Duke Ellington's "jungle music," Baker's hybrid dance routines, the graphic design and illustrations of Aaron Douglas, and the many literary articulations of the primitive demonstrated the kind of artistic control associated with formalism and modernism. The aesthetic

discourse known as primitivism was, in fact, highly sophisticated. Why, one might wonder, did a wide range of self-consciously modern artists embrace the primitive? Certainly, financial gain motivated many of those operating in Harlem and elsewhere, but the primitive seemed to attract as many artists operating on the fringes of consumer society—and highly critical of it—as profit-seekers.

In this chapter I analyze the artistic discourses produced out of this modern fascination with the primitive and the psychic fantasies on which they were built. I am particularly interested in the ambivalence surrounding primitive representation as people were made, or made themselves, into glamorized and primitive objects. The ambivalence is spoken through the oscillating artistic responses that moved from the recognition and critique of commercial exploitation and incipient racism, to the complex and deeply felt pleasures offered by primitive aesthetics. Baker's pleasure, for example, in her on- and offstage displays of primitive aesthetics might seem to contradict her self-fashioning as primitive (and colonized) object. Her apparent delight in performing as the primitive object is generally overlooked in any discussion of modern uses of primitive form; in fact, primitivism has generally been viewed as a damaging fascination, particularly for those black writers who engaged it, encouraged by white patrons such as Charlotte Mason and Carl Van Vechten.[8]

Despite the obvious help Van Vechten offered to young black artists (in the form of publishing contracts, social contacts, and so on), he remains a figure of some controversy in the histories surrounding Harlem of the twenties, largely due to the publication of his novel, *Nigger Heaven,* in 1926. In the same year, Van Vechten had published numerous articles and reviews on various African American art forms, many of which appeared in *Vanity Fair;*[9] yet most of the critical attention was focused on the novel, whose scandalous title largely determined public response, despite the clear (and often ponderous) critique of racism the novel extends. The novel had an enduring, and largely negative, influence, at least according to contemporary critics such as Benjamin Brawley, Allison Davis, and W. E. B. Du Bois, who blamed the book for misguiding both black and white writers into stereotypical images of the exotic and primitive, including their suggestion of sexual license. So says Amritjit Singh, who generally agrees with their sentiments:

> If the fad of primitivism cannot be blamed entirely on Van Vechten or on the group of whites who wrote about the Negro in the twenties, it is reasonable to conclude that the book seems to have had a crippling effect on the

self-expression of many black writers by either making it easier to gain success riding the bandwagon of primitivism or by making it difficult to publish
novels that did not fit the profile of the commercial success formula adopted
by most publishers for black writers. The unusual success of *Nigger Heaven*
and later of McKay's *Home to Harlem* clearly indicated an eagerness for works
exalting the exotic, the sensual, and the primitive.[10]

The primitive, according to Singh, tempted black writers with its ready-
made formula that repeated the imprisoning discourses of racial difference
and racial essentialism. Singh's criticism clearly stems from his politically
engaged reading of the Harlem Renaissance and the ready market that
many writers found difficult *not* to exploit. Yet, here I hope to complicate
the complex *aesthetic* and arguably ethical movement, beginning with its
implications for the ways that subjects and objects were defined. If the
1920s were, as Bill Brown has claimed, the decade of profound attention to
objects,[11] what did it mean for the self-made object? Looking to the expression of primitive glamour by self-consciously urban sophisticates such as
Baker and the Harlem Renaissance novelists Wallace Thurman and Nella
Larsen, I argue that the figure of the primitive could equally be produced
as a reimagining of subject-object relations, a paradoxical critique *and* deployment of pleasures coming out of primitive license, and a picture of
arrest, despite the motion, vitality, energy and erotic frisson imagined to
be at the heart of the primitive. While much revisionary work has already
been done on the representation of the primitive,[12] I want to resituate the
term "primitive" in a more ambivalent direction by addressing its uses and
pleasures for the artist positioned outside of dominant white culture. What
did the primitive offer to those intellectuals and artists who engaged it?
Certainly it offered something more than crippled self-expression: primitive glamour does rely, as Singh suggests, on the use of personae, imper-
sonation, or a kind of eclipse of the human subject, but these possibilities,
despite being fraught with risk, also offered substantial creative results (and
with them pleasure).

The modern primitive, rather than silencing artists with the gag of stereotype or the limitations of the market, often enabled the merging of subject
and object, whereby the primitive object crossed into the modern subject:
in that transaction emerged primitive glamour. Glamour, in this articulation, draws from a crossing of attributes, an impossible longing in the form
of a fantasy of self as the object of desire able to transcend historical and
cultural time. It also refigures the self as markedly other chronologically,
historically, physically and aesthetically. Who is the primitive object? Is there

a primitive subject? For Wallace Thurman and Nella Larsen, this fantasy of crossing object with subject makes the primitive into the glamorous. Rather than simply pandering to the financial dictates of a white racist audience and its colonial fantasies, glamour—whether emerging out of orientalist or Africanist primitivism—offered a mode of objectification based in the pleasure of losing the self. Primitive glamour induced a kind of pleasure that was therefore politically and culturally significant, despite its obvious risks. These writers do not necessarily critique or denaturalize the category of the primitive, but rather find an ambivalent pleasure in which a chosen objectification, through the embrace of an exoticized other, enables a momentary release from different (racist) objectifications. Primitive glamour plays both with racial and gender destabilization as it loosens rigid boundaries and undoes, at least momentarily, the stranglehold of identity.[13]

Death and Artistic License

Wallace Thurman's novel, *Infants of the Spring*, appeared late in the Harlem Renaissance, as activities in Harlem wound down (even if artistic production did not) and the realities of the Depression set in. The novel stages the intellectual debates surrounding the production of African American art during this period and centers on what Thurman sees as the failures of the movement, among them the compromises arising from too-high expectation and the over-zealous interest in any Harlem-produced art. No one escapes Thurman's critique: he takes aim at the patronage of the white establishment motivated solely by its fetishizing gaze, at the black artists who exploit that interest and demonstrate little talent, as well as those artists whose talent is lost to flasks of gin and endless parties; finally Thurman castigates the book industry and Harlem-based journals that will publish and celebrate even the most mediocre writing. The novel ends with a symbolically realized and theatrical death that stages a version of primitive glamour that might seem to corroborate Singh's views about the damaged self-expression of black artists.

Paul Arbian, the "debonair, Paul the poseur, Paul the irresponsible romanticist" is found dead in a tub of water, a result of suicide, leading the narrator to ask, "Was this merely another act, the final stanza in his drama of beautiful gestures?"[14] Paul Arbian has been a shadowy figure throughout the novel, a member of Niggeratti Manor, the subsidized house intended to be a center of community and artistic production but in reality a house with only empty pretensions to art. No one has more pretension than Paul, whose delusions of grandeur increasingly concern the novel's protagonist. Thurman leaves it unclear whether Paul is among the talented or talentless; the reader knows only of his decadent aestheticism, cynicism, and dissipation. Paul models himself, as Monica L. Miller notes, on the figure of the dandy, bringing the Harlem Renaissance into conversation with the Baudelairian tradition of self-fashioning: "Dandy style in the modernist period highlights the presences of a cultural condition in which the binaries that unnecessarily limit identity can be and are being challenged."[15] Paul's aesthetic interests are clearly coded as queer, and the black dandy stands out as the glamorized figure whose interests are decadent, aesthetic, and deathly.

Paul has been the site of excess, of "cultivated artificiality," of extravagant disregard for convention, and when his body is found, it is a poetic and "fascinating spectacle":

> he had locked himself in the bathroom, donned a crimson mandarin robe, wrapped his head in a batik scarf of his own designing…and carpeted the floor with sheets of paper detached from the notebook in which he had been writing his novel. He had then, it seemed, placed scented joss-sticks in the four corners of the room, lit them, climbed into the bathtub, turned on the water, then slashed his wrists with a highly ornamented Chinese dirk. When they found him, the bathtub had overflowed, and Paul lay crumpled at the bottom, a colorful, inanimate corpse in a crimson streaked tub.[16]

The bohemian artist is now represented by a slash of color, an exotic abstraction at the bottom of the tub. This death is self-consciously, and successfully, ornamental: Paul has carefully aestheticized his final scene, creating himself as the brilliant, orientalized object who becomes himself a text, positioned amid and as part of the arrangement of pages from his novel. The attention to detail in this tableau is remarkable, particularly for the singularity of its style: from the Chinese robe, to the batik scarf, to the incense, and finally the knife that would be the instrument of death, Paul has created a picture of deathly orientalism. Certainly the detail betrays something more than a desperate act of despair and one imagines the pleasure with which Paul orchestrated his final and greatest scene.

The narrator carries on cynically: "What delightful publicity to precede the posthumous publication of his novel, which novel, however, had been rendered illegible when the overflow of water had inundated the floor, and soaked the sheets strewn over its surface. Paul had not foreseen the possible inundation, nor had he taken into consideration the impermanency of penciled transcriptions." All that is left is the book's title, "Wu Sing: The

Geisha Man," its dedication to his idols, Joris Huysmans and Oscar Wilde, and a drawing of

> a distorted inky black skyscraper, modeled after Niggeratti Manor, and on which were focused an array of blindingly white beams of light. The foundation of this building was composed of crumbling stone. At first glance it could be ascertained that the skyscraper would soon crumple and fall, leaving the dominating white lights in full possession of the sky.[17]

And so the novel concludes in a flourish of beautiful prose, forecasting the end of the movement known as the Harlem Renaissance and predicting the continued dominance of white culture, figured as the blinding white beams of light.

Is Paul's suicide the ultimate aesthetic statement and "final stanza," or is it the inevitable outcome of a literary world that operates through violence and can be countered only through suicide? The final passage of the novel presents the aestheticized body whose objectification through an orientalizing aesthetic and through suicide becomes the signifier of the Harlem Renaissance and precipitator of its own demise. Thurman's irony is ambiguous, leaving the artist figure somewhat illegible: he may be suggesting that the fictional author's reliance on white, decadent models ensured his ruin, that white literary models would not provide a solid foundation for a black literary movement, or that the dissolution of the Harlem Renaissance would inevitably follow from the dissipation of its glamour-seeking followers (Thurman, perhaps most notably).[18] Thurman's passage raises crucial questions concerning the subject *as* object, the objectifying effects of identity, and the pleasures and risks that attend these processes. One such pleasure appears in the prose of the final passage alone, which is markedly more poetic than any found in the preceding pages. As David Levering Lewis comments in his seminal history, *When Harlem Was in Vogue:* "The novel's ending is conceptually well done and exhibits its most skilled, unencumbered prose."[19] As he constructs the beautifully realized death of Paul through the veil of exoticized aesthetics, Thurman finds his best artistic expression. Paradoxically, then, Thurman's use of an exotic and ritualized death does not stifle the writer but gives him the material for his most skillful prose. Thurman achieves artistic power as he presents the subject as object, the subject who takes the body as material for art, even if this art is self-destructive. It is as if Thurman has discovered something about pleasure and aesthetics that he might apply to his own work. Paul Arbian makes of himself, strategically and consciously, an object and finds refuge there, escaping the enforcement of normative identity, although such escape will require his death. In creating himself as the gorgeous dead object, Paul has finally succeeded as an artist. Does death, then, offer the only aesthetic possibility to the glamorous and glamorizing subject? How, in other words, are we to read this process of self-objectification in narrative and aesthetic terms?

Thurman's aesthetic decisions concerning the fate of Paul Arbian echo some of the insights that Frantz Fanon offers in *Black Skin, White Masks* about the processes of objectification, self-objectification, and its compensations that accompany black identity in a colonized world. Fanon also will figure himself as object, explicitly the object of racist discourse: "I came into the world imbued with the will to find a meaning in things, my spirit filled with the desire to attain to the source of the world, and then I found that I was an object in the midst of objects."[20] His idealistic belief in origins and his own agency is replaced with the devastating knowledge that he circulates as an object in a world of objects. At the moment he understands he is the object of the words "Dirty nigger" or "Look, a Negro," he becomes a participant in that fiction—as all subjects must—and is exposed as both outsider and object in the language of the colonizer. In an effort to survive, he writes, "I took myself far off from my own presence, far indeed, and made myself an object. What else could it be for me but an amputation, an excision, a hemorrhage that spattered my whole body with black blood? But I did not want this revision, this thematization."[21] Fanon describes a psychic division with the power to rend his body; using the language of agency, he describes himself as an object to survive the humiliations of being marked as a racial other in a white world that insists its dominance in overt and subtle ways. Fanon figures his body *as* text in this passage, his blood like black ink spattered on the page, his identity revised, given a different meaning, a "thematization," conforming to the logic of the master narrative that writes him into its self-serving story. Fanon understands that race is itself an ideological fiction, a trope that, while arbitrary, can nevertheless produce real and painful effects. Created in and through language, Fanon will answer in language, figuring himself as a narrative whose plot and authorship he cannot entirely control.

There is, however, at times relief that is left unexplained and ambiguous as Fanon turns to objecthood to find some compensation for the pain he experiences: "Sealed into that crushing objecthood, I turned beseechingly to others. Their attention was a liberation, running over my body suddenly abraded into nonbeing, endowing me once more with an agility that I had thought lost, and by taking me out of the world, restoring me to it."[22] Fanon turns to the other, whose attention runs over his body and renews his agility: his language reflects the tension between mobility—as he imagines himself removed and restored—and the stasis of an object. Only within the space of fantasy can these others provide liberation; in Fanon's language, this fantasy is, paradoxically, erotically charged, although disembodied. He no longer feels crushed, sealed in, and static but cleansed of his body and finally renewed. Fanon describes the painful loss of subjectivity through crushing objecthood, yet how does one account for the fleeting pleasure he recounts, the humanizing moment that defies the overdetermination of racist ideology?

In the fantasy of nonbeing within the symbolic realm, a fantasy of losing his identity status, Fanon can find satisfaction and sustenance, even if only momentary exhilaration is possible. Of course, there is no being without identity. There is no subject before identity, and thus the substitution of a new vision is necessarily a substitution of one identity for another, a fantasy that one can escape the repetitions of identity that both enact and negate one's difference. It is the incongruity of identity—its centrality to the subject who is through identity made into an object—that underwrites the writings of many modernists who observe and enact, in their texts, the collapsing of subject and object. This collapse, in fact, structures the very category of identity. The *Oxford English Dictionary* provides the simplest illustration of the paradox of identity when it defines the noun as denoting first, "absolute sameness," and then "individuality." The absolute of sameness only lasts until the comma, at which point it must make room for difference. Difference, of course, both allows and requires us to claim any identity, since who we are must be defined against who we are not. Lee Edelman complicates this definition when he adds the term "language": "To enter into language is always…to be sundered into identity and to be imbued with a need to defend that identity as a bulwark against the negativity, the endless differentiation, of the language (in which) one has become."[23] As Edelman suggests, it is in language that subjects are created and this is not a peaceful operation; the acquisition of identity is violent and divisive, although it will provide the subject some necessary stability, or at least the fiction of stability. Edelman concludes his essay on the rhetorical structures of identity: "Identity—including racial and sexual identity—depends upon the fracture or *refraction* of unarticulated sameness into the language of difference that would compensate for, and disavow, its partiality; it depends, that is, on the totalization that misrecognizes part for whole in order to create the fiction of the ego, and the subject, as fixed and real."[24] That process of refraction, then, happens in language, draws on deflection and the visual realm, and is rooted in fracture: its root, *fract*, means break and it is the break that expels and inflicts pain, yet provides the possibility of a moment—even if it is an illusory moment—freed from identity when one vision can be substituted for another.

Paul, it would seem, has entered this fantasy and paid for it with his life. Thurman, however, as artist, has not. He achieves a vision of escape, of aesthetic possibility outside the narrow structures of identity. He has used primitivist discourse as a way to open up new possibilities for being and for art. Gorgeous in death, Paul achieves both his and Thurman's artistic dream and this is glamour fully realized: Paul sinks into a state of object-hood, exoticized, created by the ornaments with which he chooses his death yet paradoxically finding in death the self-expression he had not found in life. If death is the logical extension of this state of objectification, it may also, then, be the only outcome to creating oneself as the beautiful, exotic object. Of course, this offers one little choice. Fanon chooses life, and Thur-man, by contrast, follows the logic of the blood-spattered body through to its end, in the ritualized scene of Paul's death. Paul uses the exotic, the other, the primitive rite to provide a vision of self that is enduring, even as the self itself does not endure. Paul controls the plot and its conclusion but does not survive it: rather, he sacrifices himself to become the object, no longer touchable, but lasting in its art, in the narrative it will leave behind.

Primitive Identification

Fanon and Thurman interrogate the possibilities of objecthood as a means to find temporary relief from the harsh realities of everyday life. They each, nevertheless, recognize the obvious dangers of the subject made object. No Harlem Renaissance novel more thoroughly plays out the costs and benefits of self-creation as beautiful object than Nella Larsen's *Quick-sand*. Yet Larsen turns these relations inside out. Rather than emphasizing the objectification of an interior self, Larsen's novel, through its attention to the object world, offers a critique of interiority; rather than interrogat-ing notions of psychological depth, the novel looks to the realm of the surface as Helga defines herself through the beautiful things she gathers around her.[25] In this way, Helga attempts to retextualize her body, to make it signify differently: she rebels against being made into a fetishized object while at the same time constructing herself, with fetishistic attention, as an object.[26] Helga ambivalently embodies desire as she wanders insatiably through the narrative, swept into the fantasy and fetishism of others. She remains impulsive, idealizing one version of herself, while rejecting those versions that conflict with her ideal identification as elegant, tasteful, and perfectly packaged. The struggle in *Quicksand* is ultimately over control of this representation: Helga wants to author her own image (as Paul Arbian has), to produce herself on a stage that she controls, and to create herself as the glamorous other. In this narrative, unlike Paul's, the act of self-creation allows her to escape the immobilizing effects of the objectifying and death-bestowing gaze, at least for a time. Helga, the narrative repeatedly illustrates, *needs* the promise of the exotic, even as the category of the exotic itself has her in a stranglehold, leaving her breathless and perilously close to death.

Hazel Carby persuasively reads the novel as a text about the objectified body in capitalism—a body objectified through its perceived exoticism and its consumption by whites.[27] Yet I wish to account for an aspect of this issue that Carby does not address: the question of aesthetics and the pleasure Helga takes in her own erotic self-presentation and self-objectification. In the conservative setting of Naxos, the school with a philosophy of racial uplift or assimilation where Helga teaches, she dresses to outrage her fellow teachers. Helga will do the same in New York, where her style invites and excites the visual attention of her friends, all of whom, unlike her Naxos colleagues, are urban sophisticates. Deborah McDowell asks, "How to write about black female sexuality in a literary era that often sensationalized it and pandered to the stereotype of the primitive exotic?" She offers an answer: "We might say that Larsen wanted to tell the story of the black woman with sexual desires, but was constrained by a competing desire to establish black women as respectable in black middle-class terms."[28] Helga, however, we know, is not comfortable as a member of the black middle class and objects to its normativizing demands through her eccentric and attention-grabbing dress and behavior. Her attempts to escape from the constraints of what is determined to be acceptable are aesthetic. Yet she will repeatedly be placed back in her body whether by the racial politics of her Harlem circle, the exoticizing attentions of her Danish community to whom she eventually flees for comfort and acceptance, or by the material reality of pregnancy and childbirth. In other words, Helga's attempts to escape the demands of race and gender through her own erotic self-representation are repeatedly thwarted by their repetition by forces outside her that insist on a singular signification—black woman as sexualized object—that eradicate her will to produce herself according to her own desires. In the end, she gives in to the logic of reproduction, moving from the urban societies of Harlem and Copenhagen to the religious South, where she will die in a dusty room, thinking nostalgically of "freedom and cities, about clothes and books, about the sweet mingled smell of Houbigant and cigarettes in softly lighted rooms filled with inconsequential chatter and laughter and sophisticated tuneless music."[29]

Helga continues to dream of objects—even her children are "like rare figures carved out of amber" (122) that she cherishes as perfect objects—and superficial pleasures. She knows that these are the things that provide definition to her fantasy-self, rather than the more readily analyzable taxonomies of race, gender, and class.[30] In fact, Larsen introduces Helga as a beautiful object among beautiful objects: her protagonist cares for aesthetics more than any of the categories (such as race, gender, and class) that define and thwart her. Larsen introduces her in a room noteworthy for its attention to detail; it is dramatically lit, with a spotlight illuminating its occupant and designer:

> Only a single reading lamp, dimmed by a great black and red shade, made a pool of light on the blue Chinese carpet, on the bright covers of the books which she had taken down from their long shelves, on the white pages of the opened one selected, on the shining brass bowl crowded with many-colored nasturtiums beside her on the low table, and on the oriental silk which covered the stool at her slim feet. (1)

Helga's introduction in her carefully arranged space at Naxos defines her better than any psychological profile could: she surrounds herself with gorgeous things and sits, not with an open book in her lap, but at her side. The open book is significant in its role as aesthetic object, highlighted amid the shadows that fill this opening scene. The emphasis on books with their brightly colored covers, the blankness of the white page pooled in the light, suggests the self-consciousness of Larsen's novel as a material item and the luminous potential of the page. Like the book, with only its white pages visible (and in this, like Thurman's white beams of light, gesturing toward white dominance in the pages of history and literature), Helga tries to evacuate her own subjectivity in favor of a surface of blankness, to become an object onto which (even her own) fantasies can be projected. She hopes thereby to recede not from view but from participation in the social and professional world she unhappily inhabits at Naxos. Only after offering us the materiality of the book does the novel disclose the book's identity as Marmaduke Pickthall's *Saïd the Fisherman*. McDowell describes Pickthall as an "English orientalist novelist" and writes that the novel "has Eastern color, movement, and sharp authenticity."[31] The reader understands that this is counterpoised to the whiteness—the exoticizing colonialist viewpoint—that informs its fascination. The role of the book is both prop and signifier not just of the "eastern" country (Syria) where its action takes place, not just of the whiteness whose ideology underwrites those fictional pages, but of Helga's fantasy of herself as a fantasy image.

It is, of course, important that we meet Helga in the context of books (books will appear throughout the novel, always eliciting Helga's admiration), since books allow multiple identifications across boundaries of identity and since they also self-referentially mark Larsen's own artistic expression. In her opening (and closing) pages, Larsen has Helga inhabiting an imagined exotic landscape through the book she reads; yet Larsen also gestures toward the orientalism of the period in her representation of Helga's slim feet, the silks, carpet, and red and black lighting she borrows from the turn-of-the-century fascination with the perceived mystery of the Far East. Helga arranges these objects around her, as if to forge a shape for herself that might be beautiful, mysterious, and distant from the world of mundane concern. Rather than investigating an internal psychological profile of Helga, Larsen here seems particularly interested in the external objects that shape her self-image. Helga, she repeatedly shows us, is drawn to the foreign, the exotic, and the "upsetting" that might disrupt her enchantment.

A more fully experiential and upsetting scene of primitive otherness eclipses Helga when she makes an excursion to a Harlem jazz club with her sophisticated circle of New York friends; here, the contradictions that structure her ambivalent creation of herself as exotic become fully visible. Glamour, in the images of Harlem after-hours (peopled with pimps, chorus girls, jazz musicians, drunks, and slumming whites), depends on an encounter with alterity, an alterity figured as both external to the reading public and as anxiously internal. This dangerous relationship, in many Harlem novels, takes the form of a prim woman with class aspirations who meets a dangerous figure of otherness (Helga, Mary in *Nigger Heaven,* Irene in *Passing,* Emma Lou in *The Blacker the Berry,* and so on) and is mesmerized and changed in the encounter. Borrowing from the popular version of the primitive that links blackness and eroticism, Larsen adopts the understanding of primitivism as a powerful expression of sexuality. She also employs the primitive as a means to escape dominant constructions of the subject. The escape is enabled through an imagined loss of self that accompanies what might be described as the erotic fascination with the primitive.

Employing the primitivist language of the day, the narrator (focalized through Helga) describes the "black giant" who seats them at their table, and the waiter, described as "indefinitely carved out of ebony" (59) like an African sculpture, who serves them:

> For a while, Helga was oblivious of the reek of flesh, smoke, and alcohol, oblivious of the oblivion of other gyrating pairs, oblivious of the color, the

noise, and the grand distorted childishness of it all. She was drugged, lifted, sustained, by the extraordinary music, blown out, ripped out, beaten out, by the joyous, wild, murky orchestra. The essence of life seemed bodily motion. And when suddenly the music died, she dragged herself back to the present with a conscious effort; and a shameful certainty that not only had she been in the jungle, but that she had enjoyed it, began to taunt her....She wasn't, she told herself, a jungle creature. (59)

The only language of sexual desire available to Helga uses the jungle as the rightful arena for wild animal longings, untempered by a structuring super-ego that would police and restrain such impulses. Helga understands herself as temperate *and* sensational; she craves only those sensations she finds in the safe and secluded world of reading. When she is face to face with her desire, her composure—and the image she has tried to project—shatters. The repetition of the words "oblivious" and "oblivion" in this passage suggest the degree to which the self, and the self's hold on rationality, might be compromised in this environment of open sexuality. Further, Helga's fascination with and quick revulsion for the primitive indicates the complicated processes at work in her self-representation and the desire that she resists and attempts to control.

Dr. Anderson is, throughout the narrative, an audience for Helga's various self-projections. He is the fickle object of her desire, and when she spots him across the dance floor, she recognizes an opportunity to reframe her image in his eyes. Yet, quickly her attention is captured by his dance partner, a beautiful woman who Helga learns is disliked by the young African American elite of Harlem for her willingness to "ignore racial barriers" (62). Audrey Denney is rejected by her peers not because of her mixed race but because she refuses to disavow her whiteness, embracing her difference instead. The biracial or multiracial Audrey, with her lovely skin and beautiful clothes, becomes an object of identification and desire for Helga, who watches the beautiful woman intently, studies her as she might herself in a mirror, admiring her "brilliantly red, softly curving mouth" "pitch-black eyes, a little aslant...veiled by long, drooping lashes," the "extreme decolleté" of her dress that showed a "skin of unusual color, a delicate, creamy hue" (60). The woman is figured as the perfectly glamorous object: Helga first sees her indifferently smoking a cigarette. She appears melancholic, her pale complexion is "deathlike" (60) and her hair short and severe. As she gets up to dance, we see through Helga's fascinated gaze: "Languidly the girl followed [Dr. Anderson's] movement, a faint smile parting her sorrowful lips at some remark he made. Her long, slender body swayed with an eager pulsing motion. She danced with grace and abandon, gravely, yet with obvious pleasure, her legs, her hips, her back, all swaying gently, swung by that wild music from the heart of the jungle" (62). The passage is structured through contradiction as it frames the glamorous woman in primitive terms: Audrey smiles with sorrowful lips; her languid sway is also a pulsing motion; she is at once a study of grace and abandon; grave and eager, she is sophistication itself, yet figured as a part of the primitive. The beautiful woman is the figure for a fascinating glamour, a glamour that relies on the tensions between motion and stasis, object and subject, restraint and abandon.

Helga's gaze is arrested, at least for a moment, by this vision of primitive grace: here the primitive is both an expression of the music that induces movement and also Helga's fascinated gaze, fixed on the glamorous Audrey and allowing for a momentary loss of the racial structures that would equate the primitive with the animal world. Instead, fascination with the primitive, the fascination that is itself primitive, opens up to possible modes of self-expression that are not fixed and do not rely on the erasure of the aestheticized self (as in Paul Arbian's death). The primitive sexuality that had disgusted Helga earlier is now replaced in the pleasure of watching the controlled and suggestive movements of Audrey, who inhabits her body without the inhibitions that constrain Helga. The pleasure appears to be amplified by Audrey's overt sexuality and her confidence in the motion of her body and her sexual power. She is everything Helga believes she is not and holds her gaze; the reader sees that they share a great deal. That moment of identification enchants Helga as she watches this possible version of herself, the light-skinned and scandalous woman.

Glamour, as this passage suggests, depends on the other, figured as outside normative discourse. In other words, the transformation of the body into something glamorous will take place only when something outside it intervenes; to be glamorized, the object requires the glamorizing subject to transform it, one who will project her dematerializing and rematerializing fantasies onto it. Audrey becomes the object of the gaze yet an object constructed through contradiction, and through the tensions between motion and stasis, object and subject, control and abandon. Audrey is here the glamorized object of Helga's gaze, a gaze suffused with identification, awe, and desire.

As if uneasy with the transaction it describes, the narration then shifts Helga's gaze to a different and apparently more suitable object: "Helga turned her glance to Dr. Anderson. Her disinterested curiosity passed. While she still felt for the girl envious admiration, that feeling was now augmented by another, a more primitive emotion. She forgot the garish crowded room. She forgot her friends. She saw only two figures, closely clinging. She felt her heart throbbing" (62). While there is nothing "disinterested" in the image of Helga drinking in the erotic energy in the image of Audrey Denney, the narrator here distances Helga's participation in the scene, reducing her fascination to mere curiosity. What was a complicated and glamorizing vision structured through the frame of the primitive becomes mere "envious admiration" that soon will be transformed by the narrator into a "more primitive emotion" directed toward Anderson. As if to delimit Helga's character, the narrative marks out clearly defined boundaries of who Helga can and cannot desire, and where she may draw the lines of identification. Erasing the use of the primitive in the depiction of Audrey, the narrator suggests that Helga's primitive emotion arises only in the vision of Anderson, an emotion that in its clear reference to sexuality must necessarily horrify, leading Helga to bolt: she hastily exits the club and returns home "feeling cold, unhappy, misunderstood, and forlorn" (62).

The reader of *Quicksand* watches Helga watch herself, her terror evoking that of the Freudian primal scene, her fixation at the sight of Audrey's movement recast as the horror of her own desire directed toward its male object. This erotic fascination evokes a kind of primitivism as timeless, existing outside of history, and as holding the power to immobilize its viewer that the narration is unwilling to acknowledge. Here again, then, the reader witnesses the violent encounter between the disciplined, civilized subject and the discourse of the primitive where desire exceeds its boundaries and threatens the coherence of its understanding of the subject. And here again the reader sees those lines of the subject refracted and dissolved in its encounter with the other. Audrey Denney is the object of Helga's fascinated gaze, attaining a glamour that Helga repeatedly attempts to embody and repeatedly achieves in all eyes but her own.

Primitive identification, then, for Helga is dangerous and must be externalized, contained in the objects with which she surrounds herself. This is the conceptual knot that Larsen presents and works to untangle: the sexual energy that charges the primitive encounter threatens to obliterate Helga's careful self-presentation (thus the stress on the words "oblivious" and "oblivion" in the passage above); yet that presentation feeds on a terrifying erotic energy, an erotics necessary to satisfy longings for a self that might transcend the ugliness of everyday life. The scene with Audrey oscillates between the vital motion of sexual desire and the stasis that would contain it, a struggle that drives the narrative forward and then back again, in an unending circuit of desire and its sublimation. Similarly, the objects that surround Helga in the novel's opening provide her with the primitive charge of desire made safely distant. It is as if she can feed from their glamour without experiencing the overwhelming emotion that eclipses her in the cabaret. Primitive identification, then, may be experienced through the object world, or more dangerously, in the world of experience. Either way, the crossing of the modern subject with a force outside itself, with a force perceived to be dangerous and compelling, produces a new vision of self, one that for Helga, as for Paul Arbian, is glamorous, yet unsustainable. As if to underscore this for the reader, Larsen will trace the circuit again: after escaping from the cabaret, Helga embarks for Copenhagen, where once again she makes herself (and is made) the object of the exoticizing attentions of those around her. Again she experiences pleasure as she outfits herself as the object of the exoticizing gaze, and again she becomes restless, returning to New York after a marriage proposal by the famous Danish artist whose portrait of Helga scandalizes her with its explicit eroticism.

Helga's movement suggests a striving for something, but something she cannot articulate: "There was something else, some other ruthless force, a quality within herself, which was frustrating her, had always frustrated her, kept her from getting the things she had wanted. Still wanted.... But just what did she want? Barring a desire for material security, gracious ways of living, a profusion of lovely clothes, and a goodly share of envious admiration, Helga Crane didn't know, couldn't tell" (10–11). Desire remains opaque to her. Disgusted or nauseated by any expression of sexual desire, Helga seeks satiation through those things that seem to satisfy her aesthetic wants, although she will still want more. Finally deciding to act on her desires, Helga makes herself available to Dr. Anderson, who will misunderstand her attentions and rebuff them. Helga, whose position as desiring subject is terrifying to her, breaks down, finding herself at a storefront church where she will be "saved" (the congregation seeing in her a fallen woman). Her marriage to the Reverend Pleasant Green quickly follows, and Helga discovers the physical pleasures of a sexual relationship without fantasy, finding "rank weeds" (122) where she used to imagine the jungle. Weeds cannot sustain the appetites of Helga, however, and she repeats the now-familiar circularity of the novel.

That motion illustrates the Lacanian paradox of desire that Slavoj Žižek narrates: "We mistake for postponement of the 'thing itself' what is already the 'thing itself,' we mistake for the searching and indecision proper to desire what is, in fact, the realization of desire. That is to say, the realization of desire does not consist in its being 'fulfilled,' 'fully satisfied,' it coincides rather with the reproduction of desire as such, with its circular movement."[32] This "circular movement" captures the structure of *Quicksand* itself and represents an inescapability as powerful as that of the quicksand for which the novel is named. It is important to recognize the ways pleasure is expressed in Helga's projection of glamour: it seems attainable only when her environment is unfamiliar and her desires remain at a safe distance. Once she has exhausted the newness of her terrain—Naxos, Chicago, New York, Copenhagen, even Alabama—she retreats, following the circular motion of the closed circuit. The novel's concluding scene reframes its beginning as we return to an albeit less beautiful room that is, nevertheless, suffused with Helga's glamorizing imagination.

Sustained pleasure is located in the condition of objecthood for Helga where she may remain—at least on some level—undisturbed, removed from the ugliness of an unglamorous world. Close to death, Helga reclines in her room, dreaming of more beautiful things and of aesthetic escape. Life for Helga consists in fantasy, in the pleasures of imagined cigarettes, perfume, and superficial chatter. She is the object of her own fantasy, creating glamour in the scenes she infuses with beautifully remembered things. Helga refuses to learn any lesson provided by the events of the novel and for this we should be thankful; she turns into neither the moralizing Jane nor the pious Dr. Anderson. Instead, she holds onto her narcissistic vision, along with her green and gold negligee and the books that inspire her exoticizing imagination. The novel understands the price Helga pays for her commitment to those objects that reflect and refract her ideal image yet withholds its judgment, neither condemning nor condoning the choices she makes (unlike many of the book's critics). *Quicksand* begins and ends in the fantasy of escape, in the dream of restoration, the circular logic of desire spiraling back to where it began. Glamour has a price, according to Larsen (a fact played out in her personal life as well), but is, perhaps, worth it, offering as it does the pleasures powerful enough to enchant the everyday, to provide a different, and better, if only transitory, sense of uplift.

Primitive glamour may be an effect of the arrested image for Helga, who is motivated by aesthetics and lives in a world of ugly politics and narrowly defined identity, but it also makes possible her reconception of identity, a difficult shattering and recomposition that is painful yet, for her, vital. The last pages of the novel tell us that there is no future for Helga, only a thinly rendered present composed of fragments of the past. The veil is descending and the reader's final view of *Quicksand*'s protagonist, as she clings to her lovely fragments—shoring them against her inevitable ruin—is one that Larsen wants us to inhabit and remember: she leaves us at the precarious edge of existence, on the boundaries of subjectivity, thinking of beautiful things. The novel's conclusion, echoing that of *Infants of the Spring*, does not apologize for the protagonist's choice; instead, both narratives place their dying characters among beautiful things, easing their way out of disappointed lives. Glamour, in the scenes of primitive pleasure, has no place in the future; instead it emerges out of a fantasy of what is irrevocably past, in the present only able to freeze time with those objects that suggest something better.

The Future of Glamour and the Fate of Civilization

The ambivalence that defines Helga's relation to the primitive is nowhere visible in the exuberant performances of Josephine Baker, whose embrace of the primitive was, in turn, embraced the world over. Baker held to no boundaries, combining the ornate feathery and sequined costumes with the physical contortionism (the mugging she made her trademark) that delighted audiences and produced, nevertheless, a hybrid glamour. Baker positioned herself, through her mode of artful self-caricature, as the object of desire who fed on the public's fascination with the primitive. The stance may not appear to have been in her own best interest, relying as it did on colonial fantasies about the savage other, yet she took it up again and again, framing herself in the ornamental cage of the primitive. This is overtly rendered in *Zou Zou*, the 1934 film that features her, lithesome and feathered, in a birdcage, singing of her faraway island home, and finally leaving the cage to jump into the arms of several men who await her below. Many critics have read her performance of the primitive as strategic parody or subversion of the very codes that would attempt to contain her.[33] Baker did effectively mock the classes from which she would be excluded, made them laughable, and laughing, carried on with the show.

The biographer Phyllis Rose puzzles over Baker's decision to continue the comedic mugging that complicated her indisputable glamour:

In her films, she is an unsophisticated 'native' who becomes a glamorous creature of the city. In her nightclub acts, she emerges from an egg or appears as a fledgling creature with wings. To put it another way, her glamour is concealed inside her humble, unpolished, and invariably colonial shell. The shell splits to reveal the ravishing creature inside. The question is: Why can't she just show the ravishing creature? Why does she need to keep dragging her shell along? ... For the audience, the insistence on the poor little girl she had been was a way of desexualizing her glamour. ... For Baker, compulsively displaying the poor little girl she no longer was constituted a way of holding on to her racial identity while enjoying a glamour that transcended color.[34]

Glamour, in this construction, cannot be burdened by identity, that is, cannot have a race or at least a race that is not white. Glamour here then is the fantasy of uplift without the politics: rather, it offers an escape from the ugly realities of social (and here explicitly racial) injustice.[35] Of course, the transcendence of color—and indeed of all identity markers—is exactly what Paul Arbian and Helga Crane seek. Yet that seeking leads not to a glamour unburdened by identity but only to the death that attends the impossible task of giving over one's identity. Does Baker, in her relentless self-objectification, escape the moribund aesthetic of glamour? Does her glamour come without a price? Perhaps the bifurcation of identity she maintains allows this escape, the childish exuberance and vitality marking some protection against the lamé-clad constrictions of celebrity and stasis.

An explicit demonstration of Baker's refusal to give herself over to glamour comes in the 1935 film *Princesse Tam Tam*, which investigates, or flirts with, the mobility of identity. Baker, in the character of a "savage" child-woman, Alwina, is taken in by a French Henry Higgins-esque novelist and "civilized." Again, the movie does not deviate from the primitive script: even in her elevation to royal status as Princess Tam Tam (her name a seemingly feminized reference to the "tom tom beat" of the music that moves her to dance), the Tunisian free spirit cannot be repressed. During her royal visit to France, Alwina will burst into dance, revealing the untamed and uncontainable savage, much to the delight of the Western eyes who gaze on her and celebrate her authenticity. The film predictably dichotomizes civilization and nature, the contrived and the authentic, and Baker, it would seem, relishes her earthy position. The elaborate jewelry, high-heels, and lamé gown will have to come off, peeled away and thrown into the audience, who looks on with glee, as Princess Tam Tam becomes Alwina, the primitive girl, her hips shuddering to a tribal drumbeat as she shakes off the pathetic physical constraints of modern Western civilization.

Where Larsen complicates the painful ambivalence of self-objectification, Baker stylizes it, borrowing and emphasizing the vocabulary of primitive otherness and civilized glamour. Just as caricature itself reduces the subject to its elemental lines, the features abbreviated to achieve expressive force, so does Baker.[36] The film in fact employs, as a kind of shorthand for Princess Tam Tam's swift rise to fame, a series of seven caricatures, representing her in various forms but always recognizable as Josephine. The progression of caricatures is in itself interesting, beginning with a conventional portrait, its representation realistic and undistorted, then moving further away from detail until the celebrity is figured by a few thick black lines, recognizable nevertheless by the curl of hair on her brow. Her status, the series of pictures tells us, is unquestioned, her celebrity so well understood that mimesis is no longer necessary. Superimposed behind the series of drawings is a simple marble or stone bust, the defining hair style just barely visible on the sculpted head: this is classical (high) art, smooth, serious, and dignified. The drawings signify popular (or low) art, as they move over the elegant bust, identifying Baker/Princess Tam Tam by the curl of hair on her forehead or at her temple, and the exuberance of her expression in the wide eyes or smiling mouth (without, surprisingly, falling into racial typing). The celebrity of the princess plays off the celebrity of Baker, reproduces and calls attention to it. When we see her powder her nose for photographers, it is Baker we see, just as it is Baker we see in the caricatures. The illustrations will reduce the star to her elemental features, exaggerating them and thus simplifying their interpretation: the complications and ambivalences of identity are thus removed for the sake of strong visual impact and easy digestion.

From the flurry of celebrity images, the film moves to the stillness of a bedroom, a concert of Oriental music playing on the radio, and here we seem returned to a room like Helga Crane's, and in it, her air of quiet dissatisfaction. Baker has the cool pose of sculpture as she reclines on the bed, one knee raised; she is languid, beautiful, the picture of Garbo-esque boredom. This is, for the moment, the transcendent Baker who has achieved the deathly stasis of the perfected image. The camera lingers on her as she rests, for once motionless, seemingly timeless, an aesthetic object fusing North Africa to France. This is, we will learn, an act: Alwina performs a version of Garbo's trademark line, "I want to be alone," and then uses the opportunity to go slumming at a sailor's bar where she can move freely without the constraints of the mannered world. Here we understand the clash of lively vitality and the arresting gaze that so potently drives the style of primitive glamour. This scene, with its sense of static calm, seclusion, and emotional remoteness, might conclude the glamorous text, but Alwina will return to Tunisia, marry the villa servant, bear a child, and turn the villa over to the animals in a comedic ending that undercuts the film's glamour. The final shot frames a donkey's head as it nibbles at the corner of a book, then consumes the whole cover, pulling between its masticating teeth the title "Civilization." While Paul Arbian's novel within a novel will remain unreadable, unknown, obscured by his death, this book holds no mystery: we already know its plot and are happy enough to see it returned to organic material.

The year after *Princesse Tam Tam* debuted, *Vanity Fair* published its final issue, acceding at last to the Depression's financial blows. The magazine did not close its covers, however, without one last look at the glamour that defined its pages: against a bright yellow background, the figure of Josephine Baker smiles, her pearls fly, her feathers just grazing her willowy body.[37] Wendy Wick Reaves notes that "Sparkling with humor, color, and glamour, it was a dramatic farewell gesture for Nast's and Crowninsheld's great, dying magazine."[38] There was something apropos, it seems, in the vivacity of the illustration and the knowledge of death. The magazine understood that in its impending death it could still nod to life, and in that move, it sealed its own glamour.

6 : CELLOPHANE

These new materials are expressive of our own age. They speak in the
vernacular of the twentieth century. Theirs is the language of invention,
of synthesis. Industrial chemistry today rivals alchemy! Base materials
are transmuted into marvels of new beauty.

—Paul Frankl, *Form and Re-form* (1930)

Under Cellophane Skies

As the curtains opened on the avant-garde opera event of 1934, Virgil
Thompson and Gertrude Stein's *Four Saints in Three Acts,* the audience
faced a vast sign of the production's cutting-edge modernity: fifteen hun-
dred square feet of sky-blue cellophane was draped from the sides and
ceiling of the stage, creating a semitransparent cyclorama, glittering under
bright white lights. The stark artificiality of the stage design proclaimed its
relationship to the modern world and its unsurpassed hold on the new:
"The cellophane set, brilliantly lit to evoke a sky hung with rock crystal,
defied comparison to anything the audience had ever seen."[1] The set and
costume designer was Florine Stettheimer, a New York painter whose close
friends included Marcel Duchamp and Carl Van Vechten, and whose paint-
ings were characterized by their light-infused surfaces and whimsical approach to their subjects (her style was sometimes called "primitive *moderne*").[2] Stettheimer had never ventured into the world of stage or costume
design before *Four Saints* (and wouldn't again), but her efforts were met
with critical acclaim for her spectacular vision: "Some thought that [her]
costumes outdid the Ziegfeld Follies, and one quipped that the sets were
'Botticellophane.'"[3] Plastic, that most twentieth-century of materials, here
transformed the stage into a powerful blend of art, glamour, and the latest
technology.

We've lost, in the intervening decades, the ability to read the early-
century semiotics of plastics, and particularly of cellophane. Stettheimer's
stage today, rather than looking sleek and streamlined, appears hung with

the cheap plastic that wraps mattresses or other bulky household items for shipping. But what did cellophane signify? Why was it taken up not only by Stettheimer but by the designers of lavish Hollywood musical sets and their promoters? Cellophane appears throughout popular culture in the 1920s and 1930s, generally signifying the slickly modern. Cellophane tablecloths glitter in an upscale nightclub in the Astaire-Rogers blockbuster *Swing Time* (1936); cellophane also appears in an earlier Joan Crawford film, *Dancing Lady* (1933), in the transparent swags at the back of a dance set, and again in the Broadway musical staged within the film. In this film, the cellophane also appears in costume form: a group of black-attired old women, complete with bonnets, lace collars, wire glasses, and bent-over backs make their way into a futuristic beauty parlor and emerge as modern bombshells, perfectly artificial with cellophane outfits and what might be plastic hair. Cellophane similarly appears in a swanky Chinese nightclub as the "The Girls in Cellophane" take the stage in W. C. Fields's *International House* (1933). The pages of *Vogue* magazine also mark cellophane as haute couture, here as the "cellophane toque" that makes a "deceptively simple"[4] garment cutting edge by newly framing the model's face in the most artificial of head covers; and again, as an arresting sight in this newspaper photograph of an urban street. Cellophane fashion staked out a turning point: cellophane was chic and, above all, *now*.

How could this plastic sheeting have connoted glamour for 1930s audiences? From its first American appearance in 1931 as the revolutionary new moisture-proof wrapper of Camel cigarettes, cellophane was an undisputed success, standing out "as the lone spot of brilliance in the otherwise dismal commercial landscape of the Depression."[5] Cellophane served as a cultural reference with greater significance than the mere freshness of cigarettes: it inspired a new packaging aesthetic as well as an intensified relationship of desire between consumer and product. And the aesthetic clearly went beyond the mundane glamour of such luxuries as tobacco products. Cellophane proved to be a cultural force: besides appearing on the avant-garde stage, the MGM musical set, and as a backdrop to celebrity photographs, it evoked commentary of one sort or another in the pages of magazines such as *Fortune, Esquire,* and *The New Yorker*. Even Cole Porter equaled it to Spanish nights, great art, and Garbo's salary in his 1934 hit "You're the Top" ("You're the purple light of a summer night in Spain / You're the National Gallery / You're Garbo's salary / You're cellophane!"). Cellophane was linked with glamour in its earliest marketing; one of its first advertisements announced "glamorous new transparent cellulose sheeting." Somehow, this tag line fails to convince, but historian Stephen Fenichell writes that

"cellophane was defining itself as a carriage-trade product, a shimmering jewel in sheet form, the epitome of elegance and glamour in the new commercial art form called packaging."[6] And customers were buying.

The development of plastic coincided with the Machine Age interest in streamlined design, clean lines, and the spareness that characterized modern buildings, furniture, industrial design, and so on. The prevailing design aesthetic of the early 1930s was "low, horizontal, sculptural, flowing, [and] evocative of speed"; the "streamlined design reflected the desire for frictionless flight into a utopian future whose rounded vehicles, machines and architecture would provide a visually uncomplicated protective environment...closed off from the Depression and marked by static perfection."[7] Plastics seemed to offer a thoroughly modern medium with the magical power of transmuting and perfecting form. Paul Frankl, one of a group of self-proclaimed industrial designers and author of several books based on the principles of Machine Age design, exclaimed: "The new alchemy! The very name invented by twentieth-century necromancers rival those mystical elixirs of the Middle Ages! Cellophane, pyroxolia, karolyth, aladdinite, pyrolin, amerith, durez!...They are truly the founders of a new language of industrial design."[8] The language of synthetic chemistry—the plastics that inspired the designer's imagination—borrows its vocabulary from shape-shifting, magic, and the plasticity of language itself in a mélange that connotes glamour.[9] Frankl exhorted the public to employ this "new idiom," this "new alphabet" in order to learn its "unprecedented syntax."[10] Plastics, or "materia nova,"[11] provided a modern vernacular that could speak directly to the twentieth century and its miraculously transforming technologies. In speaking this language, one participated in its mysterious alchemy and helped to ensure its utopian results. The new plastics made one, above all, modern. American leisure, Frankl exuberantly proclaimed, must be "wrapped in cellophane!"[12] Leisure, the time made available by machine labor, should be aesthetically brilliant, impervious to the elements, artificial in all the best senses of the word. *Fortune* magazine declared that "the synthetic plastic...is a glamorous substance and a tribute to the powers of man"[13] and Frankl exhorted his readers to wrap themselves up in those powers, make themselves over in a shiny new substance, and celebrate the virtuosity of a transparent plastic coating.

I am interested in cellophane as pure surface, as the plastic without depth that provides the transparent gloss and promises to perfect one's leisure, at least aesthetically. The paper-thin, impermeable layer of cellulose sheeting offered the modern imagination new ways of seeing the mundane world: the glassy sheen of cellophane provided a protective veneer from dusty reality, and, like lightweight and mobile glass, cellophane could wrap anything and thus transform it into a sparkling play of light. Cellophane arrests the gaze at its glittering surface, becomes a version of the photograph, emptied of content or form. This would be a photograph without any representative function, but rather a blank surface that is endlessly appealing, seductive, though it transmits little beyond the wonder of its alchemy. Perhaps it was this blankness that Stettheimer wished to exploit as she planned her cellophane sky and the cellophane robes that some of the actors would wear. Reviewer Joseph Wood Krutch corroborates the empty effects of Stettheimer's cellophane set, claiming that "*Four Saints in Three Acts* is a success because all its elements—the dialogue, the music, the pantomime, and the sparkling cellophane décor—go so well with one another while remaining totally irrelevant to life, logic, or common sense....One will find [like *Ulysses* and *The Waste Land*]...the tendency toward form without content and toward a kind of intelligibility without meaning characteristic of surrealism and the Dadaists."[14]

The comment is directed toward the combined effects of the opera's elements, but it certainly speaks to the function of cellophane on the stage itself. Empty of anything but the barest form, the draped cellulose film is irrelevant to life or logic and offers nothing in the way of meaning. The empty effect was emphasized by the bright white lights that Stettheimer insisted should illuminate the gathered cellophane and made it shine like some artificial and otherworldly sky. Krutch deftly makes the link, then, between the work of cellophane and the more lofty literary modernism that emerged in the preceding decade. As pure form or form without content, cellophane stands in, at least superficially, for some modernist formal ideals. Crisp, smooth, clear, hygienic, even icy in appearance, cellophane was a wonder wrapping and metaphor for language remade, removed of all its "words worn thin."[15] While Stein had nothing to do with the concept behind the set design, the cellophane seemed to suit, perfectly, her approach to writing.

For Stein, neither memory nor representation had any place in writing; instead her writing would gather its force from vibrant word juxtapositions in the flattened moment of what she termed the "continuous present."[16] Flatness was a consistent aesthetic priority for Stein, from the time she wrote *Three Lives* in 1913 to her lectures presented on her return trip to the United States in 1934, just following the opening of *Four Saints*. In one of these lectures, "Plays," she refers to *Four Saints* as a sort of unmoving landscape: "A landscape does not move nothing really moves in a landscape but things are there, and I put into the play the things that were there."

She continues: "Magpies are in the landscape that is they are in the sky of a landscape...they hold themselves up and down and look flat against the sky."[17] The reader, or audience member, would be invited, then, into this flattened landscape to experience a single plane or flattened moment rather than the progressive diachronic demands of typical dramatic narrative. Stein asserts, again in keeping with the formal innovation and transparent surface of cellophane: "After all, my thought is a complicated simplicity. I like a thing simple, but it must be simple through complication."[18] Cellophane offers one version of this complicated simplicity, its empty surface reflecting a complex synthetic chemistry and an experimental history that spanned decades. Formal experiment defines more generally the early decades of twentieth-century literature, and certainly no figure looms larger than Gertrude Stein's.

The production of *Fours Saints in Three Acts* thus offers a unique opportunity to consider the relationship between modernism and the new synthetic materials of the twentieth century. One might even think of cellophane as the objective (and material) correlative to many of the aims of modernism: as an almost substance-less substance, it resonates with Stein's project to drain the signifier of its signification. It harnesses a new generation to consider the impact of the surface through an attention to form (rather than a singular focus on content). It also speaks to an increasing concern with hygiene, both in the realms of public health (preventing the contamination of food) and aesthetics (encouraging the clean line, shorn of all superfluous words).[19] Cellophane, then, as a sign of the new, offered modernists a material with all the plasticity and possibility of language; Stettheimer's set design and Stein's text together spoke in the century's new vernacular, insistently contemporary, to an audience delighted to hear the message.[20]

Plastic and "Limitless Control"

To understand the excitement generated by Stettheimer's set, it helps to understand something of the drama that produced it. Cellophane is, of course, first and foremost a consumer item whose role has been largely played out *not* in the world of design, literature, or avant-garde opera, but in the manufacturing sector and marketing campaigns of such companies as Camel, Lucky Strike, Coty perfumes, and Whitman's chocolates. Its history begins in 1904 when a Swiss chemist worked to invent a waterproof tablecloth. This particular venture failed, but in the process Dr. Jacques

Brandenberger created a method of producing transparent sheets of viscose film. He would form a company in 1913 called La Cellophane (a combination of the Greek *kellon* for "wood" and *phaino,* or "to be seen")[21] with the goal of producing a new film stock, an alternative to the highly flammable cellulose nitrate. Again, this venture would fail (the film was not, after all, impervious to heat), but Brandenberger would continue to develop his synthetic film as a wrapping material, first selling it as an expensive luxury wrapper to Coty perfumes in the early 1920s. The company began production in the United States in 1924 and became a familiar household product with the breakthrough development of the humidor pack for cigarettes in 1930.

The development of cellophane occurs against the broader backdrop of a rapidly expanding plastics industry. Plastics were nothing if not diverse—they ranged from thermosetting plastics (phenolic resins, cast phenolic, urea resins), thermoplastics (cellulose nitrate, cellulose acetate, acrylic resins, polystyrene), and protein plastics (made from casein)—and included such revolutionary materials as celluloid, Bakelite, nylon, and cellophane. Plastics offered industrial designers a new material with unlimited opportunities unhampered by the various challenges of designing in wood, metal, or glass, as one enthusiastic commentator on the development of plastics writes: "From all these limitations, imposed by the nature of materials, the designer is now free. Plastics have given him a new and almost unbelievable liberty for experiment and expression." Now a "limitless control of material"[22] defined the designer's idiom and created a utopia of infinite design potential. The idea of infinity bedazzled the growing numbers of modernist designers, whose art would no longer be made to suffer the tyrannical control of natural materials. The materia nova offered unfettered access to the creative imagination without the limits imposed by the bends and warps of wood, its narrow range of color, or its limited availability as a natural resource; in this way, plastic was the most impersonal of materials, unmarred by any idiosyncrasy, even untouched by human hands. It epitomized another kind of modernist ideal, then, in its cool, aloof distance from the subjective world of craftsmanship.

By the late 1920s, plastics production incorporated modernist design principles, although the history of plastics long predates modernism. The earliest patent of a plastic material was granted in 1855; celluloid proved to be an excellent material for fabricating billiard balls, piano keys, and various other items to resemble ivory, bone, horn, marble, or tortoiseshell. This penchant for imitation aligned celluloid with a distinctly Victorian aesthetic; not only could the nitrocellulose material be formed into highly ornamented household objects that previously only the wealthiest could afford, but its disguise preempted any anxiety around the newness and radical innovation of the product.[23] Plastics, in the guise of age-old natural products, threatened no one and thus conservative public tastes would not bar its financial success. It was not until the 1920s, writes Jeffrey Meikle, that the "modernist disdain for imitation as dishonest and immoral"[24] influenced the way that celluloid was produced and promoted. Those household objects such as brushes and combs were now characterized for consumers as "so radically different, so smart and so modern"[25] and did not hide the fact of their industrial production. Instead they were streamlined, designed according to function rather than according to what modernists perceived as the fussy standards of nineteenth-century ornamentation. The aesthetic of spareness (Ezra Pound suggests a kind of poetic hygiene in his principles of imagism)[26] becomes visible a decade later then on the vanity table and in the pantry.

Celluloid would soon lose ground to the multiple new kinds of plastics that were emerging. Meikle writes that "celebration of an approaching 'plastic age' reflected the euphoria of the industry's executives in the 1920s and 1930s. In a few short years they had witnessed their field's expansion beyond the limited materials and methods of celluloid."[27] A 1929 plastics directory, he continues, lists eighty-four trade names, in 1933 that number doubles, and more than triples by 1939. The amazing growth in the patenting and manufacture of plastics provided a new alphabet indeed for those interested in creating a new aesthetic, which would become particularly relevant for a culture making the transition from the economic boom times of the 1920s to the tightly constrained financial climate of the 1930s. Plastics offered radically democratized access to the products of cutting-edge design: with improved manufacturing processes, plastics could be affordable for a great section of the population who wanted to share in, or speak with, this new and luxurious vernacular. Elite design and middle-class incomes coincided for perhaps the first time as the Plastic Age was ushered excitedly in.

Glamour continued to be linked with plastics, both in the world of elite design and in the more everyday world of consumer goods. A 1940 issue of the trade magazine *Modern Plastics*, for example, makes this connection in an article titled "Vending Machine Glamour." Plastic pulls the "silent salesman" (that is, the vending machine) out of awkward adolescence and into a mature and sexy adulthood: "To the vending machine industry the plastics have given the color and brightness which is helping to transform its products from the awkward appearance of yesterday into the *glamour boys* of today and tomorrow."[28] The article declares the incipient manifest destiny of this industrial marvel:

> In the ingenious and sometimes spectacular applications of plastics to more and more diversified groups of products and uses, each invasion into a new industry constitutes a chapter of singular importance. Frequently, in fact, an entire industry may gravitate in their direction and the plastics find themselves established in a new field almost overnight. That such annexation of new territory sometimes occurs in exposed and unexpected fields only makes the advance more colorful and interesting.[29]

As the language indicates, plastics were sweeping the landscape, conquering new and unexpected lands in a mission to liberate and beautify. The colonizing metaphor is not, in retrospect, so far-fetched: the "freedom" and "limitless control" celebrated by Frankl reappear here in the gleeful tone of an industry recognizing the potential for limitless expansion and therefore limitless profit. The partnership of glamour and the colonial impulse, like that of glamour and the primitive, becomes a recognizable trope in the 1930s. Just as the age of colonial empire was coming to a close, an age of global industrial expansion was opening up. A universe of commercial possibilities came with it, including at times—despite Frankl's excitement about a new vernacular—a borrowed vocabulary from the more tarnished language of empire (though polished up for its new medium). *Modern Plastics* recognized the industry's bright future with its "glamour boys" advancing on the front lines, poised to bring home the sale.

The Race for Plastics

Enter into this climate of euphoric executives, ecstatic designers, and an emergent consuming public the collaborative Thompson-Stein (and I will add Stettheimer) venture, *Four Saints in Three Acts*. Exploiting the vogue for everything African, Thompson had decided to use an all African American cast for the production, claiming (somewhat disingenuously) that the superior diction of African Americans made them the best choice for the difficult language of Stein's libretto: "They alone possess the dignity and the poise, the lack of self-consciousness that proper interpretation of the opera demands. They have the rich, resonant voices essential to the singing of my music and the clear enunciation required to deliver Gertrude's text."[30] Van Vechten, surprisingly, given his penchant for all things Negro (he was, after all, situated at the center of the Harlem Renaissance as patron, cheerleader, photographer, and a writer of some infamy after the publication of his novel *Nigger Heaven*),[31] disapproved of Thompson's choice, believing that Stein's text had nothing to do with African Americans. Stettheimer also expressed her apprehension on aesthetic grounds, worrying that the "varied brown skin tones would sully the brilliant colors of her costumes"; she consequently (and apparently seriously) "proposed painting the cast white or silver."[32] The artist, whose aesthetic interests ranged from extravagant Victorian landscapes of lace to the more austere modernity of cellophane (her own apartment was decorated in draping lace and cellophane), would incorporate both materials, creating formal costumes against the wondrous vacancy of the surrounding cellophane skies.

When Stein herself heard of the plan to costume the black actors in cellophane, she also expressed grave doubts about maintaining the integrity of her text: "I suppose they have good reasons for using negro singers instead of white, there are certain obvious ones, but I do not care for the idea of showing the negro bodies, it is too much what the English in what they call 'modernistic' novels call futuristic and do not accord with the words and music to my mind."[33] Stein apparently worried about the clash between the false futurity of the falsely modern, and her own truly modern prose of the "continuous present," a prose that had brought literature, she claimed, into the twentieth century. She made this claim about the appearance of *Three Lives*, its central story "Melanctha," of course, exploiting the fascination with African masks and African American stereotypes (the story explicitly circles around Melanctha's insatiable desire as she learns to gather "wisdom" or sexual knowledge). Stein was certainly invested in representations of race—as many critical works on her explore—but in *Four Saints*, she claimed, her interest was elsewhere.

Carl Van Vechten's assertion that *Three Saints* had nothing to do with African Americans seems reasonable. The opera focuses on two sixteenth-century Spanish saints, Ignatius and Therese, and is, like much of Stein's work, difficult to paraphrase neatly. The four saints of the title number more like twenty, and there are four or even five acts rather than the promised three. The word "negro" appears twice within the text, though the use is arguably glancing: "Saint Therese. Could a negro be be with a beard to see and to be. / Saint Therese. Never have to have seen a negro there and with it so."[34] Stein distinguishes seeing and being, producing categories of difference, and opposing ontology to superficial appearance. The negro, with visible beard, is *there* to see, embodied and ontologically unquestionable, despite the question form of the line itself. Eight lines later the scene ends with "Saint Therese come again to be absent." While the negro emphatically, or at least doubly, is said to "be," Therese herself comes again (in the voice of the continuous present), reappears, but only in her absence, derealized in the visual realization of the negro. The embodiedness of the negro, in these lines, is counterpoised to the absent body of the saint (who is paradoxically there and not there). In this sense, one sees that being is bestowed on the African American (who is not absent) here; Stein uses the idea—that is, borrows the popular stereotype—that the African American is all body, closer to nature, and thus becomes the figure for embodiment altogether (as she had when she created the character of Melanctha). The body of culture, however, is represented by the saint, who is present only in her absence, in the luminosity of her halo, and who occupies the space of idea rather than any sort of solid physicality. Thompson may have reflected on these lines as he made his casting decision, but it seems more likely that he was working within a milieu that appreciated the avant-garde implications of using a cast of African American opera singers; he was also banking on the guaranteed notoriety this would bring to the production (*Porgy and Bess,* George Gershwin's opera featuring an African American cast would premiere the following year, in 1935).

It has been suggested that it was the prurience, if not the notoriety (she seemed comfortable with this), of showing bodies beneath cellophane that concerned Stein in the Stettheimer design, although these robes would, in the end, be worn over richly ornamented costumes (even the hands of the cast would be chastely covered with white gloves, combining two popular images of African Americans as minstrels and devout churchgoers). According to Steven Watson, "Only in the opera's 'sniplets,' as choreographer Frederick Ashton dubbed the two fleshly *divertissements,* did the dancers reveal flesh. One of these, a dance in the second act about six angels learning to fly, featured women with bare midriffs, the shortest of skirts, and bare-chested, bare-legged men."[35] Watson adds a comment on the overall effect of the casting and set design: "At just the right moment, *Four Saints in Three Acts* offered a casting revolution, daring and inevitable, at once libidinous and prim, wrapped up in a gauzy candy box of a setting." This, the aesthetic of primitive moderne, best characterized the opera's overall look: if there was a race for plastic, it was the African race, and in that juxtaposition the production achieved a winning effect, at least as far as the artistically minded of 1934 were concerned. The black body, at least for avant-garde audiences, signified some proximity to nature and the *feeling* that modern culture (that is, "civilization") denied its subjects. The cellophane stage, then, represented a sort of reality principle: its cold swags, reflecting the bare bright lights, produced a riveting and modern blankness.

The cast members, in all the ontological *presence* accorded the African American, appeared in relief against the modern and deeply compelling absence of the set (and against the disembodied *absence* of the "civilized" and thus white modern subject who did not appear at all on the *Four Saints* stage). The modern script that accepted the civilized/primitive binary held true, then, even on the avant-garde stage. Modernity, represented by the manufactured plastic sky, is here aligned with death or stasis, in contradistinction to the life force of the African American cast on stage.

Here we see glamour as both depending on and rejecting the other, recognizing difference as the thrill of transgression. Glamour, emerging from the new technologies signified by the appearance of plastic, the sexual availability that glamour promises and withdraws, and the implicit exclusions on which it is based, is thus founded on a paradox. The racial dividing line on the *Four Saints* stage marked a distinction between life—represented in the casting decision—and death, here associated with civilization and its industrial production. Cellophane, invented in an exhilarated rush of entrepreneurial energy and embraced by a generation of artists who recognized in it the sign of the new, works in conjunction, then, with death. If, as Freud succinctly claimed in 1920 when he introduced his theory of the death drive, "the aim of all life is death,"[36] the mass of cellophane hanging over the stage was a harbinger of that inevitable return to an earlier state of matter. Death was thus inscribed on the stage, presented against the vitality of the opera's performers, singing against the chasm, or the void that defines human life.

Regarding Nothing

While blankness, absence, and transparency are not unique to the text and staging of *Four Saints*, they produced a particularly timely demonstration of its impact on the modern stage, and on the modern subject. Absence, and its suggestion of a greater Nothing, appears repeatedly in the literature of the period as a defining trope of the modern. Modernist literature often swirls around a central and structuring abyss: one thinks of the meaning-collapsing darkness of the Marabar Caves in *Passage to India,* Caddy's painful absence in *The Sound and the Fury,* the circular wandering and central lack of *The Sun Also Rises,* the missing main character of *Jacob's Room,* or the terrifying Nothing that characterizes the work of Beckett and Kafka. This structural emptiness reflects the anxiety of a world no longer able to rely on reason, a world in which, as Heidegger characterizes it, "we hover in anxiety"[37] against a defining Nothing. Nothing is the formless void, yet even "void" suggests its status as object. It is without form, without status in our world of nouns. "Nothing" may be interpreted in numerous registers, from the psychoanalytic (one thinks of Lacan's Thing, that zone around which desire endlessly circles, the vortex or vacuole linked to the failure of language and representation, the space that stands for all we have lost in the transition from infancy), to the existential, to the metaphysical and theological. Even a generation after Nietzsche, the modernist age continued to be characterized by the *nihil* and the death of god. In god's place, as Marxist theory argues, was the growing fetishization of the commodity: plastic, produced in the magic of synthetic chemistry and met with the public's perpetual wonder, takes up its place as fetish, then, despite the blankness of its surface.

But blankness isn't, after all, identical to nothing. Blankness, particularly the blankness of cellophane, merely comes to represent the nothing through the emptiness of its surface. It is not nothing but signifies, or better gestures toward, the nothing that generates so much anxious modernism (Eliot's paradigmatic line, "I can connect / Nothing with nothing" comes to mind).[38] Rather than ask cellophane to bear the weight of these significant philosophical enquiries into the nothing, I simply want to invoke its power on Stettheimer's stage as metaphoric, as speaking through its shallow and shiny surface to a culture quietly hovering in the anxiety of historical change, a questionable hold on reason, and dizzying technological development. This affective response, one might note, echoes the effect of the sublime, characterized by the bewildered response to something incomprehensibly vast, outside the individual's powers of reason to contain it. Blankness, without the delimiting detail, presented the vastness of scope that the sublime generally indicates.

In his work on the sublime, the artist and art critic Jeremy Gilbert-Rolfe points out the growing use of blankness as a signifier in the early twentieth century:

> The passage from the Victorians to modernism and beyond is one which leads from a *horror vacui* to a displayed blankness.... Transparency was also close to the idea of the instantaneous, whereas detail is a matter of duration, and this is the sense in which the kind of modernism grounded in an absolute substitution of transparency for detail and plenitude may be seen as a transitional period between what it despised and what takes it for granted. Before modernism, accumulation and detail, after it, blankness.[39]

Gilbert-Rolfe suggests that transparency, here synonymous with blankness (a point to which I will return below), becomes a wider cultural ideal and signifier for all that is modern. Transparency provides a new way into time itself, which was being newly and constantly theorized during the modernist era. "Duration," in Gilbert-Rolfe's usage, is not to be confused with the Bergsonian "durée," which describes the experience of time as outside of chronology, overlaying past, present, and future in a single and simultaneous moment. The modernist moment, the arresting of an instant in the rush of the crowded events of historical time, provided a way to open up and understand experiential time outside the tyranny of chronology. Like the instantaneous, Stein's continuous present and James Joyce's "fluid succession of presents"[40] (a concept much like Stein's notion and produced at roughly the same time) bespeak an intimate relationship to the modernist experimentation with and theorization of the "fourth dimension."[41] Captured in the transparent skies of Stettheimer's set was a vision into a complexly realized and dramatically flattened time. Her billowing sky, then, suggests this multiply constituted nothing, the window that offers no information except the gleam of its own blankly transparent surface.

Transparency and blankness, although apparently analogous, in fact operate in different registers. Transparency relies on the logic of consumer desire: the clean, see-through material that appeared to consumers in the early thirties offered both an unimpeded view of the product and an additional sheen that improved its appearance; its smooth, glossy surface created a relationship of desire, acting as tantalizingly flimsy barrier, between consumer and good. Transparency thus encouraged consumption through a series of promises, from the cleanliness and good health of the product to the style and modernity of its package.[42] Blankness, however, works on a much vaster scale and does not engage the desires produced by consumer goods; rather, blankness points to absence and to the terrifying and exhilarating void that eighteenth-century theorists elaborated in their works on the sublime. Gilbert-Rolfe is most interested in charting the shifting significations of blankness through the Victorian period up to the contemporary moment. He writes: "Where [blankness] once marked the absence of the sign by being a sign for absence, it is now the sign of an invisible and ubiquitous technological presence."[43] He describes the meaning of blankness at both ends of this short historical spectrum from the realm of crowded visual detail to the silent hum of the electrical (or digital) current: for the Victorians, blankness was absence, the space to be (anxiously) filled. Blankness was not a desirable condition but one to be addressed (thus the ubiquitous wallpaper of the era). In the contemporary moment (Gilbert-Rolfe is writing in the last breath of the twentieth century), blankness itself is the sign, blankness speaks, it is eloquent rather than silent. Blankness today, he argues, finds expression in excess (an excess linked to the electronic and digital age) rather than absence.

Modernism is importantly situated between these two understandings of blankness. Gilbert-Rolfe uses the modern period in its transitional importance, as a moment of shedding the earlier demand for detail and an increasing desire for the blank surface. Yet the point should not be skimmed over lightly: hardly a passive transitional period, modernism defiantly took up the empty, the blank, or the transparent, projecting it as a historical condition and aesthetic ideal. Particularly fascinating is how in the modern period, blankness was *both* the absence of any variety of things—spanning a vast categorical range from ornament to metaphysical values—*and also,* in the figure of cellophane, the sign of a newly ubiquitous, or a swiftly becoming ubiquitous, technological presence. It is the both/and that fascinates me here—how blankness during the modern period signified absence (in the form of things lost or cast off) *and* presence in the form of the overwhelming recognition of technological power. Gilbert-Rolfe refers to the pervasive technopresence associated with the age of computer technology; cellophane, rather, and particularly on Stettheimer's stage (and also on the Hollywood set as I will discuss below), suggests the overarching, all-encompassing presence of the technologies born out of synthetic chemistry—these audiences could have no idea just how thoroughly plastic would permeate their lives, even eventually their bodies—via its consumer-driven products. Nevertheless, its blank surface, shimmering innocently (that is, as if to bear no message) in the bright lights, one might experience the vastness of its import, a recognition of the exponentially increasing power of technology over the puny human subject and in this sense a sublime in which, as Gilbert-Rolfe argues, the infinite nature of technology replaces the formerly infinite nature of nature itself.

In the twentieth century, nature is outdone by the velocity of technological development, as Walter Benjamin has famously noted;[44] caught up in the tremendous surge of its power, the modern subject experiences a newly revised sublime. The power, one should remember, comes from chemistry, the science that shares in the magic of alchemy and shape-shifting. With the recognition that the physical universe was alterable through the new capacity to change its physical properties, anything seemed possible. The force of this revolutionary technology overtakes and carries along everything in its path—nature will not look the same again, once the industrial world has allied itself with sweeping technological change, and a new era of mass production has begun. This is more visible to us now, having the whole of the century to observe at once, but in the 1930s, technological potential was thrilling (as was the idea of conquering nature), though mixed with the anxiety that accompanies any such sweeping change and encounter with magic.

Art deco design worked to maximize the tension between the blank quiet of smooth lines and white surfaces and the impending explosion of the technologized world. Van Nest Polglase, the designer behind the beautifully stark sets of the Astaire-Rogers films, developed "the fixed architectural institution that soon became known as the B.W.S. (Big White Set)."[45] The signature look was one of white on white to emphasize the smooth harmony and open space of the set: "Bodies, or rather costumes, which also formed an essential part of this environment, had to be streamlined even when standing still" which added to the "total, smooth environment" of the set.[46] Gloss was a premium feature of the design, and Polglase employed plastics (particularly Bakelite) to produce gleaming dance floors. The result was a calmly static set, although Polglase also exploited the effect of circles against angles to "suggest the springs and spokes of a machine, or, more abstractly, the contrast between movement and stillness."[47] Polglase featured cellophane in the 1936 film *Swing Time,* as I mentioned earlier, creating a set that was clearly artificial (even ironically so with the cellophane-clad glamour girls) and streamlined to heighten the effect of the dancers. Technology was quietly visible on stage, although the expanses of cellophane suggested calm stasis over the noise associated with industry. This was Hollywood magic at its purest, combining the beautifully engineered with the veneer of impenetrable beauty.

Perhaps one of the greatest displays of Hollywood alchemy, and one that explicitly linked technology with the infinite, was the extravagant sixty-five-hundred-square-foot set constructed for the final dance sequence of the Fred Astaire–Eleanor Powell musical, *Broadway Melody of 1940.* This was the largest set ever constructed for a dance sequence and gathered all the forces of Hollywood technical wizardry. Ann Miller recalls its massive, mirrored-glass floor and "midnight blue cyclorama wired with 10,000 light bulbs for stars."[48] Thirty-foot mirrors multiplied the set's effect as they reflected the light, the dancers, and produced an effect of infinite depth. A giant curtain of thinly sliced cellophane hung toward the back of the set, and through it the seemingly innumerable stars shone. Twenty-five-foot palm trees, also constructed from sliced cellophane, completed the effect of a desert oasis, their cellophane fronds hanging sleekly over the whole set. The Merrill Pye art deco design emphasized the seemingly infinite space, the palm trees, and stars visible on every surface, producing an effect that was clean, slick, and entirely comprised of shimmering surfaces.

The final extended dance sequence begins as a woman in sarong and head-wrap sings Cole Porter's *Begin the Beguine* in a sultry style of music appropriate to the tropical setting. The actress here is Carmen D'Antonio, though the singing is dubbed (the vocals are by Lois Hodnett). D'Antonio's filmography indicates that she worked, for the most part, as a secondary player, cast as a dancer and "harem girl," "native girl," servant to Salome, the "treasure of Kalifa," and an "Oriental dream"[49] (she even once played the Puerto Rican love interest of Uncle Bill on the 1960s television series *Family Affair*). She offered Hollywood a pretty and generic otherness that could authenticate its fantasies of Singapore, Arabia, or Morocco. In this Astaire-Powell vehicle, D'Antonio provides an exotic and old-world counterpoint to the sleek Plastic Age features of the set. A chorus of women appears like a dreamy harem in beautifully flowing costumes, their midriffs bare as they sway to the sensual music. A gauzy curtain parts to reveal the cellophane trees, and behind them, the shimmering cellophane swag. This gigantic MGM set is designed to produce the utmost effect of glamour, with its infinite reflections, its glassy surfaces, and the exotic dancers who, like Thompson's African American cast, provide a shorthand sign for authenticity, a measure of the distance modern culture has come, and an expression of the modern desire to preserve the vision of a simpler and more sensual life (the women, swaying in unison and singing softly suggest beautiful field laborers, picturesque in their servitude). The visual spectacle, resulting from the combination of cellophane and this picture of ethnic authenticity literalizes the movement of the sublime from the awesome power of nature to the cool distance of glamour. The physical embodiment, or the weightiness of the authentic or natural is displaced, replaced by the physical transparency, the sleekness of the manufactured product.

The Carmen D'Antonio character quietly disappears as the real star, Eleanor Powell, rises before the cellophane curtain, her white costume a variation on a belly-dancer's seductive garb but made for the athlete's body, as Powell's movement quickly demonstrates. The set gives a sense of infinite depth: Powell's figure is reflected in the mirrors, she dances on the shimmery image of palm fronds, there are lights shining everywhere. Fred Astaire appears and together their feet tap in swift and complicated harmony, the exoticism of the piece undiminished in its passionate choreography. Considered "the greatest tap duet ever filmed,"[50] this choreography does not fail to awe in its technical mastery and dazzling design: the sound alone is stunning, the deftness of their tapping feet imperceptible to the eye. This is the body made machine. One might say that here is the sublime, re-realized for an eager moviegoing public: the infinite sound, the depthless

lights, the reference to otherness, the glassy impenetrability of the set produce an echo of the sublime in its glamour, bolstered by the explicit use of streamlined technology.

But before the audience can quite make out the complex desire initiated by this sequence, it comes to a close as the couple dances offstage and soon reappears, recostumed for the next segment in all-American clothes. Powell is in a ruffled knee-length day dress, Astaire has shed his toreador costume for a comfortable suit, and the music has shifted to a more recognizably American swing tempo. They are the picture of go-to Americans, engaged in friendly competition on the dance floor. It is good clean fun as goofy smiles replace the serious expressions and erotic overtones of the preceding segment, and the cellophane set recedes from view, as each dancer shows, again, a staggering—and this time individual—tap virtuosity. Finally, in a flurry of spins they dance offstage, are reunited with a friend (played by George Murphy), and the three return to the stage, the image of happy, wholesome, American friends.

In the background, significantly, remains the chorus of women in their Easternized costumes, immobile and statuesque against the cellophane curtain. Here we see the image of American vitality against the beautiful static glamour of the background, and here the film ends. While one may argue that cellophane has played the smallest of roles here, offering some style in the form of a shiny accent, I argue, rather, that it stands for the beckoning emptiness of the modern age, the transparent reminder of the absence at the heart of, or especially at the heart of, the most innocent American pleasures. The cellophane curtain and palm fronds, hanging like icicles, offer the cold artifice of glamour, a stillness in the background that arrests the eye, despite the athleticism and hard-working effort of the film's tap-dancing stars.

Nudity and High Buildings, or, Cellophane Rising

> Chicago in the summer of the Century of Progress…a confused impression of gaiety and boob-baiting…of Bible-belt citizens coming to gasp—and gape…and returning, after a wondering examination of the multitudinous exhibits of science and the arts, with only this one memory sharp and clear: nudity and high buildings.[51]

The giddy use of the new plastics and particularly of the candy-wrapping cellophane had its detractors. *Esquire* published a satirical image called "The Cellophane Gown" (by Gilbert Seehausen) in 1933, the first year of the magazine's publication. The 1933 Chicago World's Fair (branded as "The Century of Progress") was the instigator of the image, as the above caption makes clear. In the image, a shapely model smiles as she poses in high heels wearing an extravagant and entirely transparent cellophane gown. Richly gathered folds of cellophane fall behind her, a ruffle of cellophane fans about her shoulders, and what looks to be a cellophane tiara tell us that this outfit is a version of the modern ball gown: she is a fairy queen, though an immodest one. On closer inspection, one notices some complicating details: the gown's full skirt resembles a grass skirt belted with flowers, a flower lei is draped about the woman's neck, a bra or bikini-top is visible. Is this another modern-day primitive posed against an ultramodern setting? Behind the smiling model, an array of skyscrapers fan away from her. She balances like a beauty queen, rising up in the metropolis in all her plastic glory: Jane of the urban jungle. The image captures the recognition that plastics are on the rise, taking the city by storm, and by seduction.

If cellophane connoted everything modern, it shared all the failures of the modern age, including its vulgar consumerism, its reliance on the rhetoric of progress, and its overt commodification of sex. E. B. White, in the same year as the *Esquire* image appeared, wrote an impassioned pamphlet called *Alice through the Cellophane* that bewailed the shallow commodity culture that had seemed to enwrap the public's mind and threatened society with a kind of consumer-culture asphyxiation: "The revolution began with cellophane," he complains; people are "intrigued with its new transparencies," and driven to accumulate, egged on by the empty promises of ambitious industrialists. White makes clear that "[he] should like to propose a society based on the assumption that nobody is going to buy anything, ever again."[52] Cellophane, for White, stands in for all that has gone awry in a society recently impoverished and nevertheless obsessed with its purchasing power: "I can imagine no more tender or healthy sight than a group of little children making the cellophane plant rewind all the little rolls of transparent wrapping material at the end of the day, like a spider eating his own rope."[53] White imagines children, presumably untouched by the corrupt influence of plastic (unlike today's children, whose toys seem exclusively made of plastic) to be the disciplinary parents, making the cellophane plant rewind all its glittery, candy-like product for the good of the adults.

The glamour of the new products could not last. Plastics entered into a new phase of mass production during the war and a dawning recognition of the environmental costs of the explosion of cheap disposable products chilled the utopian dreams once inspired by the alchemical marvel. What

THE CELLOPHANE GOWN *by* **GILBERT SEEHAUSEN**

Chicago in the summer of the Century of Progress . . . a confused impression of gaiety and boob-baiting . . . of judges declaiming against "those who would put pants on a horse" . . . of other judges insisting upon "if not pants, then at least something" . . . of Bible-belt citizens coming to gasp—and gape . . . and returning, after a wondering examination of the multitudinous exhibits of science and the arts, with only this one memory sharp and clear: nudity and high buildings.

had seemed the magic of its immortal qualities now acquired new meanings as the nondegrading plastic waste claimed more and more space. The sublime delight at the universe of possibility associated with plastics production became sublime terror at the sheer magnitude of disposal. And the semiotics shifted: what once appeared new, glamorous, and a link to the modern design world, was now cheap, disposable, and a sign of impoverishment, ranging from that of the natural world to the world of culture. Of this fall from the giddy heights of early production to the backs of our cupboards and the garbage dumps, Roland Barthes remarks: "Plastic has climbed down, it is a household material. It is the first magical substance which consents to be prosaic."[54] Like the aging star, cellophane could not hide its defects (its toxicity, its yellowing in time), nor maintain its glamour.

Sylvia Plath would put this in more extreme terms in her *Ariel* poem "Paralytic," which presents the patient lying in a modern hospital, gripped by the past:

> Dead egg, I lie
> Whole
> On a whole world I cannot touch,
> At the white, tight
> Drum of my sleeping couch
> Photographs visit me——
> My wife, dead and flat, in 1920s furs,
> Mouth full of pearls…

The prognosis is not good as the introduction of cellophane will make clear:

> Eyes, nose and ears,
> A clear
> Cellophane I cannot crack.
> . . . .
> The claw
> Of the magnolia,
> Drunk on its own scents,
> Asks nothing of life.[55]

Here is glamour in its most deathly guise, drawing on past images of 1920s fashion, the flatness of the photograph, the inward-turning magnolia in its perfumed drunkenness, and the stifling, life-denying layer of cellophane. The thrill of technology in the first wave of plastics production gives way here to something far more insidious.

Coda: Cellophane Futures

I close by considering three more recent expressions of cellophane fashion in dress form. Each tells us, in one way or another, how far we have come from the modernist aesthetic that celebrated the power of transparency, blankness, the dress as an empty sign. First, a Leonard Joseph design from 1968: one would not guess this dress was made from cellophane, embellished as it is with gold and laden with sequins. The dress may be made of plastic, but it appears in masquerade, hardly announcing its industrial raw material. Cellophane is mere idea here: it carries the dress but holds on to none of its identifying features. Certainly there is no celebration of plastic in this richly textured gold shift. Instead the dress connotes a kind of luxurious royalty, apropos of the royal who wore it, fashion icon Lee Radziwill. Second, a 2003 Givenchy Couture show featured a cellophane gown as elaborate as the 1933 *Esquire* image: one reviewer, clearly delighted, wrote: "[Givenchy designer Julien Macdonald] threw caution to the wind only once, when a giant gown of iridescent ruffled cellophane blew along the runway" (Sarah Mower, style.com). Yet, this gown takes up deep rich color, works with an opaque palette that resembles the rainbow of an oil slick, and does not use, for its effects, the utopian blankness of the cellulose material. Here the vision is one of excess, a colorized plastic canvas, producing an extreme combination of vamp and vampiric, darkly threatening with lacy accents. The cellophane continues to connote deathliness, mirrored in the blank indifference of the runway model's expression, yet the Givenchy gown reaches back to a prior age, literalizing in its design the threat of plastics as a dangerous seduction.

Finally, a photograph from the *Honolulu Star Bulletin* on February 12, 2002, pictures a statue of Queen Kapiolani wrapped up in what could be a plastic sarong. The caption reads: "No, this isn't the latest cellophane gown from the avant-garde designers in Paris. The statue of Queen Kapiolani was wrapped up in plastic yesterday as workmen began preparations for a flower bed." Prosaic indeed: here the plastic serves only to protect the queen from the mud that surrounds her as two men labor at her feet. The image echoes, in remarkable ways, the primitive moderne—Thompson's African American cast, the female chorus of *Broadway Melody,* and the transparently clad model of the *Esquire* image—yet it tells us that plastic as image no longer has any cultural power. As the emperor to his clothes, the queen to her plastic wrap: this time, however, the nothing is simply that, serving no metaphor, no artistic movement, no galvanizing aesthetic. The Nothing,

the conceptual abyss that motivated so much of the work of modernism, disappears in these more recent uses of cellophane. Modernism had attempted to respond to the gaping center with its insistently gorgeous prose, its attention to the effects of a carefully contrived surface, and its own deployment of a glamour that might transfix the reader and thus transform an age. We might remember Stein's words: "And each of us in our way are bound to express what the world in which we are living is doing."[56] In 1934, when she said this, she referred to the sweeping effects of the cinema on human subjectivity. She might also have been referring to the plastics that were coming to redefine the meaning of "continuous present."

When Anthony Patch, one of Fitzgerald's failed heroes, learns that "desire cheats you," he refers to a phenomenon we now recognize as the power of glamour: "It's like a sunbeam skipping here and there about a room. It stops and gilds some inconsequential object, and we poor fools try to grasp it— but when we do the sunbeam moves on to something else, and you've got the inconsequential part, but the glitter that made you want it is gone—."[57] We may demand the sparkling surface, like a cellophane coating, yet what we are able to grasp will be of little consequence. Glamour wields the power to capture its viewer's attention as if by a spell that fascinates and arrests. It promises access to time that ignores grammatical boundaries; glamour offers a relation to the past, however, that cannot be enacted. Transfixed, one gazes at a world of possibility that is foreclosed, inaccessible, yet endlessly alluring. The pleasure of glamour thus operates on the premise of denial, on fantasy, and on a willingness to gild the world around us with a knowledge of its necessary ephemerality and thus its inevitable loss. Yet the pleasure of the glitter offers some compensation, at least in the moment, for the thing we cannot have. It may not be sustaining, as Anthony Patch discovers, but the thrill of proximity, of living within the circle of magic, is a driving force and one that propels the aesthetics of modernism.

I return to this book's opening epigraph from Blanchot, who invokes the depthless depths, the abyss that is desire, in his definition of fascination. Yet Blanchot quickly turns from the language of depth and suggests this depth itself is an illusory one: "but the fact is that this light is alien to revelation, has nothing to reveal, is pure reflection, a ray that is still only the radiance of an image."[58] The fascinated gaze can only look back at itself, revealing nothing about the image, providing the subject only a narcissistic view that brings together subject and reflected image, collapsing their difference in the radiant and illusory moment. Light illuminates light, a grand effect with nothing serving as foundation but a desire to believe in its reflection. As

H. D. puts it in "Projector," light takes shape from nothingness, "renders us spell-bound, / enchants us / and astounds."[59] Here, as in a wide range of modernist work, we have radiant form—the pure reflection of glamour, a pure reflection that *is* glamour, enveloping, seducing, and charming both its writer and reader.

Notes

INTRODUCTION

1. On the history of smoking and its marketing in the early twentieth century, see Eric Burns, *The Smoke of the Gods: A Social History of Tobacco* (Philadelphia: Temple University Press, 2007); Sander Gilman and Zhou Xun, eds., *Smoke: A Global History of Smoking* (London: Reaktion Books, 2004), and Richard Klein, *Cigarettes Are Sublime* (Durham: Duke University Press, 1993).

2. Mick Lasalle, quoted in Noah Isenberg, "Cinematic Smoke," in *Smoke*, ed. Gilman and Xun, 255.

3. See Tanya Pollard, "The Pleasures and Perils of Smoking in Early Modern England," in *Smoke*, ed. Gilman and Xun, 38–44.

4. Nineteen-year-old Bacall's famous line comes in her first film, *To Have and Have Not* (William Faulkner was one of the screenwriters), based on Hemingway's novel of the same name.

5. T. S. Eliot, "Cousin Nancy," in *Collected Poems 1909–1962* (London: Faber and Faber, 1963), 32.

6. Richard Klein, *Cigarettes Are Sublime* (Durham: Duke University Press, 1993), 3.

7. Ibid., 10.

8. Pollard writes that "despite its reputation for masculinity and potency, the association of tobacco with pleasurable intoxication led to attacks on what many saw as the feminine passivity and powerlessness induced by its addictive and narcotic qualities" ("Pleasures and Perils of Smoking," 38).

9. An immense effort to deglamorize cigarettes marks contemporary media coverage. Nicole Kidman's smoking at a Cannes Film Festival press conference in 2003 garnered wide press coverage and brought the disapprobation of, reportedly, her director as well as her "fuming" public. The *Sydney Morning Herald* reported: "During a press conference to promote a new film…she bummed a cigarette from another actor and puffed away, despite the director, Lars von Trier, saying: 'Nicole, please don't do that—you promised'" (May 24, 2003).

10. Sander Gilman and Zhou Xun write in their book's introduction: "While smoking dissolved cultural and social barriers, it also enforced them. As smoking became more and more a part of the life of ordinary people, a problem arose, which had to do with pleasure. Smoking gives pleasure, but this was to be enjoyed by royalty, by the privileged and by the elites, not by

the self-respecting working masses, whose preoccupations were supposed to be work, productivity and discipline" (*Smoke*, 15).

11. Klein, *Cigarettes Are Sublime*, 17.

12. Of course, there is also a camaraderie to smoking: the social smoker, the group that gathers outside the doors of an office building, etc. See Matthew Hilton, "Smoking and Sociability," in *Smoke*, ed. Gilman and Xun, 126–133.

13. One could fill books with references to earlier incarnations of glamorous figures, from the magical transformation of the loathly lady in the Wife Of Bath's tale, for example, to the notorious eighteenth-century socialite (and later poet), Mary Robinson, to the nineteenth-century stage act of the "electricity fairy," Loie Fuller. See the fascinating accounts of the latter figures in Michael Gamer and Terry F. Robinson's "Mary Robinson and the Dramatic Art of the Comeback," forthcoming in *Romantic Studies*, and Rhonda K. Garelick's *Rising Star: Dandyism, Gender, and Performance in the Fin de Siècle* (Princeton: Princeton University Press, 1998). Stephen Gundle, in the only elaborated critical reading of glamour that I have found, more precisely locates its origins in Paris during the Belle Époque:

> Glamour as it is understood today emerged at a quite specific point in history that was characterized by: the shift in terms of the general order of meanings and priorities from a society dominated by the aristocracy to one governed by the bourgeoisie; the extension of the rules of monetary exchange ('commodification') into ever wider public and private spheres; the development of a new urban system of life permeated by consumerism and the importance of fashion; the closer proximity of the theatre and 'high society'; the creation of patterns of leisure experience shared by virtually all urban classes; an obsession with the feminine as the cultural codifier of modernity's tensions and promise ("Mapping the Origins of Glamour: Giovanni Boldini, Paris and the Belle Époque," *Journal of European Studies* 29 [1999]: 269–295).

Tracing the development of a "pictorial language of glamour" (291), he focuses on the portraiture of Giovanni Boldini, an Italian painter who worked in Paris from 1871 to his death in 1931: "It may be argued that precisely Boldini's subjects (society women) and the special look he conferred on them (edgy, Parisian fashionableness) placed him at the very centre of a set of transformations that were crucial to the invention of glamour" (270). Boldini, in this reading, serves up a scandalous theatricality in his society portraits, especially those depicting such modern types as the divorcée, gaily living on the edges of polite society. Yet what Gundle leaves out is the crucial *medium* of glamour, the technology and mass reproduction that inevitably shaped its popular perception. One might trace glamour's genealogy to the Parisian moment—Gundle's case is after all convincing—yet glamour had only begun to emerge as the definable force that will shape the aesthetics of modernism.

14. Regenia Gagnier, "Wilde and the Victorians," in *The Cambridge Companion to Oscar Wilde*, ed. Peter Raby (Cambridge: Cambridge University Press, 1997), 22. Harlem Renaissance writer (and dandy) Bruce Nugent cites the same anecdote ("was it Wilde who had said...a cigarette is the most perfect pleasure) and clearly revels in a Wildean delight of the senses in his story "Smoke, Lillies and Jade!": "oh the joy of being an artist and of blowing blue smoke thru an ivory holder inlaid with red jade and green." "Smoke, Lillies and Jade!" in *The Portable Harlem Renaissance Reader*, ed. David Levering Lewis (New York: Viking, 1994), 573, 576.

15. Talia Schaffer and Kathy Alexis Psomiades, *Women and British Aestheticism* (Charlottesville: University Press of Virginia, 1999), 6.

16. The novel that most mercilessly explores these risks is Andre Gide's 1902 *The Immoralist*, in which Michel, inspired by the Wildean character, Ménalque, sacrifices everything—his wife, his wealth, and ultimately his health—to the pursuit of pleasure.

17. I am thinking of studies such as Bill Brown's influential *A Sense of Things: The Object Matter of American Literature* (Chicago: University of Chicago Press, 2003); Rebecca Walkowitz's *Cosmopolitan Style: Modernism beyond the Nation* (New York: Columbia University Press,

2006); and the works of, for example, Rita Felski (*The Gender of Modernity* [Cambridge: Harvard University Press, 1995]); Simon Gikandi (*Writing in Limbo: Modernism and Caribbean Literature* [Ithaca: Cornell University Press, 1992]); and Laura Doyle and Laura Winkiel, eds. (*Geomodernisms: Race, Modernism and Modernity* [Bloomington: Indiana University Press, 2005]). Work within the field of new modernist studies has been defined by its extended range of interests, as Rebecca Walkowitz and Douglas Mao write: "The new modernist studies has moved toward a pluralism or fusion of theoretical commitments, as well as a heightened attention to continuities and intersections across the boundaries of artistic media, to collaborations and influences across national and linguistic borders, and (especially) to the relationship between individual works of art and the larger cultures in which they emerged." *Bad Modernisms* (Durham: Duke University Press, 2006), 2.

18. On the role of the marketplace in modernism, see Stephen Watt and Kevin J. H. Dettmar, eds., *Marketing Modernisms: Self-Promotion, Canonization, Rereading* (Ann Arbor: University of Michigan Press, 1996); Aaron Jaffe, *Modernism and the Culture of Celebrity* (Cambridge: Cambridge University Press, 2005); John Xiros Cooper, *Modernism and the Culture of Market Society* (Cambridge: Cambridge University Press, 2004); James C. Davis, *Commerce in Color: Race, Consumer Culture, and American Literature, 1893–1933* (Ann Arbor: University of Michigan Press, 2007).

19. Douglas Mao's book *Solid Objects: Modernism and the Test of Production* (Princeton: Princeton University Press, 1998) beautifully works out the complicated relations between the object as commodity and as symbol, arguing that neither can be understood independently of the other. While Mao's work tells us a great deal about the modernist enchantment with objects and while this bears a great deal on the idea of glamour, I add more weight to the ephemeral, the fluid, and the intangible in modernist form, rather than to the enduring and solid.

20. Angela Leighton, *On Form: Poetry, Aestheticism, and the Legacy of a Word* (Oxford: Oxford University Press, 2007), 1.

21. Ibid., 14.

22. Virginia Woolf, *Orlando: A Biography* (New York: Harcourt Brace, 1956), 124.

23. *The New Fowler's Modern English Usage,* 3rd ed., ed. R. W. Burchfield (Oxford: Oxford University Press, 1998), 333.

24. Virginia Woolf, "Modern Fiction," in *Essays of Virginia Woolf,* ed. Andrew McNeillie, vol. 4, *1925–1928* (London: Hogarth Press, 1986), 160.

25. James Joyce, *Portrait of the Artist as a Young Man* (New York: Penguin, 1992), 231.

26. Joseph Conrad was especially fascinated by this leap and makes it central to his famous preface to *The Nigger of the "Narcissus"* and to the novel itself where he evokes the transcendent power of aestheticized language to lift words to new and magical heights. Conrad suggests the modernist interest in tapping into unfamiliar modes of expression that might be channeled to enchant and delight the senses. The novel is fascinated by the process of reading itself, that act which lifts us out of one reality and places us into another that is more gripping, more extraordinary.

27. Christopher Isherwood, *Good-Bye to Berlin,* in *The Berlin Stories* (New York: New Directions, 1945), 1.

28. Michael North, *Camera Works: Photography and the Twentieth-Century Word* (Oxford: Oxford University Press, 2005), 12. See also Nancy Armstrong's *Fiction in the Age of Photography: The Legacy of British Realism* (Cambridge: Harvard University Press, 1999) as a way of rethinking literary modernism with visual culture, and Karen Jacobs's study of vision and modernism in *The Eye's Mind: Literary Modernism and Visual Culture* (Ithaca: Cornell University Press, 2001).

29. North, *Camera Works,* 3–4.

30. Photographs and photography appear in *The Voyage Out, Jacob's Room, Orlando, Swann's Way, Heart of Darkness, The Great Gatsby, Howards End, HERmione,* and numerous

other modernist texts. *An American Tragedy,* Theodore Dreiser's 1925 novel that is generally associated with naturalism and not modernism, uses the camera as recorder of fact, weapon, and object of violence that literally leaves its imprint on its victim's face. In *Howards End,* twice a photograph is dropped and twice it inflicts a wound as its viewer retrieves its pieces.

31. Joseph Conrad, *Heart of Darkness* (London: Penguin Books, 1995), 90–91.

32. Laura Frost's work on the libidinal energy of fascism in modernist representation suggests the ways that glamour might be harnessed for fascist ends. See *Sex Drives: Fantasies of Fascism in Literary Modernism* (Ithaca: Cornell University Press, 2002). See also Andrew Hewitt, *Fascist Modernism: Aesthetics, Politics, and the Avant-Garde* (Stanford: Stanford University Press, 1993), and Paul Morrison *The Poetics of Fascism: Ezra Pound, T. S. Eliot, Paul de Man* (New York: Oxford University Press, 1996) for the connection between modernist aesthetics and repressive politics.

33. Theodor W. Adorno, "On Popular Music," in *Essays on Music,* ed. and trans. Richard Leppert (London: University of California Press, 2002), 437–469. See especially 448–450.

34. Laura Mulvey, *Fetishism and Curiosity* (Bloomington: Indiana University Press, 1996), 47.

35. Douglas Mao and Rebecca Walkowitz, eds., *Bad Modernisms* (Durham: Duke University Press, 2006), 4.

36. Two recent books explore the possibilities of negativity in modernism. Heather Love's *Feeling Backward: Loss and the Politics of Queer History* (Cambridge: Harvard University Press, 2007) finds powerful possibility in the negative for queer aesthetic and political expression. Sianne Ngai's *Ugly Feelings* (Cambridge: Harvard University Press, 2005) also makes an argument for the surprising aesthetic and political potential of negative feelings or affects.

37. D. H. Lawrence, *Women in Love* (Ware, Hertfordshire: Wordsworth Editions, 1992), 7. All further page references appear parenthetically.

38. Jean-François Lyotard, "Representation, Presentation, Unpresentable," in *The Inhuman: Reflections on Time,* trans. Geoffrey Bennington and Rachel Bowlby (Stanford: Stanford University Press, 1991), 121–124.

39. Glamour also emerges in the eroticized description of Walter Morel, the protagonist's father in *Sons and Lovers:* "Gertrude Coppard watched the young miner as he danced, a certain subtle exultation like glamour in his movement." D. H. Lawrence, *Sons and Lovers* (Oxford: Oxford University Press, 1995), 15.

40. Letter to Dollie Radford, June 29, 1916, *The Collected Letters of D. H. Lawrence,* vol. 1, ed. Harry T. Moore (London: Heinemann, 1962), 456.

41. Wallace Stevens, "Extracts from Addresses to the Academy of Fine Ideas," in *Wallace Stevens: The Collected Poems* (New York: Vintage, 1982), 252.

42. Immanuel Kant, "Analytic of the Sublime," in *Critique of Judgment,* trans. J. H. Bernard (New York: Hafner Press, 1951), 83.

1. PERCEPTION

1. Chanel here took her cue from Paul Poiret, who was the first to remove the necessity of the corset from women's fashion. Poiret's fashion, often heavily orientalized, tended toward the lush and ornate while Chanel pared this back, modernizing and simplifying the lines of her clothes.

2. The perfume was lucrative for Chanel's business partners, Pierre and Paul Wertheimer, who controlled 70 percent of the stock. She didn't make much money herself on the perfume, owning only 10 percent. Chanel and the Wertheimer brothers would be entangled in lawsuits for years. See Axel Madsen, *Chanel: A Woman of Her Own* (New York: Holt, 1990) and Janet Wallach, *Chanel: Her Style and Her Life* (London: Mitchell Beazley, 1990) for a history of the contractual disputes between Chanel and the corporation Parfums Chanel, over which Wertheimer had control.

3. Madsen, *Chanel,* 133.

4. On the development of Chanel No. 5, see the following histories: Madsen, *Chanel;* Edmonde Charles-Roux, *Chanel—Her Life, Her World* (New York: Knopf, 1975); Richard Stamelman, *Perfume: Joy, Obsession, Scandal, Sin: A Cultural History of Fragrance from 1750 to the Present* (New York: Rizzoli, 2006); Harold Koda and Andrew Bolton, *Chanel* (New York: Metropolitan Museum of Art, 2005). The date of the perfume's first appearance changes in various accounts—1920 in Charles-Roux, 1923 in Madsen (making it coincide with Chanel's fortieth birthday), 1922 in Diane Ackerman's *A Natural History of the Senses* (New York: Vintage, 1990). The Chanel company itself claims 1921 as the date of the perfume's introduction.

5. Chandler Burr, *The Emperor of Scent: A Story of Perfume, Obsession, and the Last Mystery of the Senses* (New York: Random House, 2002), 206. Burr's book narrates the remarkable story of Luca Turin's genius for the science and enjoyment of scent. Also see Turin's *The Secret of Scent: Adventures in Perfume and the Science of Smell* (London: Faber and Faber, 2006).

6. William Shakespeare, sonnet 5 in *The Complete Works of William Shakespeare,* ed. William Allan Neilson (Cambridge, MA: Riverside Press, 1906), 1170–1171.

7. Chanel was concerned with her lack of formal education and paid Maurice Sachs, a young friend of Jean Cocteau's, to stock the shelves of her library with books she should read. She also, throughout her life, surrounded herself with the artistic elite, including Stravinsky, Cocteau, Marie Laurencin, Erik Satie, and Colette. See Madsen, *Chanel,* 128–131.

8. Shakespeare's sonnet has often been read in terms of sexual desire and sublimation: see particularly Richard Halpern, *Shakespeare's Perfume: Sodomy and Sublimity in the Sonnets, Wilde, Freud, and Lacan* (Philadelphia: University of Pennsylvania Press, 2002). Turin sees perfume differently, as his chapter titles suggest: "What Perfumes Are *Not* About: Memory and Sex"; "What Perfumes *Are* About: Beauty and Intelligence." Turin moves perfume into the more abstract space of the intelligence and away from the body and its more earthy desires.

Wallace Stevens indeed writes against the object, or at least the objectivism of a certain strain of modernism associated with poets such as William Carlos Williams, who, incidently, also enshrines the number 5 in his 1921 poem "The Great Figure":

> Among the rain
> and lights
> I saw the figure 5
> in gold
> on a red
> firetruck…

With his concrete images, based on clear-sighted description, Williams produces a vivid, immediate, and present poetry. Williams, particularly in his early poetry, is not so interested in the insubstantial as he is in the thereness of the thing, its material presence and its visual impact.

9. Turin, *Secret of Scent,* 54.

10. These terms come from perfume reviews and columns found on the influential perfume blogs basenote.net and boisdujasmin.net.

11. Wallace Stevens, "The Idea of Order at Key West," in *Wallace Stevens: The Collected Poems* (New York: Vintage, 1982), 130.

12. Ibid.

13. Mikel Dufrenne, *The Phenomenology of Aesthetic Experience,* trans. Edward S. Casey (Evanston: Northwestern University Press, 1973).

14. In fact, Dufrenne comments that "it is clear that there are no arts of contact, e.g., of odor, taste, or touch. When one speaks of an art of perfumery or of cooking, 'art' signifies technique" (358). Despite this claim, he also argues that "perception does begin in presence, and it is precisely aesthetic experience which confirms this. The aesthetic object is above all the apotheosis of the sensuous, and all its meaning is given in the sensuous. Hence the latter must be amenable to the body. Thus the aesthetic object first manifests itself to the body, immediately inviting the

body to join forces with it. Instead of the body's having to adapt itself to the object in order to know it, it is the object which anticipates, in order to satisfy, the demands of the body" (339). The application of his theories to perfume, despite his demotion of perfume to technique, seem obvious.

15. Dufrenne, *Phenomenology of Aesthetic Experience*, 226.

16. Wallace Stevens, "Effects of Analogy," in *The Necessary Angel: Essays on Reality and the Imagination* (New York: Vintage, 1951), 118.

17. Ed Comentale writes: "Poets such as Pound and Eliot tended to use analogy in a relational sense, as a way to unite the world's disparate forms and thus forge a higher, abstract order." See *Modernism, Cultural Production, and the British Avant-Garde* (Cambridge: Cambridge University Press, 2004), 125.

18. Stevens, "Effects of Analogy," 130.

19. "Thirteen Ways of Looking at a Blackbird"; "Notes Toward a Supreme Fiction"; "The Snowman."

20. Jacqueline Vaught Brogan, *The Violence Within, The Violence Without: Wallace Stevens and the Emergence of a Revolutionary Poetics* (Athens: University of Georgia Press, 2003). Brogan usefully compares the objectivist practice of Williams and its rejection by Stevens. See particularly pages 11–16.

21. Brogan persuasively reads this poem as a response to Keats's cold pastoral in "Ode on a Grecian Urn" (ibid., 11).

22. "Imagination as Value," in Stevens, *Necessary Angel*, 139.

23. *Letters of Wallace Stevens*, ed. Holly Stevens (New York: Knopf, 1966), 434.

24. Stevens comments on the music of this poem in his essay "Effects of Analogy." Interestingly, he cites the lines of the poem that address smell, although his only stated interest is the musicality of the lines:

> A washed-out smallpox cracks her face,
> Her hand twists a paper rose,
> That smells of dust and old Cologne,
> She is alone
> With all the old nocturnal smells
> That cross and cross across her brain,
> The reminiscence comes
> Of sunless dry geraniums
> And dust in crevices,
> Smells of chestnuts in the streets
> And female smells in shuttered rooms
> And cigarettes in corridors
> And cocktail smells in bars.
> (*Necessary Angel*, 124–125)

25. Stevens, *Letters*, 443.

26. Ibid., 402.

27. Ibid., 252.

28. Wallace Stevens, "The Reader," in *The Palm at the End of the Mind: Selected Poems and a Play*, ed. Holly Stevens (New York: Vintage, 1971), 102.

29. Wallace Stevens, "Phosphor Reading by His Own Light," in *Palm at the End of the Mind*, 195.

30. T. S. Eliot, "Tradition and the Individual Talent," in *Selected Prose of T. S. Eliot*, ed. Frank Kermode (New York: Farrar, Straus, and Giroux, 1975), 41.

31. Michael Quinion, World Wide Words.org.

32. Richard Halpern, in his analysis of Shakespeare's sonnet 5, claims it as "a tiny treatise on poetic sublimation" (*Shakespeare's Perfume*, 14). "A manifestation of pure *claritas*, Shakespeare's perfume bottle is a distant ancestor of the snowy, asceptic bowl in Wallace Stevens's 'The Poems

of Our Climate.' The bottle's walls of glass are visually transparent but semiotically opaque; they reduce the image to mere seeming or appearance rather than meaning" (18). The sublimation, Halpern goes on to argue, is that of "everything [the sonnet] tries to exclude," namely sodomy in a "theologically subversive form of aestheticism" (20) that links sodomy with sublimity in what he will figure as a "counter-sublime" (31), returning it to the world of human desire and transgressive aesthetics. The work of sublimation has profound implications for the work of art and leads to an aesthetic object that is ungovernable, lawless, yet smells faintly of more earthy concerns. Halpern's analysis is compelling in its tracing of the lines of desire that emerge in the space of seeming that is liberated by the aesthetic object. The sublime, his essay asserts, is a space of contestation between competing modes of desire that direct us, inevitably, back to the human. Personality remains central to Halpern's thesis, then, as desire finds expression in the "semiotically opaque."

33. Thomas Weiskel opens his influential study, *The Romantic Sublime: Studies in the Structure and Psychology of Transcendence* (Baltimore: Johns Hopkins University Press, 1976) with the sentence: "The essential claim of the sublime is that man can, in feeling and in speech, transcend the human" (3).

34. "Dante," in *Selected Prose of T. S. Eliot,* ed. Frank Kermode (New York: Farrar, Straus, and Giroux, 1975), 216.

35. In fact, Dufrenne discusses at length the merging or reconciliation of subject and object in the sensuous. For a discussion of this effect, see the translator's introduction, *Phenomenology of Aesthetic Experience,* xxxi–xxxiv.

36. Immanuel Kant, *Critique of Judgement,* trans. J. H. Bernard (New York: Hafner Press, 1951), 97.

37. Marshall Berman, *All That Is Solid Melts into Air: The Experience of Modernity* (New York: Viking Penguin, 1988). Berman theorizes modernism as the effect of historical forces, particularly the modernization that has fed the "maelstrom of modern life" (19).

38. The doctrine of impersonality is much more complicated than I may seem to suggest here. Maud Ellman writes that "even in its early days...the doctrine of impersonality was inconsistent and eclectic. It derives from many sources, philosophical, poetic, and political: it can mean anything from the destruction to the apotheosis of self. It conceals an ideological tension as well as a conceptual instability, and for this reason it continually slips into the ethics of 'personality' it was designed to supervene." *The Poetics of Impersonality: T. S. Eliot and Ezra Pound* (Brighton, UK: Harvester Press, 1987), ix. I return to the concept of personality in chapter 4.

39. This cultural and philosophical history lies behind Rei Terada's claim that "while emotions are real experiences, the expression that supposedly conveys them and the subject that supposedly expresses them are unnecessary angels parasitical on the phenomenon of emotion" (118). In her work investigating the possibility of emotion despite the death of the subject, Terada finds emotion freed from the constraints of subjectivity, the fiction of the self that characterizes earlier eras of thought and literary production. See *Feeling in Theory: Emotion after the "Death of the Subject"* (Cambridge: Harvard University Press, 2001).

40. See, for example, Patricia Yaeger, "Toward a Female Sublime," in *Gender and Theory: Dialogues on Feminist Criticism,* ed. Linda Kauffman (Oxford: Basil Blackwell, 1989); Jean-François Lyotard, *The Inhuman: Reflections on Time* (Stanford: Stanford University Press, 1991) and *Lessons on the Analytic of the Sublime* (Stanford: Stanford University Press, 1994); Fredric Jameson, *Postmodernism, or, the Cultural Logic of Late Capitalism* (Durham: Duke University Press, 1991); Sianne Ngai, *Ugly Feelings* (Cambridge: Harvard University Press, 2005).

41. See, for example, Paul Endo's "Stevens and the Two Sublimes" in *The Wallace Stevens Journal* 19 (1995): 36–50; Rob Wilson's chapter, "Wallace Stevens: Decreating the American Sublime" in his book *American Sublime: The Genealogy of a Poetic Genre* (Madison: University of Wisconsin Press, 1991); Michael T. Beehler's "Kant and Stevens: The Dynamics of the Sublime and the Dynamics of Poetry" and Mary Arensberg's "White Mythology and the American

Sublime: Stevens' Auroral Fantasy," both in *The American Sublime,* ed. Mary Arensberg (Albany: State University of New York Press, 1986).

42. Stevens, *Palm at the End of the Mind,* 174.

43. Kant remains shadowy on the possibility of a sublime art, although he devotes the final section of "The Analytic of the Sublime" to the question of art. His only acknowledgment of the sublime in art comes in a footnote: "Perhaps nothing more sublime was ever said and no sublimer thought ever expressed than the famous inscription on the Temple of Isis (Mother Nature): 'I am all that is and that was and that shall be, and no mortal hath lifted my veil.'" Immanuel Kant, *Critique of Judgment,* trans. J. H. Bernard (New York: Hafner Press, 1951), 160 n. 44.

44. Wallace Stevens, "Description without Place," in *Palm at the End of the Mind,* stanza I, p. 270. All further page references appear parenthetically.

45. Stevens writes in 1935:

> I was on the point of saying that I did not agree with the opinion that my verse is decorative, when I remembered that when HARMONIUM was in the making there was a time when I liked the idea of images and images alone, or images and the music of verse together. I then believed in *pure poetry,* as it was called.
>
> I still have a distinct liking for that sort of thing. But we live in a different time, and life means a good deal more to us now-a-days than literature does. In the period of which I have just spoken, I thought literature meant most. Morever, I am not so sure that I don't think exactly the same thing now, but unquestionably, I think at the same time that life is the essential part of literature (*Letters,* 288).

46. Wallace Stevens, "The Emperor of Ice Cream," in *Palm at the End of the Mind,* 79.

47. Harold Bloom, *The Poems of Our Climate* (Ithaca: Cornell University Press, 1976), 239, and Helen Hennessy Vendler, *On Extended Wings: Wallace Stevens' Longer Poems* (Cambridge: Harvard University Press, 1969), 229. She actually says worse about the first section of the poem: "If this is not the unspotted imbecile revery, it is not far from it" (219).

48. Wallace Stevens, "To the One of Fictive Music," in *Palm at the End of the Mind,* 82.

49. See George S. Lensing, *Wallace Stevens and the Seasons* (Baton Rouge: Louisiana State University Press, 2001), 331–337, for an extended discussion of this question and a record of his explanations of the poem.

50. What Stevens advocates is, of course, indebted to Keats and his notion of negative capability (in a letter to his brothers on December 21, 1817, Keats writes: "I mean Negative Capability, that is when a man is capable of being in uncertainties, Mysteries, doubts, without any irritable reaching after fact & reason"). There is a strong argument for reading Keats via the glamorous rather than via the sublime, even allowing for historical distance and the pre-twentieth-century context. Every theory has its exceptions and Keats here is the exceptional.

51. Stevens, *Necessary Angel,* 141.

52. Ibid., 4.

53. Ibid., 23.

54. Stevens, *Palm at the End of the Mind,* 175. Stevens seems to claim an all-powerful role for the imagination, although he tempers this in a comment about the "cognitive element of poetry." "If poetry is limited to the vaticinations of the imagination, it soon becomes worthless. The cognitive element involves the consciousness of reality." He continues: "Someone told me the other day that Ernest Hemingway was writing poetry. I think it likely that he will write a kind of poetry in which the consciousness of reality will produce an extraordinary effect" (*Letters,* 500).

55. Dufrenne, *Phenomenology of Aesthetic Experience,* 361. Further page references appear parenthetically.

56. For Dufrenne, I should make clear, the imagination in everyday perception operates differently than that of aesthetic perception. In fact, in aesthetic perception, contrary to Stevens' beliefs, Dufrenne limits the role of the imagination. His translator comments: "This

conspicuous demotion of the place of imagination in aesthetic experience is an aspect of Dufrenne's antagonism to Romantic and idealist theories of art where imagination is given a characteristically elevated and inflated role. Even if imagination is essential to artistic creation, the relation of this act of creation to the spectator's grasp of the aesthetic object is tenuous, and in any case, no comparable exertion of imagination is called for on the part of the spectator" (xxix). Dufrenne distinguishes ordinary perception from aesthetic perception; Stevens does not divide the two; instead he sees all perception as potentially aesthetic (despite the reality of war, the Depression, etc.).

57. *Letters of Wallace Stevens*, 501.

2. VIOLENCE

1. F. Scott Fitzgerald, "Echoes of the Jazz Age," in *The Crack-Up*, ed. Edmund Wilson (New York: New Directions, 1945), 20.

2. F. Scott Fitzgerald, *The Great Gatsby* (New York: Scribners, 1925). All further page references appear parenthetically.

3. Roland Barthes, *Camera Lucida: Reflections on Photography* (New York: Hill and Wang, 1981), 18.

4. Ackbar Abbas, "On Fascination: Walter Benjamin's Images," *New German Critique* 48 (1989): 49–50. Abbas studies the way Benjamin politicizes the state of fascination by using images dialectically: "His thinking about the image, dispersed throughout his work, constitutes a manual on how to use fascination as a critical tool" (49). While Fitzgerald's novel does not proclaim any interest in social justice nor offers any judgment on the world it portrays (though it obviously favors the beautiful rich and their access to commodities), it nevertheless reveals and satirizes a world so mesmerized by images that even T. J. Eckleburg can stand in for God. Abbas counterpoises Benjaminian fascination to that in the writings of Baudrillard for whom fascination is ultimately a passive, amoral state.

5. Jean Baudrillard, "On Seduction," in *Jean Baudrillard: Selected Writings*, ed. Mark Poster (Palo Alto: Stanford University Press, 1988), 146.

6. Perkins's letter to F. Scott Fitzgerald, November 20, 1924, in *A Life in Letters*, ed. Matthew J. Bruccoli (New York: Simon & Schuster, 1995), 87.

7. Letter, December 1, 1924, ibid., 89.

8. Ibid., 126.

9. Letter, May 1925, 109.

10. Ibid.

11. Ibid.

12. Woolf, reflecting on *Mrs. Dalloway*, writes in her diary, "And I suppose there is some superficial glittery writing" (entry dated December 13, 1924, *The Diary of Virginia Woolf*, ed. Anne Olivier Bell [London: Penguin, 1981], 2:323).

13. Fitzgerald's letter to Perkins, April 10, 1924, in *Life in Letters*, 67.

14. Ibid., 48.

15. Jacques Derrida, *Of Grammatology* (Baltimore: Johns Hopkins University Press, 1998), 98.

16. See Frances Kerr, "'Feeling Half Feminine': Modernism and the Politics of Emotion in *The Great Gatsby*," *American Literature* 68 (1996): 405–431.

17. Undated letter to Frances Scott Fitzgerald, in *The Crack-Up*, 304.

18. Barbara Hochman, "Disembodied Voices and Narrating Bodies in *The Great Gatsby*," *Style* 28, no. 1 (1994): 95–118. Hochman does not develop her comments on the prioritizing of written language but focuses, for the most part, on voice and narration.

19. *Life in Letters*, 78.

20. Sigmund Freud, "Fetishism," in *On Sexuality: Three Essays on the Theory of Sexuality and Other Works* (London: Penguin, 1977), 354.

21. Gilles Deleuze, "Coldness and Cruelty," in *Masochism* (New York: Zone Books, 1991), 31.

22. Emily Apter and William Pietz, eds., *Fetishism as Cultural Discourse* (Ithaca: Cornell University Press, 1993), 3.

23. *Life in Letters*, 67.

24. F. *Scott Fitzgerald: The Critical Reception,* ed. Jackson R. Bryer (New York: Burt Franklin, 1978), 212–238.

25. See especially Michael North's discussion of "spectroscopic vision" in the novel, in "F. Scott Fitzgerald's Spectroscopic Fiction," in *Camera Works: Photography and the Twentieth-Century Word* (Oxford: Oxford University Press, 2005), 109–139.

26. In chapter 4, I discuss the modernist expression of personality in literature and in the mass media.

27. Many critics have discussed the visual aspects of the novel, including its use of visual technologies, especially the motion picture. On "seeing" in the novel, see Ronald Berman's *The Great Gatsby and Modern Times* (Urbana: University of Illinois Press, 1994). See also Laura Barrett's "'Material without Being Real': Photography and the End of Reality in *The Great Gatsby,*" *Studies in the Novel* 30, no. 4 (1998): 540–557, and Lawrence Dessner's "Photography and *The Great Gatsby,*" *Essays in Literature* 6 (1979): 79–89.

28. Michael North, "F. Scott Fitzgerald's Spectroscopic Fiction" in *Camera Works,* 113.

29. Hochman points to the entanglement of authorial and narratorial voice: "Nick's wish to separate voice from body can be related both to his motivation of telling his story in writing and to the functions, for Fitzgerald, of employing the figure of Nick as his own voice, his primary narrating presence in the book" ("Disembodied Voices and Narrating Bodies," 98).

30. Barthes, *Camera Lucida,* 27.

31. Katherine Mansfield, *Bliss, and Other Stories* (New York: Knopf, 1920).

32. Katherine Mansfield, notebook 14 in *The Katherine Mansfield Notebooks,* ed. Margaret Scott (Minneapolis: University of Minnesota Press, 2002), 2:145.

33. Jeffrey Meyers, introduction to *Stories,* by Katherine Mansfield (New York: Vintage, 1991).

34. Mansfield's dislike for the French pales in comparison to her more disparaging renderings of Germans in her first book, *In a German Pension,* where they appear as humorless, gluttonous, and arrogant.

35. Katherine Mansfield's letter to John Middleton Murry, January 13, 1918, in *Letters to John Middleton Murry, 1913–1922,* by Katherine Mansfield, ed. John Middleton Murry (London: Constable, 1951), 118.

36. F. Scott Fitzgerald, *This Side of Paradise* (New York: Scribners, 1920), 248.

37. Ibid.

3. PHOTOGRAPHY

1. Hermione Lee, *Virginia Woolf* (New York: Knopf, 1997), 463.

2. Nicola Luckhurst, "Visualizing the Feminine: Fashion, Flowers, and Other Fine Arts," in *Virginia Woolf and the Arts: Selected Papers from the Sixth Annual Conference on Virginia Woolf,* ed. Diane Gillespie and Leslie K. Hankins (New York: Pace University Press, 1997), 77. Logan Pearsall Smith made this comment in an exchange with Woolf who writes: "I've been engaged in a great wrangle with an American called Pearsall Smith on the ethics of writing articles at high rates for fashion papers like Vogue. He says it demeans one.…What he wants is prestige: what I want, money" (*The Letters of Virginia Woolf,* ed. Nigel Nicolson and Joanne Trautmann, vol. 3, *1923–1928* [New York: Harcourt Brace Jovanovich, 1977], 154). Luckhurst narrates Woolf's relationship with Vogue, from her great friendship with editor Dorothy Todd to her enmity, two years later, 75–84. For more on the relationship between Woolf's cultural capital and the mass

circulation magazine, see Jane Garrity's "Virginia Woolf, Intellectual Harlotry, and 1920s British Vogue" in *Virginia Woolf in the Age of Mechanical Reproduction,* ed. Pamela Caughie (New York: Garland, 2000), 185–218.

3. Letter to Jacques Raverat, January 24, 1925, *Letters of Virginia Woolf,* 3:154.

4. My project here shares Jonathan Crary's view that ideas about vision are inseparably linked with processes of modernization. Crary writes in *Suspensions of Perception, Attention, Spectacle, and Modern Culture* (Cambridge: MIT Press, 1999) that "the state of being suspended, a looking or listening so rapt that it is an exemption from ordinary conditions, that it becomes a suspended temporality, a hovering out of time" (10). These "suspensions of perception" are arguably central to Woolf's exquisite moment pulled out of time.

5. Quoted in Beaumont Newhall, *The History of Photography from 1839 to the Present* (New York: MOMA, 1988), 164.

6. Ibid.

7. Whether thematically central or not, photography comes to structure and organize many of the narratives of modernism. See especially Nancy Armstrong's work on photography as a way of rethinking literary modernism in *Fiction in the Age of Photography: The Legacy of British Realism* (Cambridge: Harvard University Press, 1999), and Karen Jacobs's *The Eye's Mind: Literary Modernism and Visual Culture* (Ithaca: Cornell University Press, 2001). For work on the photographic image in Woolf's novels and nonfiction works, see *Virginia Woolf in the Age of Mechanical Reproduction,* ed. Pamela Caughie (New York: Garland, 2000); Diane Gillespie's "'Her Kodak Pointed at His Head': Virginia Woolf and Photography," in *The Multiple Muses of Virginia Woolf,* ed. Diane Gillespie (Columbia: University of Missouri Press, 1993), 113–147; Emily Dalgarno's *Virginia Woolf and the Visible World* (Cambridge: Cambridge University Press, 2001), and Helen Wussow's "Virginia Woolf and the Problematic Nature of the Photographic Image," *Twentieth Century Literature: A Scholarly and Critical Journal* 41, no. 1 (1994): 1–14.

8. Virginia Woolf, "A Sketch of the Past," in *Moments of Being: Unpublished Autobiographical Writings,* ed. Jeanne Schulkind, 2nd ed. (San Diego: Harcourt Brace Jovanovich, 1985), 76.

9. Virginia Woolf, *Three Guineas* (New York: Harcourt Brace Jovanovich, 1938), 10, 11. The connection between death and photography has been frequently theorized, perhaps most famously by Barthes in his autobiography *Roland Barthes by Roland Barthes* (Berkeley: University of California Press, 1977) and in his final work, *Camera Lucida: Reflections on Photography* (New York: Hill and Wang, 1981). Susan Sontag makes the connection in *On Photography* (New York: Doubleday, 1977) and Eduardo Cadava, in his Barthesian study of Benjamin, *Words of Light: Theses on the Photography of History* (Princeton: Princeton University Press, 1997), provides an excellent meditation on the symbiotic relationship between photography and death. Since the invention of photography in 1837, the correspondence between photography and death has provoked comment; for an especially early reading, see Pierre Marc Orlan, "Elements of a Social Fantastic," (1929) in *Photography in the Modern Era: European Documents and Critical Writings, 1913–1940,* ed. Christopher Phillips (New York: Metropolitan Museum of Art and Aperture, 1989), 31–33.

10. Marjorie Perloff, "Modernist Studies," in *Redrawing the Boundaries: The Transformation of English and American Studies,* ed. Stephen Greenblatt and Giles Gunn (New York: Modern Language Association, 1992), 157.

11. Virginia Woolf, "The Moment: Summer's Night," in *The Moment and Other Essays* (New York: Harcourt, Brace, 1948), 9.

12. Jane Goldman, *The Feminist Aesthetics of Virginia Woolf: Modernism, Post-Impressionism, and the Politics of the Visual* (Cambridge: Cambridge University Press, 1998), 1.

13. Virginia Woolf, *Mrs. Dalloway* (New York: Harcourt, 1981), 3.

14. Ibid., 37.

15. Judith Butler, *Gender Trouble: Feminism and the Subversion of Identity* (New York: Routledge, 1999), 140.

16. Virginia Woolf, entry dated October 15, 1923, *The Diary of Virginia Woolf*, ed. Anne Olivier Bell (London: Penguin, 1981), 2:272.

17. Woolf, *Mrs. Dalloway*, 4.

18. Beaumont Newhall, *A History of Photography: From 1849 to the Present* (New York: Museum of Modern Art, 1982), 119.

19. Maggie Humm, "Visual Modernism: Virginia Woolf's 'Portraits' of Photography," *Woolf Studies Annual* 8 (2002): 94–95.

20. Charles Baudelaire, "The Salon of 1859," in *Photography in Print: Writings from 1816 to the Present*, ed. Vicki Goldberg (Albuquerque: University of New Mexico Press, 1981), 124.

21. Virginia Woolf, *The Essays of Virginia Woolf*, ed. Andrew McNeillie (New York: Harcourt Brace Jovanovich, 1986), vol. 2, *1912–1918*, 290, and vol. 3, *1919–1924*, 140.

22. Virginia Woolf, *The Years* (New York: Harcourt, Brace & Company, 1965), 317. Woolf's snapshot image of nose and brow varies markedly from that of Roland Barthes' in his short essay "The Face of Garbo," which I discuss in chapter 4. Here is Barthes' description of the face: "And yet, in this deified face, something sharper than a mask is looming: a kind of voluntary and therefore human relation between the curve of the nostrils and the arch of the eyebrows; a rare, individual function relating two regions of the face" (*Mythologies* [New York: Hill and Wang, 1972], 57). Compare this to the movement from nose to brow in Woolf. These contrary images of the reproduced face in close-up may bear, however, some similarity. Barthes' reverence for the camera and his willingness to find the belated auratic effect of Garbo's face from nose to brow are clear. With an eye for the topography of the iconic face, Barthes describes an object that transcends mortality—but in the regions of the face he recognizes something human, something individual in the relationship of its features. Woolf's description is not of a person but of human remains, vacated and impervious to touch. Both images of the face hold onto a perceptible human element that deals implicitly with death—in Garbo's face it is of the order of transcendence and not the brute corporeality of a dead body that Woolf's image suggests—and both are framed by the visual apparatus of the camera.

23. Joseph Allen Boone, *Libidinal Currents: Sexuality and the Shaping of Modernism* (Chicago: University of Chicago Press, 1998), 180.

24. Ibid., 179.

25. Woolf, *Mrs. Dalloway*, 4.

26. Ibid., 37.

27. Leo Charney, "In a Moment: Film and the Philosophy of Modernity," in *Cinema and the Invention of Modern Life*, ed. Leo Charney and Vanessa R. Schwartz (Berkeley: University of California Press, 1995), 279.

28. Ibid., 283.

29. Walter Benjamin, "On Some Motifs in Baudelaire," in *Illuminations* (New York: Schocken, 1999), 194.

30. Woolf, "The Moment: Summer's Night," 9–10.

31. Ibid., 12.

32. Woolf, "Sketch of the Past," 72.

33. Ibid.

34. Benjamin, "On Some Motifs in Baudelaire," 163.

35. Woolf, "Sketch of the Past," 72.

36. Woolf, *Mrs. Dalloway*, 31–32.

37. Elizabeth Abel makes a similar point in her foundational study, *Virginia Woolf and the Fictions of Psychoanalysis* (Chicago: University of Chicago Press, 1989), when she writes:

> Woolf's language renders a passion that is actively directed toward women, and "masculine" in attitude and character, yet also receptive and "feminine"; the description of the match in the crocus, an image of active female desire, conflates Freud's sexual dichotomies. The power of the passage derives in part from the intermeshed male and female imagery, and

the interwoven language of sex and mysticism, a mélange that recurs in Clarissa's memory of Sally's kiss. Fusion—of male and female, active and passive, sacred and profane—is at the heart of this erotic experience. (37)

38. Woolf, *Mrs. Dalloway,* 32.

39. Walter Benjamin, "Theses on the Philosophy of History" in *Illuminations,* 255.

40. Woolf, *Mrs. Dalloway,* 36.

41. Ibid.

42. In his reflections on the photograph in *Camera Lucida,* Barthes writes: "I must therefore submit to this law: I cannot penetrate, cannot reach into the Photograph. I can only sweep it with my glance, like a smooth surface. The Photograph is flat, platitudinous in the true sense of the word, that is what I must acknowledge" (106).

43. Ibid., 13.

44. Jacques Derrida, *Acts of Literature,* ed. Derek Attridge (New York: Routledge, 1992), 37.

45. Maggie Humm, in fact, notes that "throughout her career as an innovative modernist writer Woolf, together with Leonard, took, developed and mounted in albums over one thousand domestic photographs" (Humm, "Visual Modernism," 95).

46. Woolf, *Mrs. Dalloway,* 10.

47. Ibid., 11.

48. Ibid., 47.

49. Ibid., 39.

50. Ibid., 47.

51. Diary entry, August 16, 1923, *Diary of Virginia Woolf,* 2:189.

52. Diary entry, June 19, 1923, *Diary of Virginia Woolf,* 2:249.

53. Derrida, *Acts of Literature,* 61.

54. Diary entry, June 19, 1923, *Diary of Virginia Woolf,* 2:248.

55. For an extended study of Woolf's iconicity, see Brenda Silver's *Virginia Woolf Icon* (Chicago: University of Chicago Press, 1999).

56. Letter to Ethel Smyth, July 14, 1932, *The Letters of Virginia Woolf,* ed. Nigel Nicolson and Joanne Trautmann, vol. 5, *1932–1935* (New York: Harcourt Brace Jovanovich, 1979), 78.

57. Kaja Silverman, *The Threshold of the Visible World* (New York: Routledge, 1996), 203.

58. Woolf, *Mrs. Dalloway,* 31.

59. Ibid., 30–31.

60. Ibid., 170–171.

61. Diary entry, April 27, 1925, *Diary of Virginia Woolf,* 3:12.

62. Woolf, *Mrs. Dalloway,* 184.

63. Ibid., 184.

64. Ibid., 185.

65. Ibid., 185–186.

66. Barthes, *Camera Lucida,* 97.

67. Woolf, *Mrs. Dalloway,* 194.

68. Diary entry, October 17, 1924, *Diary of Virginia Woolf,* 2:316.

69. Diary entry, December 13, 1924, *Diary of Virginia Woolf,* 2:323.

4. CELEBRITY

1. Virginia Woolf, "Mr. Bennett and Mrs. Brown," in *The Captain's Death Bed and Other Essays* (London: Hogarth Press, 1950), 91.

2. Virginia Woolf, "Modern Fiction," in *The Essays of Virginia Woolf,* ed. Andrew McNeillie (London: Hogarth Press, 1986), vol. 4, *1925–1928,* 159.

3. Ibid., 158.

4. Woolf, "Mr. Bennett and Mrs. Brown," 111.

5. Warren I. Susman, *History as Culture: The Transformation of American Society in the Twentieth Century* (New York: Pantheon, 1984).

6. Ibid., 281.

7. Ibid., 280.

8. Ibid., 278.

9. Sharon Cameron, *Impersonality* (Chicago: University of Chicago Press, 2007), ix.

10. Stuart Ewen, *All Consuming Images: The Politics of Style in Contemporary Culture* (New York: Basic Books, 1988), 89.

11. Richard Schickel, "Publisher's Afterword," in *Garbo,* by Antoni Gronowicz (New York: Simon and Schuster, 1990), 438.

12. Ibid., 441.

13. My information on glamour photography comes largely from the following books: John Jones, ed., *Light and Illusion: The Hollywood Portraits of Ray Jones* (Glendale, CA: Balcony Press, 1998); Robert Dance and Bruce Robertson, *Ruth Harriet Louise and Hollywood Glamour Photography* (Berkeley: University of California Press, 2002); David Fahey and Linda Rich, *Masters of Starlight: Photographers in Hollywood* (Los Angeles: Los Angeles County Museum of Art, 1987); and John Kobal, *The Art of the Great Hollywood Portrait Photographers 1925–1940* (New York: Knopf, 1980).

14. Daniel J. Boorstin, *The Image: A Guide to Pseudo-Events in America* (New York: Harper & Row, 1961), 3.

15. Ibid., 6.

16. See Richard Dyer, *Stars* (London: BFI, 1998), 17, and P. David Marshall, *Celebrity and Power: Fame in Contemporary Culture* (Minneapolis: University of Minnesota Press, 1997). There is a growing body of literature on literary celebrity that looks to the interconnections between modernism and its celebrity authors. See in particular Aaron Jaffe, *Modernism and the Culture of Celebrity* (Cambridge: Cambridge University Press, 2005); Brenda R. Silver, *Virginia Woolf Icon* (Chicago: University of Chicago Press, 1999); Faye Hammill, *Women, Celebrity, and Literary Culture between the Wars* (Austin: University of Texas Press, 2007); and Loren Glass, *Authors, Inc.: Literary Celebrity in the Modern United States, 1880–1980* (New York: New York University Press, 2004). Glass considers the tension between personality and impersonality, arguing that contradictions emerged between the statement of impersonality and the activity of literary celebrity that included very personal displays of "self aggrandizement and even shameless self-promotion" (5). I am less interested in the contradictions between writer and theory, then the contradictions inherent in the expressions of impersonal personality.

17. Walter Benjamin, "The Work of Art in the Age of Mechanical Reproduction," in *Illuminations: Essays and Reflections,* ed. Hannah Arendt, trans. Harry Zohn (New York: Schocken 1969).

18. Ibid., 223.

19. H. D., *Close Up, 1927–1933: Cinema and Modernism,* ed. James Donald, Anne Friedberg, and Laura Marcus (Princeton: Princeton University Press, 1998), 106, 107.

20. H. D., "An Appreciation," in *Close Up,* 145.

21. H. D., *Bid Me to Live (A Madrigal)* (New York: Dial Press, 1960), 124.

22. H. D., *Close Up,* 119.

23. "The Cinema and the Classics III: The Mask and the Movietone," *Close Up* 5 (November 1927), quoted ibid., 117, 119.

24. Ibid., 116.

25. "The Cinema and the Classics I: Beauty," *Close Up* 1, no. 1 (July 1927), quoted ibid., 107.

26. Roland Barthes, "The Face of Gàrbo," in *Mythologies* (New York: Hill and Wang, 1972), 56–57. For an excellent discussion of Garbo's face as object, see Paul Morrison's "Garbo Laughs!" *Modernist Cultures* 2, no. 2 (2007): 153–169.

27. An added dimension emerges when one considers that philtre is a term for the receptacle into which saints' relics were put during the Middle Ages.

28. Barthes, "The Face of Garbo," 56. All further page references appear parenthetically.

29. Robert Dance and Bruce Robertson note that Garbo had, already by 1927, a female impersonator, whose photographs are archived at MGM: "These images are amazing on two counts: first, because they were adopted by MGM publicity at all, but also because their adoption came so quickly: *The Temptress* was only Garbo's second American movie. But by then, she was already a star" (*Ruth Harriet Louise and Hollywood Glamour Photography*, 104).

30. For an account of the technical difficulty of shooting the enormous close-up and Mamoulian's conversations with Garbo about the final frame, see Mark A. Vieira, *Greta Garbo: A Cinematic Legacy* (New York: Harry N. Abrams, 2005), 188–189.

31. Thomas Weiskel, *The Romantic Sublime: Studies in the Structure and Psychology of Transcendence* (Baltimore: Johns Hopkins University Press, 1976).

32. Jacques Lacan, "Courtly Love as Anamorphosis," in *The Ethics of Psychoanalysis*, ed. Jacques-Alain Miller, trans. Dennis Porter (New York: Routledge, 1992), 139–154.

33. Gilbert Seldes, *The Movies Come from America* (New York: Scribner's, 1937), 296.

34. Charles Affron, *Star-Acting: Gish, Garbo, Davis* (New York: Dutton, 1977), 105.

35. Bert Longworth was the stills photographer; the photographs were shot in September 1926 and reproduced in *Photoplay* in January 1927. See Robert Dance and Bruce Robertson for further information on the film's still photography, *Ruth Harriet Louise and Hollywood Glamour Photography*, 228.

36. Affron, *Star-Acting*, 168.

37. Hortense Powdermaker, *Hollywood the Dream Factory* (New York: Little, Brown, 1950), 187.

38. Schickel, "Publisher's Afterword," 442.

39. Jim Tully, "Greta Garbo: An Estimate of the Swedish Film Actress Who Achieved Her Greatest Success in America," *Vanity Fair*, June 1928, 67.

40. Ibid., 67.

41. Canfield's letter was originally published as "Letter to Garbo," *Theatre Arts Monthly*, 1937. Quoted in Betsy Erkilla, "Greta Garbo: Sailing beyond the Frame," *Critical Inquiry* 11, no. 4 (1985): 595–619.

42. Garbo seemed to play a role in many modern imaginations: Ernest Hemingway (another artist known for employing spareness to achieve greater expressive power) creates a dreamy scene featuring Garbo in *For Whom the Bell Tolls* (New York: Scribner, 1995), when he brings her into erotic proximity to his protagonist, while acknowledging her remote physicality:

> But he could still remember the time Garbo came to his bed the night before the attack at Pozoblanco and she was wearing a soft silky wool sweater when he put his arm around her and when she leaned forward her hair swept forward and over his face and she said why had he never told her that he loved her when she had loved him all this time? She was not shy, nor cold, nor distant. She was just lovely to hold and kind and lovely and like the old days with Jack Gilbert and it was as true as though it had happened and he loved her much more than Harlow though Garbo was only there once while Harlow—(137)

This is the Garbo of the silent era, when her dramatic presence went unbothered by verbal communication, and when her power, many agree, was at its greatest. The impossibility of this fantasy is, of course, what feeds it. Garbo resides at a different level than even that of screen icon Jean Harlow, who is there, in his dreams, to be taken again and again. For Robert, Garbo is a one-time affair, exquisite, not to be repeated, even in fantasy. One hears the pleasure in his words as he recounts the impossible meeting, the emphasis on certain words such as "loved" and "lovely," the poignantly sweet and painfully sensual, all the more so for the battle that follows on the next day.

43. Djuna Barnes, *Nightwood* (New York: New Directions, 1937), 46.

44. Ibid., 148.

45. Georg Simmel, "The Metropolis and Mental Life," in *On Individuality and Social Forms,* ed. Donald Levine (Chicago: Chicago University Press, 1971), 329.

46. Mercedes-Benz advertisement, *New Yorker,* December 1997.

5. PRIMITIVISM

1. *Vanity Fair,* March 1925.

2. Walrond writes that "people like the Charleston because it satisfies an instinctive urge in them. In a measure it is for this very reason that there is interest in the primitive songs and music of the black slaves and their descendants. It certainly is the spirit preeminently responsible for the vogue of the black and brown revues....Now, after a reign of five intense years, the Charleston, so far as the dusky high-flyers of Harlem are concerned, is a glamorous ghost." *Vanity Fair,* April 1926, 116. See also "The Adventures of Kit Skyhead and Mistah Beauty: An All-Negro Evening in the Coloured Cabarets of New York," *Vanity Fair,* March 1925, 52, 100.

3. Covarrubias collected his Harlem drawings in *Negro Drawings* (New York: Knopf, 1927). For excellent discussions on Covarrubias and modernism, see Adriana Williams, *Covarrubias* (Austin: University of Texas Press, 1994), and Kurt Heinzelman, ed., *The Covarrubias Circle: Nickolas Muray's Collection of Twentieth-Century Mexican Art* (Austin: University of Texas Press, 2004).

4. Quoted in Phyllis Rose, *Jazz Cleopatra: Josephine Baker in Her Time* (New York: Vintage, 1989), 23.

5. Anthea Kraut, "Between Primitivism and Diaspora: The Dance Performances of Josephine Baker, Zora Neale Hurston, and Katherine Dunham," *Theatre Journal* 53, no. 3 (October 2003): 433–450.

6. A wider range of meanings fell under the rubric "primitive" in the early part of the century than is understood today. On the connections between primitivism and "japonisme" in modernist art, for example, see William Rubin, ed., *"Primitivism" in Twentieth-Century Art: Affinity of the Tribal and the Modern,* vol. 1 (New York: Museum of Modern Art, 1984).

7. Harlem Renaissance novels with cabaret scenes include *Quicksand* (Nella Larsen), *Nigger Heaven* (Carl Van Vechten), *The Blacker the Berry* (Wallace Thurman), *Home to Harlem* (Claude McKay), and *Not without Laughter* (Langston Hughes).

8. Mason, known as "Godmother" to the group of artists and writers she supported, was patron for a time to Langston Hughes, Zora Neale Hurston, Alain Locke, and Countee Cullen. Mason encouraged those she supported to represent what she saw as the primitivism of black cultural roots. Her domineering attitude and attempt to control particularly the literary works of these writers often destroyed, not surprisingly, the relationships she tried to foster.

9. Leon Coleman writes: "During a twelve-month period from June 1926, Carl Van Vechten published ten articles and five book reviews concerning African American music, theater, and literature. Eight of the articles appeared in *Vanity Fair;* one in *Theatre Magazine;* and one in the *Crisis.* All of the book reviews, with one exception, were published in the *New York Herald Tribune.*" *Carl Van Vechten and the Harlem Renaissance: A Critical Assessment* (New York: Garland Publishing, 1998), 83.

10. *Harlem Renaissance Re-examined,* ed. Victor A. Kramer and Robert A. Russ (Troy, NY: Whitson Publishing, 1997), 69–70.

11. Bill Brown writes in "The Secret Life of Things: Virginia Woolf and the Matter of Modernism": "I will in fact be preoccupied by the 1920s, the decade when things emerge as the object of profound theoretical engagement in the work of Georg Lukàcs, Heidegger, and Walter Benjamin, and which is the decade after objects and things are newly engaged by (or *as*) the work of art for Pound, Marcel Duchamp, Williams, Gertrude Stein." *Modernism/modernity* 6, no. 2 (1999): 1–28.

12. See, for example, Marianna Torgovnick's seminal book, *Gone Primitive: Savage Intellects, Modern Lives* (Chicago: University of Chicago Press, 1990); also, Elazar Barkan and Ronald Bush, eds., *Prehistories of the Future: The Primitivist Project and the Culture of Modernism* (Palo Alto: Stanford University Press, 1995).

13. Glamour derives from a paradoxical indulgence in an aestheticizing distancing of the primitive through formal control and brings into relation orientalist and Africanist primitivism. I may risk collapsing the vastly different traditions of ancient Asian and African cultures here, yet in the modern period they were exploited in similar ways and under the same rubric of the primitive. Africanist primitivism came later, after the trend of chinoiserie, the slumming in Chinatown that would turn to slumming in Harlem.

14. Wallace Thurman, *Infants of the Spring* (New Hampshire: Ayer, 1972), 283.

15. Monica L. Miller, "The Black Dandy as Bad Modernist," in *Bad Modernisms*, ed. Douglas Mao and Rebecca Walkowitz (Durham: Duke University Press, 2006), 184.

16. Thurman, *Infants of the Spring*, 284.

17. Ibid.

18. Thurman would die at the age of 32, impoverished and alone. The writer, whose bisexuality was commonly known, expresses his ambivalence about homosexuality in this passage, with its evocation of Huysmans and Wilde as dangerous models.

19. David Levering Lewis, *When Harlem Was in Vogue* (New York: Penguin, 1997), 281.

20. Frantz Fanon, *Black Skin, White Masks* (New York: Grove Weidenfeld, 1967), 109.

21. Ibid., 112.

22. Ibid., 109.

23. Lee Edelman, *Homographesis* (New York: Routledge, 1994), 73.

24. Ibid., 75 (my emphasis).

25. Barbara Johnson notes in "The Quicksands of the Self: Nella Larsen and Heinz Kohut," that "critics often praise Larsen for her psychological sophistication, but then go on to interpret the novel in social, economic, and political terms." She then asks, "How…can one account for the self-defeating or self-exhausting nature of Helga Crane's choices?" ("The Quicksands of the Self: Nella Larsen and Heinz Kohut," in *Telling Facts: History and Narratives in Psychoanalysis*, ed. Joseph H. Smith (Baltimore: Johns Hopkins University Press, 1992), 187. Johnson argues that Heinz Kohut's theory of narcissism as hollowness can explain what she interprets as Helga's lack of self: "She learns to identify with the rejecting other, to desire her own disappearance. Intimacy equals rejection; the price of intimacy is to satisfy the other's desire that she disappear" (190). Yet, it is equally important to note Helga's insistence on visibility and repeated efforts to *appear*, to make a mark on the eye that encounters her.

26. George Hutchinson writes that "*Quicksand* marks the threshold where a woman whose being forms the radical 'other' to the racial order disappears—or rather, is perpetually sacrificed on the altar of the color line." *In Search of Nella Larsen: A Biography of the Color Line* (Cambridge: Harvard University Press, 2006), 239.

27. Hazel Carby, "The Quicksands of Representation: Rethinking Black Cultural Politics," in *Reconstructing Womanhood: The Emergence of the Afro-American Woman Novelist* (Oxford: Oxford University Press, 1987), 76–90.

28. Deborah McDowell, ed., introduction to *"Quicksand" and "Passing,"* by Nella Larsen (New Brunswick: Rutgers University Press, 1986), xvi.

29. Nella Larsen, *Quicksand*, in *"Quicksand" and "Passing"* (New Brunswick: Rutgers University Press, 1986), 135. All further page references appear parenthetically.

30. Claudia Tate, in *Psychoanalysis and Black Novels: Desire and the Protocols of Race* (New York: Oxford University Press, 1998), rightly criticizes the narrowly identity-focused readings of the novel that interpret Helga exclusively in terms of one repressive discourse or another. She considers how the exclusive attention to race (what she calls the "racial protocol") has marginalized desire as a critical category of black textuality, demanding "manifest stories about

racial politics." She levels similar charges against narrowly feminist readings that insist on seeing Helga as a victim of an unforgiving patriarchal order. Tate emphasizes the complicating factor of desire in any text and reads Helga's conflict "as not simply the demand of black bourgeois sexual repression but as the overdetermination of female fetishization, self-alienation, racism, and abandonment" (20). Reading sadomasochistic pleasure in the narration of *Quicksand,* Tate offers a textually rich reading of simultaneous narrator/charactor gratification throgh the implied death—a death aligned with pleasure—at the novel's end.

31. McDowell, *"Quicksand" and "Passing,"* 243n3.

32. Slavoj Žižek, *Looking Awry: An Introduction to Jacques Lacan through Popular Culture* (Cambridge: MIT Press, 1991), 7.

33. See Wendy Martin, "'Remembering the Jungle': Josephine Baker and Modernist Parody," in Barkan and Bush, eds., *Prehistories of the Future,* 310–325. Janet Lyon reads the "surface phenomenon" of Baker's cabaret act and the ways she "flouted the interpretive paradigms of colonialism" in her essay "Josephine Baker's Hothouse," in *Modernism, Inc.: Body, Memory, Capital,* ed. Jani Scandura and Michael Thurston (New York: New York University Press, 2001), 41.

34. Phyllis Rose, *Jazz Cleopatra: Josephine Baker in Her Time* (New York: Vintage, 1991), 163.

35. Sianne Ngai, in a brilliant reading of the interrelations of stardom in Josephine Baker and Marlene Dietrich, comes to a different conclusion, reading Africanness as central to Dietrich's success: "But if it stands that becoming 'African' also paradoxically enables Helen to become Marlene Dietrich (reversing the conventional trajectory from reality to fiction in which actors are perceived to 'become' their characters), becoming an 'African queen' seems not only the way for a white immigrant to become a good modernist or a good American but a way for her to become a star. 'Africanness' equals stardom—at least, if not especially, in the cabaret." "Black Venus, Blonde Venus," in *Bad Modernisms,* ed. Douglas Mao and Rebecca Walkowitz (Durham: Duke University Press, 2006), 156.

36. Some of the most famous images of Josephine Baker were created by Paul Colin, who captured, in particular, the movement of her body and rhymed a self-conscious primitivist painting style with his subject. See Karen C. C. Dalton and Henry Louis Gates Jr., "Josephine Baker and Paul Colin: African American Dance Seen Through Parisian Eyes," *Critical Inquiry* 24 (1998): 903–934.

37. Paolo Garretto, *Josephine Baker,* collage with handpainted and airbrushed watercolor and gouache, crayon, colored pencil, wood veneer and feathers on yellow and brown woven paper, 1935. Reproduced in *Vanity Fair,* February 1936. National Portrait Gallery, Smithsonian Institute, Washington, D.C.

38. Wendy Wick Reaves, *Caricature in America* (New Haven: National Portrait Gallery, Smithsonian Institute in association with Yale University Press, 1998), 246.

6. CELLOPHANE

1. Steven Watson, *Prepare for Saints: Gertrude Stein, Virgil Thompson, and the Mainstreaming of American Modernism* (Berkeley: University of California Press, 1998), 4.

2. Stettheimer has only recently been claimed as an important modernist painter, and critical work on her career is still fairly limited. See *Florine Stettheimer: Manhattan Fantastica,* ed. Elisabeth Sussman and Barbara J. Bloemink (New York: Whitney Museum of American Art, 1995) for a critical evaluation of her work.

3. Ibid., 276.

4. Vogue, March 15, 1930, quoted from Condé Nast Store.com

5. Stephen Fenichell, *Plastic: The Making of a Synthetic Century* (New York: Harper Business, 1996), 110.

6. Ibid., 126.

7. Jeffrey L. Meikle, "Materia Nova: Plastics and Design in the U.S., 1925–1935," in *The Development of Plastics*, ed. S. T. I. Mossman and P. J. T. Morris (London: Royal Society of Chemistry, 1994), 45.

8. Paul T. Frankl, *Machine-Made Leisure* (New York: Harper & Brothers, 1932), 115–116.

9. See the introduction for a discussion of glamour's etymology (which includes necromancy, alchemy, and magic).

10. Frankl, *Machine-Made Leisure*, 112–113.

11. Meikle, "Materia Nova," 38–53.

12. Ibid., 177.

13. "What Man Has Joined Together…," *Fortune*, March 1936, 69.

14. Joseph Wood Krutch, "A Prepare for Saints," *The Nation*, February 28, 1934, reprinted in *The Critical Response to Gertrude Stein*, ed. Kirk Curnutt (Westport: Greenwood Press, 2000), 74–75.

15. Joseph Conrad, in the preface to *Nigger of the 'Narcissus,'* exhorts his public to remake language and literature through a reinvigorated relationship to the "old, old words, worn thin, defaced by ages of careless usage." *Nigger of the 'Narcissus,'* (New York: Dover, 1999), vi–vii. Conrad and Stein share a fundamental interest in shaking up the relationship between reader and word.

16. Stein elaborates on this concept in "Composition as Explanation," reprinted in *Selected Writings of Gertrude Stein* (New York: Vintage Books, 1990), 513–523.

17. Gertrude Stein, "Plays," in *Lectures in America* (Boston: Beacon Press, 1985), 129.

18. Gertrude Stein, "A Transatlantic Interview 1946," in *A Primer for the Gradual Understanding of Gertrude Stein*, ed. Robert Bartlett Haas (Los Angeles: Black Sparrow Press, 1971), 34.

19. As metaphor for modernization, then, cellophane figures a whole range of social preoccupations, from the benign (the freshness of food) to the more malignant forces that would gather strength through the thirties with the message of racial hygiene. See Alexandra Stern, *Eugenic Nation: Faults and Frontiers of Better Breeding in Modern America* (Berkeley: University of California Press, 2005), and Stefan Kuhl, *The Nazi Connection: Eugenics, American Racism, and German National Socialism* (New York: Oxford University Press, 1994). The "foreign threat" was explicitly invoked in some advertising: "Dust, dirt and the germs on inquisitive hands are *kept out* by…Cellophane. It keeps out *foreign odors* too" (emphasis in original). And again: "Strange hands. Inquisitive hands. Dirty hands. Touching, feeling, examining the things *you* buy in stores" (Fenichell, *Plastic*, 114, 115).

20. Virgil Thomson's music, writes Carl Van Vechten in his introduction to the play, "is as transparent to color as the finest old stained glass and has no muddy passages." *Four Saints in Three Acts* (New York: Random House, 1934), 6. Even the music, it seems, shared some of cellophane's virtues.

21. Fenichell, *Plastic*, 125.

22. John Gloag, *Plastics and Industrial Design* (London: George Allen & Unwin, 1945), 32, 30.

23. Jeffrey L. Meikle, *American Plastic: A Cultural History* (New Brunswick: Rutgers University Press, 1995).

24. Ibid., 13.

25. Ibid.

26. Pound's criteria for imagism included "to use absolutely no word that did not contribute to the presentation," a form of technical hygiene that kept poetry spare and efficient. "A Few Don'ts by an Imagiste," *Poetry* 1, no. 6 (March 1913): 200–208.

27. Meikle, *American Plastic*, 89–90.

28. Peter Muller-Munk, "Vending Machine Glamour," *Modern Plastics* 17 (February 1940): 26–27, 66–68.

29. Ibid., 26.

30. Van Vechten quoting Thompson in his introduction to *Four Saints in Three Acts,* 7.

31. Van Vechten often used cellophane as a background for his graphic portraits of the cast of *Four Saints.* Stein wrote to him in April 1934: "The photographs are wonderful I have never seen such photographs, and the background what wonderful stuffs and paper and flowers, and the black one of Saint Ignatius, it has completely upset everybody.…You know they are the first time that photographs are rich things instead of poor things." *The Letters of Gertrude Stein and Carl Van Vechten 1913–1946,* ed. Edward Burns (New York: Columbia University Press, 1986), 1:306.

32. Watson, *Prepare for Saints,* 206.

33. Stein, quoted in John Malcolm Brinnin, *The Third Rose: Gertrude Stein and Her World* (Boston: Little, Brown, 1959), 320.

34. Stein, *Four Saints in Three Acts,* act 1, scene 2, reprinted in *Selected Writings of Gertrude Stein,* 589.

35. Watson, *Prepare for Saints,* 208.

36. Sigmund Freud, "Beyond the Pleasure Principle" (1920), *Standard Edition of the Complete Psychological Works of Sigmund Freud,* trans. James Strachey, vol. 18, *1920–1922* (London: Hogarth Press, 1955), 38.

37. Martin Heidegger, "What Is Metaphysics?," in *Basic Writings,* ed. David Farrell Krell (New York: Harper, 1977), 103.

38. T. S. Eliot, *The Waste Land,* in *T. S. Eliot: Collected Poems, 1909–1962* (London: Faber and Faber, 1963), 74.

39. Jeremy Gilbert-Rolfe, *Beauty and the Contemporary Sublime* (New York: Allworth Press, 1999), 112–113.

40. James Joyce, "A Portrait of the Artist" (1906), in *Poems and Shorter Writings,* ed. Richard Ellman, A. Walton Litz, and John Whittier Ferguson (London: Faber and Faber, 1991), 211.

41. Joyce uses the phrase "continuous present" in his essay "A Portrait of the Artist." The fourth dimension was a subject of some fascination for philosophers and writers of the early part of the century. One of its most succinct definitions appears in H. G. Wells's *The Time Machine:* "Any real body must have extension in four directions: it must have length, breadth, thickness and duration.…There are really four dimensions, three which we call the three planes of space, and a fourth, time. There is, however, a tendency to draw an unreal distinction between the former three dimensions and the latter, because it happens that our consciousness moves intermittently in one direction along the latter from the beginning to the end of our lives." H. G. Wells, *The Time Machine* (1895; New York: Penguin Classics, 2005), 4.

42. Fenichell narrates the remarkable success of transparency in creating consumer desire: "A national grocery store chain reported a 2,100 percent increase in doughnut sales in *two weeks* after wrapping its doughnuts in cellophane. Market surveys confirmed that housewives felt no compelling urge to buy doughnuts before walking into the store but snapped them up strictly on impulse 'because they looked so inviting in transparent packages'" (*Plastic,* 112).

43. Gilbert-Rolfe, *Beauty and the Contemporary Sublime,* 111.

44. Walter Benjamin, "The Work of Art in the Age of Mechanical Reproduction," in *Illuminations: Essays and Reflections,* ed. Hannah Arendt (New York: Schocken, 1969).

45. Arlene Croce, *The Fred Astaire and Ginger Rogers Book* (New York: Outerbridge and Lazaard, 1972), 25.

46. Ellen Spiegel, "Fred & Ginger Meet Van Nest Polglase," *The Velvet Light Trap* 10 (fall 1973): 17–22.

47. Ibid., 19.

48. Ann Miller, quoted in "Begin the Beguine" (supplementary material to *Broadway Melody of 1940*), a documentary in the DVD series *Cole Porter in Hollywood,* director Peter Fitzgerald (Burbank, CA: Turner Entertainment and Warner Home Video, 2003).

49. Internet Movie Database, IMDb.com.

50. Ann Miller, "Begin the Beguine."

51. Gilbert Seehausen, "The Cellophane Gown," *Esquire,* autumn 1933, 45.

52. E. B. White, *Alice through the Cellophane* (New York: John Day, 1933), 24.

53. Ibid., 29.

54. Roland Barthes, "Plastics," in *Mythologies* (New York: Hill and Wang, 1972), 98.

55. Sylvia Plath, *Ariel* (New York: Harper & Row, 1961), 77–78.

56. Gertrude Stein, "Portraits and Repetition," in *Lectures in America,* 177.

57. F. Scott Fitzgerald, *The Beautiful and the Damned* (1922; New York: Scribner, 1995), 341.

58. Maurice Blanchot, "The Essential Solitude," in *The Gaze of Orpheus and Other Literary Essays,* ed. P. Adams Sitney, trans. Lydia Davis (New York: Station Hill Press, 1981), 75–76.

59. H. D., "Projector II," in *H. D.: Collected Poems, 1912–1944,* ed. Louis L. Martz (New York: New Directions, 1983), 355.

Index

Page locators followed by an *i* indicate illustrations.